The London Year

A novel by

Stephen Jerrome

Copyright © 2025 by Stephen Jerrome.

Stephen Jerrome asserts the moral right to be identified as the author of this work.

Cover image by Stephen Jerrome.

Cover designed by Spectrum Books.

ISBN: 978-1-915905-67-3

All rights reserved. No part of this book may be used or reproduced, transmitted, downloaded, decompiled, reverse engineered or stored in or introduced into any information storage and retrieval system, in any form or by any means without the express written permission of the author or of Spectrum Books, except for brief quotations used for promotion or in reviews.

This book is a work of fiction. The names, characters, places, and incidents portrayed in it are the work of the author's imagination. Any resemblance to actual persons, living or dead, or events, is entirely coincidental..

First Edition, Spectrum Books, 2025

Discover more books at www.spectrum-books.com

Thank you Vanessa, Christine, Peter and Patricia.

AUTUMN

It was the early 1970s, now a lifetime ago.

I was a twenty-three-year-old Californian in, of all places, Russian-occupied Czechoslovakia. And suddenly, all my dreams were up in smoke.

Crying on the phone to my parents in L.A. the only thing I knew for certain was that I couldn't go home, tail between my legs to face my friends—not after all my big talk.

I'd spent two years of fierce dreaming, saving my part-time-job money cleaning operating rooms at a local hospital; enrolled in rather sad "cinema" courses at Los Angeles City College. I even studied the Czech language with a private tutor, all with the determined intention of being accepted to the Prague Film Academy. Because at the time FAMU was reported to be the best film school in the world. Jan Kadar went there. Milos Forman! I'd been seeing the world through cinematic eyes since I was in the *sixth grade*! When I finally learned that movies had "directors", it was the only thing I wanted to do besides writing the movies I also hoped to someday direct.

But Czechoslovakia? Everyone but me seemed to think I was biting off more than I could chew. In the end, the three short films I submitted were too arty and not well crafted.

Then I didn't get in.

I was shattered.

There was no Plan B.

I didn't know what to do or where to go.

Looking back, I can say the FAMU judging panel made the correct decision. I was brave, I'll give myself that, but in actuality I faced challenges way over my head. For starters, I was never a good student. I didn't have unpleasant school years; made only average grades. But by the time I finished my senior year at high school I said that's all the school I can stand, thank you *very* much. Then to go study in Prague? Learn the Czech language with its very complicated grammar? Make my movies in Czech? *What was I thinking*?

Also, I didn't know what it *really* took to be a movie director, which, before camera angles and working with actors, required is a single-minded, almost obsessive self-confidence I *didn't* have to rally troops around a personal vision. I didn't *have* a personal vision—which is not entirely true. The formative ideas I had (and presented rudimentarily in the films I submitted), I know now, were more in the genre of commercials or music videos. But MTV and YouTube were still ten and twenty years away, respectively. The Neo-realist and New Wave films coming from Europe were a world away from anything I grew up with going to afternoon movies in L.A. I was more influenced by Andy Warhol's films (especially *Lonesome Cowboys*) than anything that came out of Hollywood. But to say I was ahead of my time is just being generous. I was no different than any young artist taking their first steps on a life of creativity—that feast or famine ride.

I was a multi-directional Aries juggling three creative aspirations: writing, filmmaking and photography. I was actually a pretty good amateur photographer, which I felt was a natural segue into cinema. But along with everything else, I had little confidence and almost no guidance on how to take my "visions" to the marketplace. Self-promotion (the *business* of being an artist) was not my strong suit. I was still trying to figure out what job I might go after that was at the very least kindred to *one* of my creative leanings. I have since come to the conclusion that in a pre-birth state I impulsively decided that I was such a smarty pants I'd try juggling numerous creative balls at once. Not a path I'll choose next time round.

After the defiant Prague Spring of 1968, followed by Russia's full-on invasion of Czechoslovakia, the occupiers naturally muscled in a presence at the national film school. I'm sure they thought having an American student among them would be a propaganda coup. During one of several interviews I was even asked what I thought about "revolution". The guy was probably some apparatchik the real directors of FAMU had to grin and bear. But he was barking up the wrong tree. What the hell did I know about revolution? I was from the California suburbs! I had nothing to rebel against!

Meanwhile, I saw the grey pall of Communism first hand. I spent too many weeks in Prague, staying with friends of family friends who were more generous to me than they could afford. I was forced to chip away at my savings on weekly visa extensions at offices where the counters were above eye level, forcing the applicant to also be a supplicant. A lively, educated population were being squelched and deprived in the name of blanket corruption described as some high-minded ideology in service to the common man. People talked in whispers; everyone had to obey. That kind of restraint was completely foreign to me, and I wonder how long I'd have been able to keep my mouth shut the way everyone I encountered was cowed to do. No wonder the Commies were worried about revolution. The system was as untenable as it eventually turned out to be.

Even the Czech national composer, Smetana, had been silenced since the invasion because of a single line in one of his nineteenth century operas. I was in the ornate National Opera House (opposite FAMU's own beautiful building) on an historic night when "The Bartered Bride" was finally allowed to be performed. Sure enough, the full house was waiting for that single line when the character Marenka sings: "She'll gladly settle for her freedom back again." Several brave voices, anonymous in the darkened theater, shouted out in response.

A visit to my host family's country dacha included a stop to buy pigeons for that night's dinner. Well off the main highway, we headed for a tiny village on a gently sloping hillside against the wall of a huge forest. We pulled into the courtyard of a small farm. An elderly woman, no doubt alerted by the sound of our tires on the gravel ground, emerged from a thatched barn. She was heavyset with a plump, weathered face, bulging bust under an old, baggy cardigan and a long farm-worn skirt.

Our purpose stated, the old woman went back into the barn and returned holding a plastic woven bag. We followed her to a granite block in the center of the courtyard. As we gathered around the woman pulled a live pigeon from the bag, pressed it against the stone and in a merciless second cut its throat with a small knife. Then she gently squeezed out its blood, drip by life-ending drip, as we all watched in silence.

I was stunned. Not by the act itself, which, to a city boy like me, was unnerving enough, but by the whole scene. This was Bruegel's paintings come to life. This was "The Painted Bird" (which I'd just read), except Kosinski was not describing a lost world. The peasant woman, her thick, sure hands, the dozen sand-colored, mud brick structures that comprised the ancient village were timeless, untouched by regime change or everything we proudly call "advances". Here, time had stopped.

One by one the pigeons were taken out, and fresh blood flowed onto the executioner's stone, seemingly its only purpose. Then the birds were wrapped in newspaper and the bundle exchanged for a few crown notes. That night we ate roasted game with delicious *knedlíky* dumplings and, in a phrase I'll never forget, *velké pivo*—a large beer.

Those and other memorable moments afforded me by my kind hosts, whom I never properly thanked again once I departed Czechoslovakia, were all quickly put behind me after the teary phone call home.

I'd never thought beyond my post-adolescent nose. Was far too young to grasp that my history was ahead of me, that one's life is a whole life's work. In time, the most obvious bruise of crushing disappointment would disappear as bruises do. Still, an inner scar would remain for years, making me afraid to want anything too badly, especially my long-imagined career as a film director.

In the end, it was my dear father who came up with a plan—or at the very least a direction—because truly, in that moment I was without one. The only bridge to my future had burned to the ground.

"Go to London," he said. "You have your New Zealand passport. There'll be no problem getting in; you can probably work there, too. You've saved enough to land on your feet. Just go! See what happens!"

He was right on every count. We'd all been born in New Zealand and lived in the US as legal "resident aliens" for nearly twenty years. The only restriction, short of full citizenship, was that we couldn't vote. As a family, me, my parents and my younger brother Walt were still members of the British Commonwealth.

As a side note, it's interesting to consider that I am the very last of a generation—a thousand generations!—to have traveled the world by ship. In 1957, international air travel was still a decade off. From Auckland we boarded the mid-tier luxury ocean liner *Orcades*, and after stops in Fiji (where Walt fell into the fishpond in front of Government House, retrieved, covered in green slime, by a tall, red-jacketed policeman), and Hawaii (where my mother felt a Lemurian connection that brought her back there many times), until, several weeks later we landed in San Francisco. I still remember the shipboard experience. Then within days my father bought a car, and we drove the coast road south through the Red Wood forests of Big Sur to our final destination in L.A. I was six years old.

~

Two days after the tearful phone call I was stamped into England on a one-year, renewable visa. I knew no one; had no preparation for being in London at all. But there was no turning back.

I carried my bags (before wheeled suitcases and moving sidewalks) down the long, long causeway at London-Heathrow Airport. Took a taxi to the Strand Hotel, which was the only one my parents knew to recommend. The plan was to stay there a few nights until I got my bearings and found more permanent lodgings.

Coming down that first night from my room to the hotel restaurant, I was asked if I'd mind sharing a table because the dining room was so crowded. As I waited, I saw a group of four being seated by the restaurant's host. I could tell at a glance they were American. The only woman among them, a big-boned, big-smile gal, was wearing a head-to-toe ensemble of purple suede with fringes dangling from arm seams, down the side of her long legs and across the back of her jacket. And a purple suede cowboy hat just in case the statement wasn't clear enough. She was going to make a splash on *her* first night in London and boy, she and her friends thought she was the cat's meow.

Then, as if to underscore everything, I heard one of the woman's dinner companions announce to their waiter: "Werr Amurricans; werr in a hurry."

I hadn't been in England six hours and I was already embarrassed by my countrymen.

When I was seated, apparently with permission of the other solo diner, I found myself on the chair side of a banquet table introducing myself to a handsome English businessman I guessed to be about forty years old. I remember nothing of our conversation except that as I talked about my unexpected circumstances, I realized I had no enthusiasm for staying the old course, least of all to start barking at the door of London's two notable film schools in hopes of winning entrance there. The sudden shift in my priorities was actually quite remarkable. I felt relief. For years I'd closed myself off to all but one possibility: getting into the Prague Film Academy. With that door closed, I looked up to see a whole new world of options.

Toward the end of our meal, as my dinner companion ordered each of us an aperitif, he said this: "Don't get into the habit of using alcohol to relax."

His words suggested he was talking from experience: a word to the wise for the young man across the table just entering the grownup world. I took his counsel in the spirit it was given and have kept it as a talisman all my life. Funny how little things can stick.

Within days, with the help of a placement agency, I found a room to rent with a family in North Acton, a suburb just outside central London. The Langers were Janice and Ted and their two kids, Sally, ten years old, and five-year-old Tom. The house was one in a tidy neighborhood of post-war, two-story row houses. I had a room with a big window above the front door. There was a small desk where I wrote letters home.

Ted Langer was about forty, square-jawed and extremely fit. Janice was plain, plump, with creamy English skin and a charming Dorset accent. She was smart and kind, with a quietly wicked sense of humor. In the sitting room, there was a twelve-year-old wedding picture on a side table. Janice was on the plump side even then, standing next to handsome Ted. I imagine she felt she'd landed quite a catch, beaming, victorious amidst her prettier bridesmaids. Against all odds, she'd got her man.

And Ted was a good provider. Janice did her part raising sweet kids, keeping a very clean house and managing temporary lodgers such as myself for extra money. She brought up tea in the morning. It seemed like a perfectly neutral launching pad to begin my new adventure. That is, until Ted Langer came home from his job as a guard at Wormwood Scrubs Prison.

The last thing I expected arriving in England was to be thrown back to 1950s-era American-style racism. The shock was actually twofold. First was dealing with Ted's intolerant attitudes, which I'd never encountered up close. The other shock was how *this* reality contrasted so sharply with the picture of England my post-Victorian New Zealand parents had painted.

As kids, my brother and I had the Queen and her very proper etiquette—especially table manners—rammed down our throats. England was the gold standard for all things right, proper and correct. My mother even once said that they didn't swear in the British navy. My father, a soldier in the New Zealand Air Force during World War II, laughed out loud at this. (He never flew a plane or even saw fighting in Guadalcanal, British Solomon Islands, but told the story of having to drive around one night looking for a film they hadn't seen in one of the base's three movie theaters. "It was hell on the canal," he often joked.)

While the Colonies had held tight to their founding customs, the Mother Country had moved on. London, I discovered, was a gritty, multi-cultural melting pot with a whole underclass of West Indian and South Asian Pakistanis, Indians and Bangladeshis, who owned most of the small shops and local markets.

I had no idea how long this "colored" face of Britain (yes, they used that term) had taken to emerge, but it was status quo by my arrival. All in all *not* the portrait England painted for the world—or even to herself in the posters and brochures at the travel agencies or in glossy magazines. In that world, everything was white.

"Immigration has ruined this country, and we're paying for it with every black conductor on the bus," Ted Langer said, citing the "colored" population of Scrubs prison to prove his point.

The specious arguments he used to shore up his racist rants were all old news in America. The main difference was that the US, born with slavery of the negro as one of its three foundational stones (along with religious fanaticism and the nineteenth century genocide of its Native People—and the buffalo) was reckoning with its racial history and, albeit haltingly, confronting racism head on.

The England I found in the early 1970s was still surprisingly racist just below the surface—and in denial. The then US Ambassador to the United Nations, Andrew Young, a Black man, made the mistake of pointing out the exact impression I had about racism in the UK, and it got him into serious diplomatic hot water. But the realities were too obvious to sweep under the rug.

This was also true for the once lionized royal family. They were under siege from London's tawdry tabloid press who were having an unrelenting field-day following Prince Charles' love life—even before Diana. *The Sun* tabloid, owned by Rupert Murdoch, was the trashy worst with some new made-up scandal every day splashed in blood across the front page and a bathing-suited pinup on the back. It was all bottom-common-denominator stuff targeted at the working class.

But there were numerous other news papers as well, each seemingly class-specific. I settled on the Daily Mail in the morning and The Evening Standard later, both of which suited my middle-range leanings. I'd have read The Times, but it was more expensive and its big pages weren't easy to open or fold on the bus or riding the Tube. All this being further example of how class—the unwritten class system—trickled down to a thousand little things, which I would discover along the way.

But the most deciding class indicator was accent. The writer and modernist painter Whyndham Lewis said "The English are branded on the tongue." A beautiful (if somewhat horrific) expression but totally correct. How one spoke, the phrases and tone one used not only indicated where one was from (sometimes one's university!), but even more to the point, one's *station*. This was not necessarily a bad thing.

While Londoners had a great affection for the quick and colorful Cockney accent, it indicated a provenance very different from the "posh" accents of the upper class, to say nothing of the dozens of mid-range variations depending what region throughout the entire United Kingdom one was from. Accent rather locked one in. Of course, things *did* change in the 1960s when working class musicians, artists, photographers and models rose to the status of cultural heroes, bringing "common" accents with them. Their new dominance actually redefined England, softening its snobbery. But in general, one's linguistic anatomy was still one's societal destiny, and it was hard to talk your way out of it.

Barely a week into my three-week stay with the Langers, talking a lot more with Janice than I ever did with Ted (who tended to make pronouncements that ended conversation), I began to see their life below the surface. I was witness to the creeping disappointment of a wife whose picture-perfect husband was being twisted by the knee-jerk suspicion and control that he brought home every day from his job at the prison. The door locks weren't strong enough. He didn't like the color of new neighbors down the road. His xenophobic skepticism made even me suspect. The Bach I listened to on the radio was derided as "church music". He scoffed at the notion that little Sally and Tom might actually find something to enrich their lives in London's great museums. He'd never take his kids there, he said. They'd be bored to death.

What became the biggest event in the time I was there was the purchase of a color television. Janice was determined to have some reward as she watched with quiet dread while Ted grew moody, opinionated and less of a man in her eyes for all the macho posturing. (Once she hinted that the sex was disappointing because he had such a small penis... truly more than I wanted to know!)

When the television arrived, a few of Janice's girlfriends came over to see it installed. I was surprised at the to-do. Color TVs had been common in the States for at least five years, but in England it was still a big deal. Plans were already in the works for a football-watching party the following Saturday, and Janice was determined to do her own controlling so everything was just right. When Ted's mates arrived with their prettier wives and kids, food and drinks laid out, everyone excited, Janice became, for an afternoon, that victory-savoring bride in the photo.

~

During those first weeks, I would take day visits to central London, catching the subway—the Tube—at North Acton Station. This form of public transportation was common enough for most people in big cities worldwide, but car-centric Los Angeles was still decades behind having any subway system at all. In fact, they'd removed a surprisingly functional tramline in the late 1950s, the Red Line, in deference to the auto, tire and oil companies who wanted an entire city dependent on them. And they got their way, reshaping the city's destiny in a stroke.

So, riding the Tube in London was my first experience with mass transit. It was exhilarating to think there was an entire big city up above as the carriages rattled through dark tunnels at full speed. Coming in from the suburbs, and never at peak hours, I always had a seat where I could study the instantly recognizable map of London's sprawling Underground constellation.

From North Acton, the Central Line was direct to Oxford Circus, which put me in easy walking distance to all the introductory sights. I listened to lunchtime organ concerts at the Church of St Martin-in-the-Fields in Trafalgar Square, where I saw a homeless man sleeping on one of the empty pews. I visited the National Gallery and saw my first Turner and Monet paintings. Familiar from books, I had no idea how huge they were. Exploring room after room of our world's most enduring treasures, I left the museum in tears.

Of course, honoring the instilled admiration with which I' been brought up, I made a special visit to the gates of Buckingham Palace. It was a big ceremonial day: Trouping of the Colors, and the one and only time I saw Queen Elizabeth II in person. She was on horseback, amidst the royal pageantry. I heard a loud popping sound coming from the sidelines. The Queen's horse jolted, and Her Majesty took a quick look over her shoulder before cantering bravely on. I was struck by how anachronistic it all was, yet how important in the way heirlooms are important: precious things one brings out just for special occasions. By all means bring out the shining jewels, the braids of gold thread, the horses and colorful uniforms. Honor tradition by giving the past its due. Yet, even in the 1970s, I could foresee the monarchy's quick demise once the reigning queen eventually passed. The world was moving inexorably past the adoration of "those greater than ourselves". Kings and popes and emperors—even dictators—would one day join history's treasure box of relics. But really, as I saw it, the arc of history was already moving in a decidedly new direction. As never before, I was ready to move on, too.

In my walking around central London I also stumbled upon one of London's less glorious attractions. At one point I was taken by the urge to pee and found myself following the Toilets sign in the ever-bustling Piccadilly Circus

Underground Station. Finding the gents, I sidled up to one of the urinals and was quickly distracted by a line of men, mostly older, all ever-so-discretely playing with their semi-hard cocks. Right beside me was a dark-haired ruffian, maybe a few years older than myself, with an exceptionally impressive piece of uncut meat that he was showing off for all to see. The brazenness as much as the cock itself took me by surprise. But stare I did along with the others.

"Where you from?" he asked me as my own cock began to swell.

"L.A." I whispered.

"Nice," he said. "'ere to earn a few quid."

I thought it was a question: *Was I in London looking for a job?*

"I suppose," I replied.

Then he leaned back slightly to give me an even better look.

"Same 'ere," he said, showing off the full extent of the goods.

Slow on the up-take, I finally realized from his accent and cheeky manner that he wasn't asking about *my* job prospects, but offering up his own. That big cock was his money-maker!

I had no reply. The whole scenario—a male prostitute working the stalls in a public facility—was completely new to me. Of course, I'd heard of Grand Central Station in New York (a city I'd never visited). It was famous for its hustler trade. But as noted, I was from a city that had no subway, let alone the century-old institution of a notorious public men's room. Mostly, I was enthralled by that impressive tool.

Eventually, seasoned salesman that the young man was, he knew I was only window shopping. The goods were put away, and his spot was quickly taken by someone who, for all I knew, might have been eyeing me as prospective merchandise. Once I gleaned the big picture, I knew it was time to leave. As I headed for the exit, a very pleasant man in his early thirties approached.

"Excuse me," he said, then reached in his jacket pocket, pulling out what looked like a wallet. Then he flipped it open to reveal a badge. It was Old Bill! I'd obviously lingered long enough to draw attention, and suddenly I was being detained!

"Where are you from?" he asked.

The question was rote; any copper would have seen at a glance that I was fresh off the boat.

"Yeah, I'm from Los Angeles," I said, all American-like.

Fortunately, this stopped the conversation in its disaster-leading tracks. No need causing an international incident over this hapless tourist.

"You'd best not 'ang around 'ere," he said. There was almost a kindness about him—another word to the wise. I considered this a quick lesson learned.

"You're right," I said. "Sorry."

"Be on your way, then."

And with heart pounding I found the stairs and headed back up to the street.

One day I was sightseeing on Kensington High Street and found Biba. I remembered the name from the Swinging London days. It had once been the hippest store in town, frequented by the likes of Bowie and Jagger as well as every mod schoolgirl who wanted to look like Twiggy. But by the early 70s, the dark, Deco-inspired interior was just a quirky tourist trap, its trendy days—to say nothing of the uber-trendy clientele—a thing of the past.

On another day, I was on busy Oxford Street when I found myself again with the need to pee. Selfridges was right there, so I went in and asked directions to the men's room. It was on a quiet top floor, and as I approached the door, a handsome young guy, Hispanic looking, casually dressed, was coming out. I caught a flirtatious eye, but proceeded in to find a toilet stall. After a moment I heard the outside door open. Someone entered, and because of the silence that followed, I assumed he went to the urinal. Then I heard a cough right outside my stall. Finishing my business, I came out to see the same guy waiting for me. The signals were clear. As I washed my hands we exchanged a few words—he was American!—and in short order took a stall together and closed the door.

After a quickie not difficult to imagine we came out and started talking in full sentences. He was from San Francisco, named Carlos, twenty-eight, living in London for nearly four years. I was invited to his flat in Earls Court, where he lived with two gay flatmates. I spent the night with Carlos, calling Janice Langer to say I'd ran into American friends and would be back in North Acton the following afternoon.

It was never a boyfriend thing between Carlos and me, but that we met at all was, well…you might say, "meant to be". Because as luck did have it, the offer of a room to rent came almost immediately; one of the flatmates was about to move out. I jumped at the timely opportunity. There was no reason to hesitate. Everything happened seamlessly. I was introduced to Carlos's other roommate, the permanent one, whose name was Burt. On the day I met him, he was still nursing a hangover from the previous weekend's birthday celebration. Burt had just turned twenty-nine and said he was feeling old. He and Carlos had been roommate pals in New York for five years before deciding to come to London.

Within a week I gave notice to the Langers and moved into the basement flat. It was opposite Nevern Square on a street lined with red-brick row houses four floors tall. It might have been up-scale in its century-old day, but Earls Court generally was a bit run down, known more as a first stop for new arrivals exactly like myself. Not quite shabby; not dangerous, but worn. There were probably some beautiful light-filled flats in the floors upstairs, but we lived "downstairs"—five steep concrete steps down from the sidewalk in what were undoubtedly former servants' quarters. The front door next to the rubbish bins felt more like a back door. It opened onto a very small vestibule with a small bathroom to the left. Entry to the rest of the flat was through the kitchen, where there was a stove and sink on the right, fridge and dining table pushed against the left wall, seating for four.

Past the kitchen was a view down a long dark hallway. But to the immediate right was another door. This was Burt's bedroom, which was big enough to double comfortably as the communal living room. It had the flat's only window light angling down from the street. A tall bookshelf held a stereo and Carlos's record collection. Halfway down the hall on the right was Carlos's large bedroom. My room was at the far end where the hallway made a right turn leading to the flat's private toilet.

It was my first time living away from home. First time with roommates. My room came with a standing wardrobe and heavy dresser, and a single bed that was actually too soft. There was one dirty window high on the wall where I could see the shadows of trees in some back property to which we had no access, least of all a view. The room was always dark. At first I felt deliciously in hiding, fancying myself in the land of *Performance*, one of my favorite films, and I was Mick Jagger's Turner, holed up and decadent. This lasted less than a week until Carlos hinted that I better get serious about finding a job.

As an introduction to London, Earls Court could not have been a more telling indicator of what London actually *was* as opposed to the fairytale postcard most of the world had (certainly the one I grew up with) that was little more than a dozen iconic tourist sights and some tall, fuzzy hats. Now, I had little time for any of it.

Instead, I found a buzzing neighborhood where I heard English spoken with every possible international accent. Most of the local businesses, including the supermarket, the bakery, clothing shops and off-licenses (translation: liquor stores), indeed almost every street-level business was owned and staffed by non-white immigrants, mostly the aforementioned South Asians often slurred together derisively as "Pakis". They worked much longer hours than the traditional nine-to-six, half-day-Wednesday, closed-on-Sunday Brits, who deemed the immigrants' ceaseless work ethic as somehow not playing fair. The resentment was palpable. And not entirely undeserved. The third-world graspiness had come with them, and more than once money was literally taken from my hand by the supermarket cashier before I could even hand it over to pay.

Once I was doing three loads at the local launderette: jeans, whites and coloreds. When they were out of the dryer I laid everything on a counter to fold and pack. When I got back to the flat I realized that I'd left my five pairs of jeans behind—basically my whole wardrobe! I raced the several blocks back, expecting the worst. To my profound relief, all my jeans were still where I'd left them, unfolded on the counter. A good twenty-five minutes had elapsed. In Big City America, without standing guard, my clothes might have been taken damp from the dryer! But England's—and the immigrants'— basically honest character had prevailed.

Earls Court also had its own Tube station—above ground under a vaulting 1870s glass roof, as well as underground lines accessed down long, rattling, wooden escalators—so it was very easy to get around. I stopped by employment agencies all over Central London. Most I didn't even need to enter because they posted availabilities on cards in their windows. There seemed to be a lot of factory work outside the area. I had no specific job in mind, but I knew commuting to a factory wasn't an option.

As for the instant social life that came with meeting Carlos and Burt, it is of singular importance to mention that our Earls Court flat was a very convenient five blocks—almost straight line—to one of London's few openly gay pubs, the Coleherne. Far from a cozy, wood-paneled den, it was almost barn-like, with cream-colored walls, high ceilings and windows facing Old Brompton Road. The building (perhaps even the pub) dated back to 1866. All this *convenience* seemed to be another blessing that was meant to be. The Coleherne was literally our "local", and I soon found myself there as a beer-drinking regular.

On my first visit, though, I had to chuckle. Tight blue jeans and mustaches were in fashion (I wore a tightly cropped beard my entire time in London), and it wasn't just a gay thing. Half of America sported the urban cowboy look; gay guys just put more emphasis on the crotch. That was fine with me. But there was a sameness to the style which had obviously reached all the way to jolly old England, because I swore I saw the very same people swinging pints at the Coleherne that I'd seen just months before with bottles of Budweiser at The Stud in L.A. The *only* difference was the accents!

~

I found my job at Harrods by accident—except circumstances were compounding to prove that there *are* no accidents. Good luck happens just like bad luck: in the mental and emotional climate (call it *fertile ground*) conducive to the nurturing of each. OR you might say some things are just written in the stars. Either way, as set as I quickly was, I had to find work because my savings were dwindling fast.

I distinctly remember where fate intervened. It was in the scruffy upstairs office of an employment agency on Tottenham Court Road. I was standing in a crowded reception area waiting to talk with one of the men seated in a pit of desks cordoned off, courtroom style, behind a low barrier. All their conversations were audible, and at one moment I heard a man say into the phone:

"No, we don't have anymore Christmas placements for Harrods."

My ears rang.

*Harrod*s….

I vaguely recalled that my mother had mentioned Harrods when talking about where the Queen shopped. Beyond that, I knew nothing. But heeding the voice of intuition, I immediately left the employment office, found a red phone box with a directory, got Harrods' address and took the Tube to Knightsbridge Station. After a short two-block walk, there it was—unmissable!

Harrods, the massive department store, was the anchor of Knightsbridge itself, a massive mid-19th century fortress; six floors of ornate arches crowned with a central dome dominating an entire block of Brompton Road. Feeling as if there was no time to lose, I walked in, asked the first sales assistant I saw where I'd find the employment office, and was directed to the fifth floor.

As it turned out, Harrods *was* hiring for the Christmas season, and I was given an application form to fill out. My American accent prompted a request to see my passport; discovering I was a Kiwi ended doubts as to my work-qualifying bonafides. I was told to appear for new-employee orientation the following day—or maybe the day after. Suddenly, I was in a room full of new hires, all of them looking as relieved as I was, and just like that I had a job!

I was assigned to "Frosted Foods", which had to be explained. (I remember the lady's eye-rolling *typical Harrods* expression). It was the store's fancy name for frozen food, and the department was located in the Food Halls. I didn't know what those were, either. I'd seen no more of the store than the employment office. Turns out there were four Food Halls: Grocery (where Frosted Food, Dairy and the Charcuterie were situated), Produce (fresh fruits & veg), the Bakery, and a large Wine & Spirits department. I would soon discover that even calling Frosted Foods a "department" was a stretch. More accurately, it was a single wall of refrigerated shelves which one didn't *visit* as much as pass by it on a path between the greengrocers and the Perfumery, which was an entirely different world in itself.

Actually, the Perfumery was almost out of character with the rest of the store, most of which still had, if not original details (the store opened in 1849), then decades-old finishings that maintained its original character. But the Perfumery had been recently updated with glossy marble floors and a new ceiling with concealed lighting that gave everything and everybody a beautiful creamy glow—not unlike all the overly made-up women who worked behind its many cosmetic-laden counters.

By contrast, Frosted Foods was probably the least glamorous of all Harrods' over-three hundred departments. But I would soon learn its hidden blessings. First, just working in the Food Halls meant I wouldn't have to wear a suit and tie for the polished presentation required everywhere else. Instead, Food Hall employees were issued starched white overcoats, fresh each week, allowing me to wear jeans or any casual clothes underneath. That in itself was a huge saving.

But the real bonus was our fifty percent employee discount. That didn't extend store-wide, just to Frosted Food and the adjacent Dairy and Cheese departments, but by any measure it was generous. Not surprisingly, management eventually decided it was overly generous, and the fifty percent was cut to twenty-five. But the perks lasted long enough to learn about *and sample* many little luxuries I didn't even know existed. And thus my Harrods education began!

I'll start with butter. The Dairy Department not only included samplings from local regions all over United Kingdom, but French, Dutch, Swiss and Greek butters as well. No wonder my overloaded liver eventually revolted, and I suffered a brief but painful attack of gout.

And cream! I never knew there were so many kinds: sweet cream, double cream and the ultimate decadence, clotted cream, which I'd never heard of. Who knew that heating rich cow's milk until the cream clotted could exceed the pleasure of regular whipped cream? Clotted cream changed my life!

Just across the Dairy aisle was a gourmet's world of cheeses, beautifully (famously!) displayed hanging from high racks and in long refrigerated display shelves. The array of blue cheese, alone with names like Crowdie and Blue Murder, was a revelation. There were cheddars, Swiss, Limburger and Goudas from all over Europe; brie and Camembert from various regions in France. None of them were yet common on American shelves or even at Tesco, England's ubiquitous supermarket. But Harrods had them all and I acquired a whole new vocabulary that would last for a lifetime—thanks to my employee discount!

Frosted Foods' buyer, my boss, was a tall Scottish guy named David Taylor, whom we called Mr. Taylor. (Employees were either a Mister or Miss). He was probably only thirty, but as a ten-year veteran with upwardly mobile aspirations in the Harrods chain of command, he carried himself with a haughty swagger only enhanced wearing his position-appropriate tailcoat—yes, even in the Food Halls, buyers and managers wore dark tailcoats.

On my first day I was talking to him about one of our customers referring to her as "she". Mr. Taylor kept interrupting me. I'd go on talking about "her" and "she" and he'd interrupt me again. It took a third time before I understood that he was instructing me on decorum. Female customers were always "the Lady".

Got it.

Our department's routine included visits from a chirpy middle-age woman we called "Miss Birdseye", who was the brand's own rep. She came in weekly to stock our shelves with bags of frozen Birdseye fruits and vegetables, which were the most fast-moving staples. The rest of our stock came in on refrigerated lorries by way of the loading dock.

Behind Harrods' impressive Brompton Road front face, there was a delivery entrance around the back leading into a carve-out on the building's footprint where the loading docks were located. This was Harrods' backstage. It was (probably still is) a kind of indoor/outdoor space with a large vehicle entryway that was always open to the elements, surrounded on three irregular sides by the dark, rising walls of the building. A section of the vaulting roof was open to the sky, with the rest covered in grit-caked glass that gave only a suggestion of natural light. Outside of summer, it was usually cold there all day long and the regular crew were often bundled up in jackets and wool caps. From six in the morning until after closing at five (we opened to the public at nine), all the dock's noisy, sometimes raucous comings and goings happened in a kind of perpetual, dingy twilight.

Store access to the loading docks was through a discreet passage in the adjacent Produce Hall. There were five or six guys working under the watchful eye of a stocky, hyperactive manager named Sammy. He greeted everyone with a boisterous call of, "How's your ring, baby?" It was a few weeks before I realized he was referring to assholes.

Mr. Taylor quickly assigned me the task of retrieving our

frozen stock from the loading dock—heavy cases of ice cream, fish, meats and prepared meals, all delivered in large frost-covered cardboard boxes—and get them up to our big walk-in freezer on the first floor.

My usual loading dock dealings were with a very pleasant guy named Dermot. He was two years younger than me, shy, almost cat-like, with a wide face and big brown eyes that didn't reveal much. He spoke with the gentle brush of a Scottish accent, which I found totally endearing.

Our brief but semi-regular chats revealed that he'd been hired just a few months before me, and like me, seemed to have been randomly assigned to his position in the giant store. In Dermot's case, this was grievous mis-casting. He was completely out of character amidst the scrappy environment of the dock. He had a temperament more suited to the books department. But we connected as fellow travelers. Neither of us were in our dream jobs; for the moment it was all about experience and a paycheck (not necessarily in that order) before getting on with the business of one's future. In my case, that was yet to be decided. I had no idea what Dermot had in mind as *his* future.

Unfortunately, outside of the loading dock, our paths rarely crossed. His schedule, starting at six a.m., was three hours ahead of mine. Our breaks and lunch hours never coincided. Had that not been the case I can imagine we might have been quite good friends—possibly much more than good friends as time would eventually reveal. Suffice to say that under Sammy's ever-watchful eye there was no opportunity to chat at length or skive off generally—a skill, truth be told, I would master at Harrods.

Over time, however, my casual friendship with Dermot began to change. I began to sense a pleasant tension in our brief encounters. I caught him watching me from the corner of his eye. Then I started to see him more regularly, literally in passing, when he'd walk by our wall of freezer shelves going about his own in-store business. There were other routes he might have taken if he was heading up to the employee dining room, but our paths began to cross and he'd look at me shyly, perhaps a brief greeting, barely slowing his pace, continuing on his way. I didn't want to project too much because, for one, we were co-workers, which could become awkward. Mostly though, with Dermot it was out of sight, out of mind.

Anyway, I had in-store tasks of my own, and once I leaned back my two-wheel dolly-load of frost-covered boxes, my only thought was getting them upstairs before the frost turned to dripping water.

Frosted Food's storage freezer was strategically located on the floor above our wall of refrigerated shelves. A discrete door off the furniture department led to a very small office where, besides a small desk and two chairs (for quick skiving), there was the thick, insulated door with a push-spring handle one could open from both sides so it was impossible to become locked in. The freezer itself was actually huge, with rows of old wooden shelves that held cases of frozen merchandise. A floor plan would show it as the size of a small department, but walled off and windowless, it was completely invisible to the customers. Even among Harrods' employees, I'm sure almost no one knew it existed.

As a work environment, it was even more grim and poorly lit than the loading dock; a completely inhospitable world cold enough to require an insulated coat if one was going to spend any time there, but always a pair of heavy gloves. Without them, your fingers might get stuck to things. One's breath came out in clouds, and after a few minutes icicles formed on eyebrows, mustaches and beards. There was also a steel-lined spiral chute where, to quickly re-stock store shelves below, we could send things down to our tiny workroom on the ground floor. One day after work I slid down the chute head-first just to say I'd done it.

Every day, Harrods head chef would send a list of orders to Mr. Taylor—usually veggies, blocks of uncooked shrimp and ice cream in bucket-size containers—and it was my job (after my morning break) to retrieve them from our cold storage and take them up to the clamorous fourth floor kitchens. Here was another behind-the-scenes world within the world of Harrods, where numerous areas were laid out for prepping, cooking, baking and dishwashing, all bright under long skylights, white tiles and the sound of busy clatter. The kitchens were located adjacent to Harrods' rather grand, old-world dining room. It was the perfect setting for fine lunches and afternoon tea, but I only ever saw it peeking through service doors—the servants' point of view.

I quickly discovered that the kitchen had its own small dining room where beautifully made deserts, unfinished from the day before, were laid out for the kitchen staff to help themselves. Sometimes there were as many as eight or ten different offerings: cakes, pies, trifles and colorful fruit tarts. My favorite was a luxurious four-layer Black Forrest cake, moist and rich with chocolate and raspberries. In my first days, I approached this bounty with guilty trepidation, head down as I helped myself with a cup of tea to take my second break of the morning. But as I became a familiar face, this daily treat became routine, so much so that I became truly annoyed when my Black Forrest cake wasn't on the "menu". This was first-rate skiving—with benefits!

~

Life at the flat was inextricably linked to our nightlife at the Coleherne. With or without Burt and Carlos, I was there several nights a week. I'm sure everyone had sex on the brain, but the Coleherne wasn't just a pickup bar. That's not how English pubs work. Niche groups like the leather crowd gathered in private settings. Pubs were a *public* thing, and the Colenerne was a place for everyone. I only remember two times that I actually brought someone back to the flat for sex. Mainly, I just felt lucky that the most popular queer pub in London also happened to be our "local".

Near closing time (when Drink Up was called even *before* eleven p.m.!), I'd walk the easy path back to Nevern Square, make a cup of tea and either swoon tipsily to music in the communal living room/bedroom if no one was home, or retire to my room and journal myself to sleep. But many was the night—the best times—that we all sat around the kitchen table, everyone a little drunk, and just shot the shit over cups of tea. Burt and Carlos both had their New York stories. It was from them that I learned about the Anvil bar, the Rambles in Central Park, the trucks, the piers—all the cruisy hotspots.

I never felt comfortable with the freewheeling "sexual freedom" of the nineteen seventies. That said, discovering gay bathhouses (in L.A.) had actually been a revelation. They were so nondescript on the outside if you weren't looking, you might never notice them at all. But on the inside, besides being safer than public cruising, I found the thrill was as much about the secrecy as the sex. This was where I'd go if I ever killed the president. *They'll never find me here!*

For me, the baths were less a banquet for maximum consumption than a titillating fantasy world with sex on the side. Many gay guys in those days—even into the mid-80s before AIDS-prevention laws shut them down—going to the baths was their big night out; sex all night and into the next morning…every weekend! But God only knew whose dick or ass it was in the dark maze, steamy steam room, or on the other side of a glory hole. My two bouts of gonorrhea and being told I'd given someone crabs *right after we'd had sex* were warning enough. I stayed away from crowds. On the irregular times I did indulge, my "bath times" were the afternoon off-hours. I'd be leaving just as the night shift was lining up, faces bland, belying their excited anticipation.

After Last Call was announced at the Coleherne, I'd sometimes join a casual parade heading round the corner and downstairs to a literal underground club called Catacombs. It was cheap to get in, no alcohol served, but backed up with a good beer buzz, the disco dancing was loads of fun. One of my favorite songs was the swoony *"Love's Theme"*—music only, heavy on the violins. And of course, *"What's Goin' On?"* Marvin Gaye was everywhere.

When not dancing or roaming the arched alcoves along the back wall, I took my turn with the other lads, shoulder to shoulder at the urinal—an age-old English pass-time amongst queer folk that, besides after-hours dancing, was Catacombs' *other* main attraction.

You knew you'd have to wait your turn because everyone took their time. It was a nightly feast for the eyes—seeing and be seen. Once I found myself standing beside an older man—definitely not the typical habitué—who let dangle the biggest cock I'd ever seen. Not just long, it was thick as an arm and not even hard; just this big white piece of uncut salami, which was likely difficult to hide under any circumstance and undoubtedly the center of attention all his life.

But when I looked up I saw the resigned smile of a player who knew he'd always win. Just the sight of his great schlong had the power to amaze if not utterly enslave. Blessed or cursed, however, the sport of it was gone; perhaps even the hope of romance as love would be forever upstaged by the distraction of his enormous tool.

The kid to his right reached down to bounce it in his hand, then I took my turn sampling the monster's full, flaccid weight. The man leaned toward me and whispered with a working man's accent: "You won't forget this, laddie."

He was right. But I didn't envy him at all.

~

One day a visitor arrived at the flat—and never left. His name was Pavel, an American whose parents were (curiously enough) Czech. Pavel was an acquaintance of Carlos from their hometown of San Francisco. He was traveling *slowly* around Europe, and we became his latest resting spot. He was around my age, quite pleasant looking, of smaller frame with a very cheery nature, the kind that fitted in wherever he was. Before I knew it (certainly without consulting me) Carlos announced that Pavel was to fit in permanently. The plan was that he'd sleep, platonically, in Carlos's big double bed. Meanwhile, he joined us at The Coleherne and at after-times around the kitchen table. There was something so boyishly charming about him I didn't think of his presence as an intrusion. Then, within a week, Pavel met Joot, a very cute nineteen-year-old blonde boy from South Africa. They became instant lovers, and then he moved in too!

The *new* plan was that they'd sleep in the hall. A small mattress was acquired, and the two lovebirds made their nest past the door to Carlos's room further back towards mine. What made it all palatable at first (in a bohemian sort of way) was that Joot was a genuinely sweet kid and together he and Pavel made an adorable couple. Love was in bloom, and they were always happy. Carlos, Burt and I were happy to give them their space even if we had to walk around it going back and forth to the loo. The love-making that surely went on happened discreetly after hours when the rest of us had gone to bed.

Ironically, and in relatively short order, their presence became less awkward than mine. In a much more subtle—dare I say British—way, there emerged a class difference between me and my flatmates. An *immigration* class difference that had escaped me entirely at first.

Boiled down, I was in London legally. Burt and Carlos were not. They'd long over-stayed their tourist visas, but in any case, the only jobs they could get were under the table. Carlos worked in a tiny wren of a space in the bowls of Victoria Station, a record shop that fit no more than three people including Carlos, behind the counter. He didn't own the shop (I never knew who did), but as the sole employee it was his by proxy. Yes, he chose the albums they sold (which explained the flat's very good record collection), but he breathed bad air all day and never saw the sun. In terms of a future, those subterranean ant tunnels led nowhere. He was literally stuck in a hole. Burt worked for a telephone answering service, which even in L.A. was low-status employment. They had no savings to speak of. Neither of their jobs had benefits, advancement opportunities or many perks. Even buying a one-way ticket out of England—because they wouldn't be allowed back in—would likely mean arriving home penniless. Pushing thirty and feeling it, they were trapped.

Meanwhile, I came back with stories of Lady This and Princess That and the overall swell environment of Harrods, which I found colorful and interesting. Add the tasty Frosted Food Hall perks, which I also brought home and was happy to share, without realizing it, I was putting distance between me and my American friends.

Then there was an incident at our kitchen table.

One night during an infrequent communal dinner, Carlos said, "You don't have to do that."

"Do what?" I didn't know what he was referring to.

"You know," he said, nodding toward my plate.

"I don't know what you mean."

"Your knife and fork," Carlos said as Burt looked on with a superior smirk.

I still wasn't getting it.

"The way you hold them," he said.

Then I realized: I didn't use the switch-hands-with-the-fork American style of eating. *And this bothered them!* I even had the impression they'd discussed it privately, and finally needed to call me on my "airs".

"This is how I eat," I said, truly surprised. "I always have."

Suddenly the *issue* was theirs. They were making something out of nothing.

"Ah, okay," Carlos replied by way of an awkward half apology.

There wasn't much else they could say.

But it was one more little sign I didn't fit in.

Carlos was always more discreet about his sexual escapades. Apart from the occasional one-night fling (ours had immediately morphed into a business arrangement) he dreamed of having a steady boyfriend and, thanks to his constant contact with the public, he'd meet guys from time to time. He must have taken them as hopefuls, not rushing the sex, because the serious ones he talked about, he never brought home. Instead, they'd go on actual dates: a restaurant or the movies. But for some reason things never panned out.

Burt was the opposite. He worked hard and partied harder. Over bank holidays he'd take on thirty-six-hour shifts for the double-time pay. I admired the way he pushed through. But on party nights it was *bring on the vodka and stand back!* Mostly, though, Burt liked to get fucked. There were several regulars he brought home, all leather types in their late forties—the lean kind who took care of themselves and liked a younger admirer.

On several occasions as Carlos and I, sometimes Pavel and Joot, would be home from the pub, sitting around the kitchen table, when Burt would come in with his fuck buddy. They'd go straight through into Burt's room, close the door and in a short while you could hear them going at it. There was no secret, and we'd mostly stopped taking notice except to wink at the often not-so-quiet grunts and moans. A while later they'd come out, Burt would walk his friend up to the sidewalk, then come back, eyes twinkling with mischief, to either join us for a cup of tea or go back to bed to sleep it off. Either way, it was kind of business as usual. More power to him. The queer life. No blame.

Another incident also fell into the "queer life" category, but to me it ended up verging on creepy.

There was a very handsome young guy, maybe thirty, with long, wispy blonde hair who was a semi-regular at the Coleherne. Though he usually kept to himself, no doubt everyone had their eye on him. One night we started chatting, and he invited me to his flat. I was immediately impressed with the finished state of it: a bit "grandma" by California styles, but I chalked that up to being English. Nevertheless, the place suggested someone with taste and probably a good job—whatever it might be. We weren't there to talk about work.

Anyway, the evening started with a kiss, and soon to bed where the kissing continued. But these were no ordinary kisses. Not before or since, not even in love, have I ever known such a deliciously drowning sensation. Almost otherworldly, like connecting to another dimension. Later I wondered if he even knew the extraordinarily sensual feeling his kisses imparted. Was it just me, or something kindred to the mysterious gift of healing hands, *but the person didn't know he had the gift*. Either way, I'd never experienced anything like it.

The creepy part came a week later, sitting around the kitchen table, when mention of the cute blonde guy came up—we all knew which one. Before I could say anything, Burt exploded: "Oh, my God, I couldn't get enough of those kisses!"

I cringed.

What I thought I'd shared with such memorable intimacy—as private as a kiss—was apparently a gift available to all. Suddenly, it was like I'd been kissing Burt; not something I would *ever* want to do! My sweet memory went sour. But I wasn't wrong about those kisses.

On another night, Carlos had a visitor. His name was Ron, a straight-guy friend of a friend he knew from San Francisco who was passing through London as he backpacked around Europe. Carlos invited him for dinner, and I helped with hosting duties. To be extra sociable, Carlos added a rare treat: marijuana. When he started to roll a joint, Ron looked on quietly aghast. I knew just what he was thinking. In England, I'd already discovered, they mixed tobacco with their pot! As a Californian it was positively sacrilege!

Purchasing "drugs" occasionally (speaking, now, only about marijuana and hashish—just enough for a special night out), I discovered that it was all a bigger deal—a much darker deal—than it was in the States. On the West Coast, at least, smoking pot, however illegal, was nevertheless part of the culture. It came from Mexico (practically local!), and you could buy it anywhere—cheap. In Europe, it was neither as affordable nor easy to come by—and highly *illegal*. Even a pinch could land you in jail. The product itself came from Turkey and Afghanistan, which meant that one was truly connecting to the "international drug trade" and all its dangerous connotations. An entirely different vibe than hippie tripping and the counterculture.

As for Ron, there was a kind of harmless naivety about him. Carlos and I both chuckled when he said "go to the can" for toilet, and used phrases like "do Dubrovnik" referencing his travels. Even to us, he seemed very American. Carlos *didn't* mention that he and his flatmates were gay. None of us were "obvious". We assumed Ron thought we were straight. No reason to mention any of it. He was only coming for dinner.

Then Burt came home from the Coleherne with his fuck buddy. They were in very good spirits, which added fun to the introductions. Ron rose to the occasion, saying he should join us next time he was in town as he'd never been to a real English pub. *Sure!* we said in polite agreement. After those pleasantries, Burt and his pal excused themselves and retired to the other room. Carlos and I exchanged glances. Things were about to get awkward.

In no time the grunting and groaning started. There was no ignoring it; no talking over the obvious sounds of two guys fucking their brains out right next door. If there'd been a cat in the bag before, it was completely outed now.

Time dragged on excruciatingly as we all waited for the big finish. While I fussed with a fresh pot of tea, Carlos scrambled together another joint and we all groped in vain for normal conversation. But words were totally beside the point. Our poor captive audience had only two options: walk out in disgust or grin and bear it. To his credit, Ron weathered the embarrassing storm until Burt and his friend reappeared. They walked through the kitchen, smiling sheepishly, and went up to the street to say their goodbyes. This time Burt didn't come back.

As far as our hosting duties were concerned, the evening was over. Ron made pleasantries, something about seeing us again on his way back through London. Was there any doubt we'd never see him again?

Pavel was the bigger problem. He had a remarkable disregard for boundaries. Perhaps we should have seen it immediately when he brought Joot home not a week after Pavel himself moved in. He was seemingly blind to the possibility that he (or he and Joot) might be an imposition. I don't even think it was willful disregard on Pavel's part; he was just profoundly self-centered. I couldn't say anything; he was Carlos's friend, and Carlos was top dog. But Pavel would just appropriate other people's things: food from the fridge or clean underwear from our dresser drawers, even our toothbrushes! He never cleaned his dishes, but left them in the sink "to soak". Joot did his laundry when their dirty clothes piled up on the floor by their bed. I came home once and realized Pavel had gone into my room and rifled through all my personal things. When I called him on it, dumbstruck with the gall as much as I was pissed off, he said he'd been looking for a book of poetry I'd showed him several days earlier.

"Then ask me!" I said. "You don't just go through people's stuff!"

"Well, it's the flat," he replied as if to say we're all family, so we share.

"No, Pavel. *It's my stuff!*"

A confused silence followed. I really don't think he got it.

And so I learned: inconsiderate people don't know they're being inconsiderate because...*they're inconsiderate!*

~

Harrods was more than a department store, it was its long history of devoted employees and equally devoted clientele. Over time, I had numerous regular customers, usually older "ladies", who would sometimes request that I help them personally. Our offerings were a world beyond American-style frozen dinners, and my customers oo'd and aah'd over the many unusual delectables. Frosted Foods offered a variety of boil-in-a-bag ready meals: Duckling l'Orange, Coco Vin, Lobster Bisque. Or desserts like profiteroles (from Italy) and rich ice cream from several countries. I sometimes helped plan an entire meal of frozen items for a small, hastily-arranged dinner party. I could endorse everything because they were treats at my own table—often shared with my flatmates thanks again to my employee discount.

For local customers who lived on the small streets behind Harrods—Walton Street and Cadogan Square, where the nineteenth century apartment buildings had their own discrete red brick grandeur in an architectural style called Pont Street Dutch—the Food Halls were their go-to supermarket. Strange to think of just popping into Harrods for a pint of milk, but for some it was just that way. Many had titles which I would see when I stamped their credit cards with a hand press onto carbon-copied paper.

Others came "up from the country" as a biweekly routine. Occasionally, I would help them out with their many bags of groceries, putting them in the boot of a beautiful Rolls Royce. From these sorts I would hear about their new "deep freeze", and at first I didn't know what they were talking about. Americans had had freezers for years, either built into a regular fridge or the top-opening kind kept in the garage. But apparently, big home freezers were a whole new concept...like color TVs...*oh, my God!* Was it true that England was still catching up after the war? For my older customers I suppose some of them were. Many had been shopping at Harrods all their lives, literally for generations, "from the cradle to the grave" as the store once advertised.

Harrods was the personification of England herself, a museum of cultural history, fortress of the upper class. In the old days, a working-class person would simply never enter Harrods unless they were employees. In not-so-distant times the entire store would remain open after business hours so a royal could do their Christmas shopping—as Queen Elizabeth and the Queen Mother did before and after the war—in exclusive privacy.

But times were changing. I saw Princess Ann on several occasions browsing casually in the Perfumery, a bodyguard hovering discreetly. The Duchess of Kent, wife of Prince Edward, made an announced visit that caused momentary excitement. When she and her retinue breezed by without stopping (to browse the frozen food?), Mr. Taylor took personal umbrage.

Royalty of a different stripe was also not uncommon. I hadn't been at Harrods for a week, still finding my way around four sprawling floors (and the rest), when I saw Rod Stewart shopping for color TVs. He stood back, eyeing a wall of the latest models, then pointed grandly—this one, that one, and *that* one—as the dutiful sales assistant took notes. My co-worker, Mr. Carter, told me one day that had I taken one step back, I would have trod on the toes of Jacquie Onassis. I once watched Mick Jagger walk right to left the full length of our frosty shelves, followed at a distance by his own burly security minder. It rattled me for the rest of the day.

Pop fame also came one step removed when a very sexy young guy, always in noticeably bulging jeans, came in from time to time. He'd rest his huge package, along with his groceries, on my crotch-high cash register table practically begging me to check the merchandise. Then paid with an Elton John credit card.

~

With the Coleherne so near I had a readily accessible sex life if I wanted it. Mostly, I didn't. I certainly enjoyed hanging with the boys, having a few pints of bitter, some minor flirting. But if Carlos and the guys were out I loved having the flat to myself to read, write and listen to music. Burt was happy going out getting drunk and screwing around. But Carlos went out with a mission. He was looking for a boyfriend.

One night he brought home a Dutch tourist named Pieter. He was lean, mid-twenties and handsome in a bookish way, with dark hair and intense dark eyes. Being Dutch, he spoke perfect English with a pleasing accent.

I was in the kitchen when they came in, so we all sat down for a cup of tea. I had *Naked Lunch* open on the table, which I'd found on the bookshelf in the living room. I was slowly plodding through the pages of block print waiting for the point. But the book caught Pieter's attention. He was familiar with Burroughs; likened his writing to abstract art that was beyond liking or disliking, but to appreciate for its cultural timing and conceptual audacity. This sparked a conversation about art in general which quickly left Carols on the periphery. Then Burt came home (alone), and the night became a social one, not a sexual one. If this bothered

Carlos, he didn't let on. But when Burt retired, so did Carlos. Pieter and I were getting on, so he stuck around. He was the first person with whom I'd had an intelligent conversation in months. Also, I found him very attractive. He asked if I'd like to go for a walk, and though it was nearly midnight, I had the following day off, so I agreed. I put on my duffel coat and we ventured out.

Pieter was better-read than I was, and our conversation ventured in all sorts of literary and philosophical directions. He'd been in London two days already, he said, walking all day and into the night excited to explore the city's historic nooks and crannies. We spent that first long night together walking, brisk-paced, all over central London. He had a dog-eared map, so we just rambled, not afraid of getting lost. It was with Pieter that I first saw Tower Bridge. All lit up and its leaves raised for nighttime river traffic, the two towers had the slightly grim feel of a nineteenth century prison not unlike Wormwood Scrubs. To my surprise, Pieter told me that Tower Bridge was built in the early twentieth century. We had a smoke, sitting close together on the wide steps of St. Paul's Cathedral. As the night wore on we found ourselves in Notting Hill Gate, which the map said would head us back the quickest way to Earls Court.

Notting Hill was a charming neighborhood with numerous squares surrounded by white-columned row houses. It had a casual air with gently winding streets that inclined on the hill for which it was named. One narrow road, described as a Walk on the map, had high brick walls on either side that led directly into Holland Park. It must have been a back entrance because at the distant end of the unlit path we could see the park's main gate. Between were a line of trees to our left, adding deeper shadows along the Eastside wall. It didn't take long before we realized that the shadows were alive. There were men there, more than several, standing solo or in close couplings. Quite by accident we'd stumbled upon a gay cruising spot!

But by this time I was walking arm-in-arm with Pieter, already falling in love.

We didn't have sex that night. Pieter wanted to get back

to his hotel. Instead, we said a chaste good night near the locked gate to Nevern Square, just across from the flat, and Pieter went his way.

The next day it became clear that my pairing off with Pieter had rubbed Carlos the wrong way. He'd found him first (though he didn't put it quite that way), so presumed priority even if (though *I* didn't say) it seemed clear they had little in common. Either way, it was a touchy situation. When Pieter came over the next day Carlos was at work, but we didn't feel right "going behind Carlos' back" and having sex in the flat. But no matter the circumstances, it was love—for me at least. I'd never fallen for anyone so quickly or so hard.

Before Pieter's departure the following day, and with a long bank holiday coming up, we made plans that I would visit him in his hometown of Nijmegen. Carlos wasn't pleased. At first I assumed he was jealous, which I could understand. Then I realized his moody silence was more than that. Our pairing had left him feeling abandoned and lonely.

As arranged, I bought my ticket for the boat-train trek across the English Channel to Holland. On the eve of my departure, I called Pieter's number to say I was on my way. A young man answered the phone.

"May I speak to Pieter?"

He asked who I was. He said his name was Hank, Peter's flatmate. I explained the plans we'd made.

"Is he there?"

There was a long silence. "Pieter is in the hospital."

"Hospital! What happened?"

I heard Hank groping for the most careful words.

"He's suffered a mental breakdown."

This came totally out of nowhere.

"But we made plans," I said, thinking only of myself. "He's expecting me!"

More careful silence. Finally, the story came out. Pieter's visit to London had been ill-advised. His family saw the signs of a looming mental episode even before he departed: the restlessness; listening to Carl Orff's *Carmina Burana* over and over, which even I knew was the soundtrack of madness. It wasn't the first time, Hank said. They'd all tried in vain to stop Pieter from traveling. By the time he returned to Holland, he suffered a complete collapse. Pieter was manic-depressive. He heard voices. He was off his medication.

I couldn't believe what I was hearing!

"I'd still like to come," I said, but my heart was already beginning to break.

Considering all this, I began to connect the dots. The dogged trekking was not a tourist's curiosity, but demon-driven, compulsive walking. He'd told me he had trouble sleeping. I wonder if he slept at all. Our time together was but a respite from the voices, which were gradually taking over when he was left alone. I'd misread everything!

Love, however, would not be deterred. When I finally arrived in Nijmegen after a train ride from Amsterdam, it was nighttime. Hank met me at the station and I was put up in a chilly enclosed porch, which doubled as a guest bedroom. I said I'd visit Pieter the next day in hospital, if that was all I could do.

"He'll probably see you, but he won't be well," Hank said.

After that, everything was anti-climatic.

When I did see Pieter he was lucid, smiling weakly, but extremely subdued from medication. I met his parents in the hospital room where they were helping gather his things. They were kind and appreciative that I'd come so far to see their son. I went with them to their home. I kept looking for signs that his family life was at cause, somehow crazy-making. There were no such signs. His parents were gentle people living in tidy, seemingly normal circumstances. They seemed as helpless as I was to explain what was happening and were clearly worn down. Their only son had had psychotic breaks since early adolescence.

I slept with Pieter in his large bed, but cuddling was all we could muster before he dropped off quickly into sedated sleep. Neither of us were in any shape to perform.

I left the next day, one day earlier than planned. Everyone said their comforting goodbyes as I boarded the train to back to Amsterdam. Hank had kindly arranged a place for me to stay with a friend of his there. He was very good-looking, and under different circumstances, I would have jumped at his (albeit shy) invitation to share his bed. But I was done, wrung out. All I could do was walk the beautiful streets of Amsterdam, licking my wounds until it was time to catch the ferry back to England.

~

What stays with me today, more than all of the romantic might-have-beens (and the fact that Pieter and I never did have sex), is the brief but powerful impressions I had of Holland in general and the city of Amsterdam in particular, even what little of it I saw. I found the Dutch relaxed and pleasing to look at, like the Californians of Europe. It didn't hurt that most everyone I encountered spoke perfect English. Yet they were very un-English compared to the always stand-on-ceremony Brits. That alone was refreshing.

But there was more. There was something about Amsterdam itself that touched me very deeply. I found the city uncannily *familiar,* almost as if I was remembering it at some deep level. The city's look and feel, its *ambience* ...there remains no question in my mind that I'd been part of that beautiful city in another time, maybe several lifetimes, all of which were filled with music.

As a seven-year-old in *this* life, I used to conduct a slope of ivy in our garden as if it was an orchestra. I'd never been to a symphony or any kind of theater performance. But I *had* been listening to Swan Lake on my parents' hi-fi. Somehow I knew a conductor's gestures, my place on an imaginary podium waving directions to the players left and right. I am sure these were the echoes of past lifetimes, ones I'd lived in Amsterdam. It was the same when, decades later, I visited Vienna, another city known for its vibrant musical history. I felt what I can only describe as a similar kind of—not quite memory, but a soul-deep familiarity.

I'll add here a related "bleed-through" incident that took me completely by surprise. This time in Italy. A sepia dusk was settling over Venice, which I was visiting for the first time. The Grand Canal was a breath-taking panorama. I felt a visceral sense of wonder at the spectacle of it. Imagined how, centuries ago, sailors from villages as time-stopped and isolated as the one I visited in the Czechoslovakia, might have been utterly dazzled by the Grand Canal—the wealth of Venice to engineer such beauty. It was no less dazzling in the distant present day.

One evening, after being presented with an entire pizza for dinner then scolded by the restaurant's owner for barely eating a third of it, I was led by my hosts through a winding maze of narrow streets when we were suddenly in the enormous Piazza San Marco. There were people everywhere, but my eyes were instantly drawn to Saint Mark's Basilica. Its incredible facade, built in the eighth century, was all lit up. *And I burst into tears!*

Without exaggeration, I can say that I had the distinct feeling I'd been recognized by the Basilica itself. It knew me, identified me in the crowd and touched a lost memory we nonetheless shared. It happened again the following night, and then I knew I wasn't just waxing sentimental. Indeed, that feeling, *coming out of nowhere* as they say (but I think not), had emotional validity as personal and undeniable—and as impossible to prove—as a dream.

~

When I got back to London, Carlos dropped the bomb. He and Burt had decided it was time for me to move on. I'm sure that my "stealing" Pieter was the final straw after all the little incongruencies, but the reason was put, not unkindly, in a more general way. We weren't a good fit, Carlos said, and he was right. There had been no fights; everyone (except Pavel) had kept up their end of the bargain. Our differences were more about lifestyle than anything else, but through it all we'd had some good laughs. Kindred spirits we were not, however. I took "the boot" as positive impetus to find my real niche in London.

I started picking up the Evening Standard every night at Knightsbridge tube station, which I perused on the ride home from work. The *Flat Share* ads were plentiful, and when I got home I made a lot of calls. Mostly, I was too late. Many were further out than I preferred. First priority was to be within striking distance from work, but also the Coleherne, which, at that point, was my only social life. (I had *no* idea what was to come!)

After a week of dedicated scrounging (sometimes making calls from our department phone if Mr. Taylor wasn't around), I finally connected with one cheery-sounding girl whose bright, sing-song accent I couldn't quite place. Her name was Gracie, and she said I could come by that evening to see the room and meet "everyone". The flat was on Wandsworth Bridge Road, not far from the east end of Kings Road and the 22 bus line, which would take me directly to Knightsbridge. Location-wise, it was perfect.

I raced back to Earls Court to freshen up, then back on the Tube for a quick two stops to Fulham Broadway. A ten-minute walk and I found myself on a broad, tree-lined street leading directly to the actual Wandsworth Bridge a quarter mile down. Surprisingly, it wasn't a busy thoroughfare, nor did it seem particularly residential. There certainly wasn't anything quaint or charming about it. In terms of character, it had almost none. There were very few shops or storefronts. Mainly, the buildings were old, three-story row houses all flush to the sidewalk; no gardens. The only adornment was some minimal century-old architectural flourishes around the wide red-brick windows of the two upper floors. The number I was looking for was no more than a plain door. I rang the bell and waited until a pleasant young woman answered. She was about my age, with prominent cheekbones and shy brown eyes. Her straight brown hair was cropped sharply at her jawline.

"Are you Terry?"

"That's me," I said. "Are you Gracie?"

"No, I'm Tess. You're right on time."

"Early bird gets the worm, or so I've found flat hunting."

"Welcome," she said, stepping back to let me in. She wasn't tall, nor thin, though it was hard to tell under her bulky blue pullover. But her creamy English skin glowed. (Did I sense it flushed?)

"Any trouble finding us?" she asked, scanning me discretely from head to toe.

"No, no. Just a stone's throw from Earls Court."

Looking quickly around, I clocked the word blue carpet, bare white walls and stairway leading to the upper floors.

"Well, come through," Tess said. "We're all in the sitting room."

Judge and jury time, I thought as I followed her along a short hallway to the left of the stairs. Both were covered in worn blue carpet. The walls could have done with a fresh coat of paint. The hallway led down a few steps toward a closed door. I could hear voices which stopped abruptly when we entered. More bare white walls and blue carpet in what was clearly a communal sitting room. I saw a small kitchen behind the two people standing before me. One was a bright-smiling girl about my own age who stepped forward immediately.

"You must be Terry. Welcome!" she said.

"And you must be Gracie. I recognize your voice."

"It's a Welsh accent," she said. "Glad to meet you."

But for her accent, she could have been a California girl, with a scarf entwined in her wild blonde hair and a long, colorful print blouse.

Standing back was the second person, a handsome man in his very late thirties, twitchy and proper in a grey plaid, three-piece suit. He was assessing me with a cool expression. After a long pause, he turned toward an older woman—back straight, hair severely coifed—who was seated at a small dining table in the corner behind the door. I hadn't seen her when I came in.

"I'd say we're glad, too, wouldn't you, Francesca?"

I guessed she was in her late forties, maybe early fifties, slightly horsey-looking in the way of British aristocracy, wearing what I now knew (thanks to Harrods) was a Chanel suit—dark navy with a large bow falling at the neck.

"More *relieved*, darling," the woman said with a very

posh tone. She was inspecting me with the same cool eyes as the gentleman.

"But I think you're right."

Tess exploded with exasperation. "Oh, for God's sake, Colin! He just walked in!"

Indeed, we had not been introduced, but Colin and *the Lady* seemed to have come to some kind of snap judgment already.

Tess stepped forward. "Terry, this is Colin. He's the landlord."

"Emphasis on *lord*," said a new voice.

I turned around to see yet another person I hadn't seen, a regular-looking guy, probably mid-twenties, lean with bushy blonde hair, sprawled on the sofa against the wall behind me. He sprung to his feet to shake my hand.

"I'm Finn," he said forcefully. "And *these* are Colin and the Baroness Francesca." He was clearly making the point that they *hadn't* introduced themselves, which Colin picked up on immediately.

"Yes, of course, Terry. I'm *so* sorry," he said, reaching for my hand to shake it vigorously. "I'm Colin and this is my girlfriend, Francesca." Then, as if to dismiss Finn, Colin added: "Don't mind Finn, Terry. We don't go by titles around here."

"Not like the good old days, eh, Colin?" Finn shot back.

Colin just rolled his eyes. Francesca spoke up without getting up. "How do you do, Terry? And yes, it's true I'm a Baroness, but please call me Francesca."

"Hello," I said, my head spinning but feeling less stranded now that formalities were out of the way.

Colin spoke again: "Tess, Gracie and Finn are the tenants here. I think you'll all get along famously."

"Colin, they need to vote," Francesca intoned quietly.

"*Thank you*," said Tess, still trying to manage things.

Then it was Finn again: "Tess is house mistress, Terry," he said, flopping back on the sofa. "We do what she says, and Colin does what Francesca says."

"Finn, that's enough, *really*," said Tess with a nervous laugh.

"Pay him no mind, Terry," Colin said. "Finn's an artist,

which he seems to think gives him a world of liberties."

"That's right. I don't look back."

"Like Bob Dylan," I said.

Finn brightened, victorious. "See that, Colin? Terry knows his lyrics! He has my vote already!"

"And he's American," said Gracie, apropos of almost nothing as she, too, seemed wishing to tamp down Finn.

"Yes, I am. New Zealand born but officially American," I replied. "From Los Angeles. Hollywood, to be exact."

"Are you an actor?" It was Francesca asking.

"Oh, no, I'm a…" I paused.

I was no longer feeling claim to anything. No one had asked me *what I did* since my life-changing debacle in Prague. And as I couldn't claim *filmmaker* anymore, I said: "I'm a writer—an aspiring one, at least."

"Ahh, a*spiring!*" Finn exclaimed. "Then you'll fit right in here. We all want to be something we're not, don't we, Colin?"

"Finn, *please* behave," Tess pleaded, stifling a giggle.

He flopped back down onto the couch.

"Would you like to see the room?" Gracie said quickly.

"Yes, the room!" Tess exclaimed.

Colin caught the drift. "Of course; the room! It's…" He pointed vaguely upstairs.

I chuckled. They all seemed to be on *very* familiar terms.

Colin was about to hand me off to Tess when Francesca spoke up.

"You look familiar, Terry," she said.

The room went silent.

That Francesca should find me in any way "familiar" seemed completely off target—especially to Colin.

"Darling, I doubt Terry moves in your…"

"No, I'm sure of it," Francesca said, studying me over her Gucci glasses.

I thought for a moment, then took an educated guess.

"Maybe Harrods? I work at Harrods."

"HARRODS!" she shrieked, rolling her r's with an enthusiasm I wasn't expecting. "Of course! You see, Colin, I'm not just a pretty face!"

Finn laughed out loud at this, jumping up to address

Francesca. "Which does remind me, old girl. I was hoping…"

"Yes, I know, I know," she said, rising from the table. She was much taller than I expected. "It's time we talked…ABOUT ME!" She trilled another high note laugh.

"It's about the…," Finn began.

Francesca waved him off: "Say no more, darling. Come out to the garden and we'll…"

She took her plain black Gucci handbag and Finn followed her through the kitchen where there was a back door leading outside.

Colin called after them. "We've got dinner, Francesca, don't forget."

"I know, darling; won't be a minute!"

I must have looked puzzled, because Tess said quietly: "He's painting Francesca's portrait. His studio's on the top floor."

"One of Francesca's strays," Colin said. "She's become a patron of starving artists, God help me. When the top room came available a year ago and Finn appeared…well, he couldn't be denied."

"He's actually very good," said Gracie.

"Granted," Colin conceded. "But as you see, there's a price to pay."

"It's the getting down to it that's torment," added Tess.

I caught a quick but pointed glance between her and Gracie as if Tess had just said something out of turn. For a long moment, no one said a word.

I broke the silence with an "Ahh…"

Tess didn't miss a beat: "Yes, the room! You haven't seen the room!"

"Oh, good Lord," said Colin. "Where *are* our manners?"

"It's the fall of the Empire as Finn would say," said Gracie.

Colin balked: "Oh, God, don't you start, too. You should all be wrapped around *my* fingers," he said. "I'm the bloody landlord."

"You can't win, Colin," Tess replied, then turned to me. "Come on, Terry, I'll show you upstairs."

We headed back to the entry hall then Tess led the way upstairs to the first landing.

"Bathroom and toilet here," she said. "We all share, so please be considerate."

I had the feeling my tenancy was already assumed.

We walked up another short flight to a second small landing and a door on the right.

"This is your room facing the back. The two big rooms are further up on the street side," she said, indicating the stairway that continued up.

"So, who shares what?" I asked.

"I share with Gracie on the first floor. Finn's above us. The light's great up there, but he mostly keeps the curtains closed. He put those in himself."

"So, there's a proper studio?"

"Oh, yes. It's his own world. But don't expect an invitation. We moved in the same time he did—that was almost a year ago—vacancies back to back. Colin was frantic. I don't think Finn would have been his ideal choice, but Francesca...well, as Colin said, she's become a patron of young artists."

"She seems to have a soft spot for Finn," I said.

"She does, but he doesn't make it easy—for Colin, either, poor dear."

"What's Colin's soft spot?"

"Besides Francesca? Property investment...this is just one. He has two others, including a building in Chelsea. Big plans for that, by the sound of it but...well, not here obviously," she added dryly. She was right. The whole place needed some *real* paint instead of the cheap white dusting that barely covered the worn state of things. The blue carpet was literally threadbare on the stairs.

"Anyway, this is your room," she said and opened the door.

It was raw, to be sure: the same white walls and blue carpet as everywhere else, but even at a glance I was relieved. The bed was to the right behind the open door: a single box spring and mattress on the floor. There was a bulky armoire in the left corner. It faced a writing desk and chair on the opposite wall by the tall window. Between them a five-drawer dresser and what was once a fireplace. Its long-sealed opening was framed by a wide mantelpiece with original, ornate moulding that extended across and down each side to the floor.

I went over to the window and saw Finn and Francesca caught in light from the kitchen. They were standing in what they'd referred to as a garden, but it was really just an unadorned concrete patio. There was a solid wooden gate in the old brick wall at the back of the "garden". Behind it, a long alley ran behind all the street-facing properties. I saw Francesca hand Finn something from her purse, which went straight into his pocket. I turned back to Tess.

"It's perfect."

"Great! Colin will be so relieved."

"Fourteen pounds a week?"

"Due every four weeks. I handle all that for Colin, so pay me and he comes to collect."

"So, Colin doesn't live here—just to be clear."

"God, no," Tess replied with a laugh. "This is *so* beneath him. He has a big flat in Shepards Bush—another of his properties. He's ambitious, I'll say that about Colin."

"And Francesca?"

"Very old money. I don't know if she *does* anything. But she knows a good horse even if Colin isn't a thoroughbred. They're actually a lot of fun. Don't be put off by the posh accent."

I chuckled. "I hear it every day at work."

"Oh, that's right—Harrods! That was a point in your favor, Terry, to be sure."

"Is Francesca really a royal?"

"I don't know if being a Baroness is royalty per se. I'm not sure how all that works. But her father's the fifth or sixth Baron of something. The family's so old they're simply above the fray."

"So, Colin isn't...?"

"Royalty? Hardly. Deep down he's just a regular bloke...as Finn constantly reminds him."

"Almost an odd fit."

Tess laughed. "Who's to say about couples? Not me. I'm a social worker."

I chuckled, but it *was* a bit of revealing news. Tess was a smart girl. I liked her immediately.

As we wound our way back downstairs I asked about Finn. Tess had alluded to something which they'd clearly wanted to skip over. She stopped at the first landing, speaking quietly.

"Finn's complicated," she began, "Fragile as glass under the bravado. It took us months to get the full picture. I might not even be interested if I weren't a psychologist—but I am, and it's interesting. Anyway, you'll get to know him yourself. He's English but was raised in Toronto, which explains the mid-Atlantic accent. Very wealthy family, but by the sound of it his father's just plain cruel. Hates that Finn won't go into the family business—even worse, that he wants to be an *artist* of all things."

"So he's an actual working artist?"

"Yes, portraits—when he gets commissions like Francesca's. Meanwhile, instead of supporting Finn in lean times, which his father could do in a stroke, the old bastard teases him with money. Makes Finn beg for it, and Finn hates himself for begging."

"Christ," I said. "That's a full plate."

"He paces at night, berating himself. You probably wouldn't hear it down here, but we have, and it's a little frightening—not a selling point for would-be tenants, which is what that little moment was about downstairs."

"And Gracie?"

"She's a dear friend. Wants to be an actress, but works at a theater doing their publicity. Getting in on the ground floor, you might say. I keep telling her it's like anything: you just have to stick at it."

When we returned to the sitting room I took a second look around. The long couch to the left of the door was nearly as worn as the carpet. A wood coffee table had permanent rings. There was an old television in a built-in bookshelf on the opposite wall. The kitchen, open to the sitting room through an arched doorway, was small but seemed bigger because of its outside access. The place was clean, and the people weren't crazy. Mainly, I was keen to be in an environment that revolved around more than sex and the pub; to be with people who weren't stuck. I knew this was going to be home—for the time being, at least.

Just as I settled on the couch, Finn and Francesca came in from the garden.

"Not even a peek, darling?" Francesca was saying.

"Not yet, my love. I'm changing the background colors; they'll bring out the blue of your eyes."

I caught Colin's quick *Oh, brother* look.

"Isn't it exciting?" Francesca went on. "Maybe Finn can do your portrait next, Colin."

"That's a good idea, Francesca," Finn replied. "I'll give him a new brain."

Even Colin laughed at this.

"Just don't make Francesca's eyes so they follow you around," he said. "The manor house is positively creepy that way. I don't like people watching when I sleep."

Francesca laughed. "That rules me out, darling; you know I sleep with a mask."

Finn flopped down beside me on the sofa. "Finish me now, oh, Lord," he whispered.

Colin looked at his watch. "We really have to get going."

"Yes, darling. Now, who is it we're meeting this time?"

"Koreans," Colin said, as if that said it all.

"Good Lord," Francesca replied, sitting back down at the dining table, taking a compact mirror out of her purse to check her lipstick.

"Sounds interesting to me," said Tess.

"And we'll be eating with chopsticks," Francesca pronounced.

Colin sighed heavily as he gathered their coats off the chair. "Last month it was Arabs." "Or were those the South Asians?" asked Francesca. "At one meeting we had to eat with our fingers; do you remember that, Colin? Truly, the lengths we go to in the name of global warming."

"I think you mean *globalization*, darling," said Colin.

"Well, whatever it is, *Poor old England* is all I can say.

We can't seem to make it on our own anymore. Daddy's ready to shoot himself every time he opens a newspaper. He says it was his generation that saw the best of things."

"Must have been nice to rule the world," said Finn.

"And now, even here!" Francesca exclaimed, gesturing in my direction, "It's *bring on the Americans*!"

"In our very own parlor, imagine that," said Tess.

Colin was starting to twitch. "We really must go, darling."

But Francesca wasn't finished.

"It's not like the old days. People looked up to us!"

"Francesca, you weren't even born in the old days," said Gracie.

She laughed ruefully. "Thank you, darling, I'll take *that* as a compliment. But a weekend with Daddy will convince you the old days never died. Why, there may not even *be* a manor house by the time I'm an aging baroness. They'll have done away with us!"

"Unthinkable," said Finn.

"*Well, it is!*" Francesca shrieked in full soprano, taking her coat from Colin. "My family is over two hundred years old! Now, what with the Koreans and the global warming…"

"*Globalization!*" we all said in unison.

"Who will I be, I ask you?"

There was a moment of silence until Gracie answered: "Just people?"

Francesca shot her a look. "Stupid girl."

Finn laughed out loud.

Colin jumped in quickly. "Well, that's it, then! We're off!"

He steered Francesca to the door, turning to me as they walked out.

"Welcome aboard, Terry. You can see Tess for all the…you know…flat things. She's head prefect around here."

"Thank you," I said, relieved for a definitive settling of matters even if there was no formal vote taking.

"*Head prefect*, Collin? Really?" said Tess, following them out. "Boarding school is over."

"Don't be so sure," trilled Francesca from the hallway. "He may never get over it!"

Then we heard the front door closed behind them.

"Oh, my God," Gracie exclaimed with a laugh once the elders had departed.

Finn slapped me on the shoulder. "You're in the deep end now, old son."

"How about a cup of tea?" Tess offered.

"I think we need it," Gracie replied.

"Not me, lasses," said Finn. "All this business is cutting into my pub time."

He stood to leave then stopped, turning to me.

"But, Terry, I did have one question."

"Anything."

"It's about your place of employment," he said with a thoughtful pause. "Which department?"

"I'm in the Food Halls. Frosted Food."

He considered that for a moment.

"So we can assume the whole Harrodian banquet: veg, meat *and* desserts?"

"Oh, yes," I replied, catching on. "And everything in between. There's little potted shrimps in butter. I have them on toast for a late-night snack. And ice cream cakes, pastries…"

Finn was all ears.

"Look at him," said Gracie. "He's positively *drooling*!"

"Even more to the point, my good man," Finn continued. "I assume there's an employee discount for this bounty?"

"Finn!" Tess exclaimed from the kitchen. "Manners, please!"

I laughed. That generous fifty percent discount had become an appreciated perk with Burt and Carlos, too.

"Allow me to surprise you."

"Do that, Terry, and the pints are on me," Finn replied.

"Fair enough."

"Well, I'm off."

"No time for a cuppa, then," Tess asked dryly as she carried in a tray with only three cups.

"Thanks, luv," Finn said, patting his pants pocket. "I've got some deposit money to quench my tortured soul." Then Finn turned to me, offering his hand. "Welcome again, old man. The girls will set you right."

And with that, he was out the door. I heard some hurried footsteps going up the stairs, presumably to fetch a coat against the cold night air, then back down a minute later when the front door slammed shut.

~

The move out of Earls Court was quick, painless and unsentimental. My belongings packed into the same two suitcases with which I'd arrived. I was hanging up clothes in my new wardrobe when there was a knock at the door. It was Finn. He said Tess and Gracie had cooked up a snack and made a pot of tea if I'd like to come down and join them. When I arrived a few minutes later Tess was laying out toasted squares of oven-baked creamed corn on a serving plate.

Gracie was saying: "You haven't even started?" She sounded incredulous.

"Lots of sketches," Finn replied. "She sat twice for those. Now I'm doodling, which is a good sign."

"Really, Finn?" Tess asked. "Doodling?"

"It's my process."

Tess just laughed.

"So that business about changing the background?" Gracie asked.

"I lied," said Finn, waving me over to join him on the couch.

Tess poured me a cup of tea.

"Help yourself to the snacks," she said. "Finn was just talking about…"

"Let me guess: Francesca."

"Talk to a woman about the color of her eyes and suddenly it's all they want to hear."

"Finn, you really are shameless."

"Come on, Gracie; you know you're all suckers for a compliment!"

"Oh, thank you very much," she replied. "I'll remind myself not to be grateful next time you say something nice."

Finn turned to me. "What do you say, Terry? What does a compliment cost, after all? Nothing!"

"That's a pretty stingy way to be generous," I replied.

Finn laughed. "Well, it got us off the subject of delivery time, didn't it?"

"All right," I said. "I'll take the bait. How *is* the portrait of Francesca coming?"

Finn looked at me, almost offended. "Not you, too!"

"He never wants to talk about it," Tess said, sitting down to join us.

"Obviously," said Gracie.

"If you must know, I'm having painter's block."

"There's no such thing," replied Tess.

"Maybe there is," I said. "Writers have blocks. I'm not sure photographers do, but…"

"You're a photographer?" Gracie said.

I stopped, lost for words again.

"Aspiring," I replied half apologetically.

This much was true. I loved photography as much as I loved writing, but I'd all but abandoned my camera; it was too tied up with filmmaking, and *that* was still very tender ground. I felt no more claim saying I was a photographer than I did claiming I was a writer.

But Finn couldn't let it go.

"That means you're a writer *and* a photographer?"

"I can do both, but…yeah, aspiring."

"My point is, as an artist, *too*, you can feel my pain."

We all groaned in unison. Tess laughed, heading back to the kitchen for table napkins. "Or maybe misery just loves company," she said over her shoulder.

"Wait, *I'm* not miserable!" I called out.

Finn turned to me with a sigh. "Tess is our in-house therapist, Terry. To her, we're all just neurotic specimens."

"*Functioning* neurotic specimens," Tess corrected, tossing a small stack of paper napkins on the table. "Just like most everyone. It's the non-functioning part that concerns us, Finn. Whatever's going on up there," she said, pointing toward the ceiling, "is entirely unhealthy."

Finn didn't reply, but took a gulp of his tea.

Then Gracie piled on. "You know we can hear you pacing."

He turned a dark gaze to her. Something had suddenly tipped too far. I caught the nervous glance between the girls; remembered what Tess had told me about Finn being complicated.

Then he softened. "Let's not sour things so soon, dear ladies," nodding my way. "Now that we're all getting along so nicely."

"Well, it's true, *dear Finn*," Gracie replied. Apparently, she and Tess were both ready to bring *something* out in the open. "All the back and forth, cursing at yourself."

"I appreciate your concern," Finn said coldly.

"We worry Finn, that's all we're saying," said Tess. "We actually do care about you."

"But the pacing scares me," Gracie said.

"I'll wear slippers," Finn snapped.

"Really, Finn, we don't even like to bring it up, but...."

"*Then don't!*" Finn shouted.

In the awkward moment that followed he reached for the teapot, but it was empty.

"I'll put some more water on," Tess said, taking the pot.

After a long silence, Finn said: "You walk in my slippers for a night, and then we'll talk."

But Tess wasn't having it, calling again from the kitchen. "That '*Pity the starving artist*' line doesn't work either, Finn."

"Alright, I admit I'm not starving. *So just give me pity!*"

Even Finn chuckled at his own words.

"I mean, she's a fucking Baroness, right? She has all the time in the world."

"But Francesca's also a friend," said Tess. "No need to try her patience."

"Francesca's a posh cow," Finn said, then turned to me in confidence. "We Brits are big on farm animals, Terry. It's best you know that early on."

Gracie chuckled. "Finn, that's so unkind."

At that point I dared to chime in: "Well, I *liked* Francesca."

"I do, too!" Finn said. "She's...she's..." He groped for the word.

"She's authentic," I said.

"Exactly," said Finn. "She can't help being one of her father's bloody portraits come to life."

Tess brought in the refilled the teapot. "Are you waiting to be inspired? Is that the problem?"

"Not exactly. It's the choices." More than Finn's words, it was his thoughtful tone that caught my attention. "Painters are guns for hire just like the rest of us. Payment for services is required. That much I accept. But I'm not a factory. I'm not a *designer*. How does one go *about* a portrait? From what angle, what starting point? The problem is everything inspires me. Everything distracts me. The world is too wondrous! And amidst all that... Picasso was right, inspiration has to find you working. You can't go *looking!*"

I didn't know Finn at all, but I could tell he was talking from the heart. By Tess and Gracie's expression I also sensed they were being made privy to uncommon revelations. Here was another side of their friend, which not only suggested his genuine commitment as an artist but also how the relentless poking at people—his prickliness—was really protection. He was guarding his heart.

Finn reached for the teapot and refilled his cup, but he didn't drink.

"What I could really use is a pint."

Yes, it was time to change the channel. I turned to Gracie.

"Tess tells me you're an actor."

"Oh, yes, she is!" said Finn, jumping back in, his snark refreshed. "Gracie's in the out-of-work actor business. I think it's going well."

"Finn, be nice," Tess said, trying to hide a chuckle.

I turned to Gracie: "So, you're aspiring, *too*," I said, hoping to soften what was teetering on unkind.

"Yes, *aspiring*," Finn replied too loudly, slapping my knee. "Now, you've got it!"

"Should I ask if you've been in a play lately?"

"Probably not," Gracie replied, hoping she didn't sound defeated. "It's been about nine months...not including auditions."

"But at least you work *in* a theater," Tess said.

Gracie looked at me and explained: "I work in the press office."

"Which gives her first chance *at* those auditions," Tess added quickly, sticking up for her friend.

"Yes, that was the original idea."

"So," I said in the awkward pause that followed, ever looking for the glass half full. "We have a little of everything here: a painter, an actress and a shrink."

"It's not official yet," Tess said. "I have another year of aspiring to do as a clinical intern before I can get my social worker license."

"Well, more power to you all." I said. "I'm officially a failed student, so I can't claim to be much of anything at all."

"You work at Harrods," Finn said. "God's work."

I chuckled. "It'll do for now."

"Just like the rest of us," Tess said. "All things being equal."

She settled her steady brown eyes on me. I looked back, holding her gaze.

Finn broke the moment of silence: "You see, Terry, we need Tess to keep our heads on straight... in case you were wondering."

"Actually, no, I wasn't," I replied, turning back to Tess. "Everything seems surprisingly clear."

WINTER

"I always knew I'd have to be pushed under someone's nose for them to see me," Tess said at one point early on. And that's sort of how it worked out, though the "push" was mutual and almost inexorably in each other's direction.

We hadn't taken the plunge yet; we were "taking it slow". But our bonding was accelerated because we *did* live under the same roof. It started with casual dinners at the flat—I'd bring home something from Harrods and asked if she'd join me. Then, when we realized the clinic where she was working part time for her internship was a stone's throw from Harrods, we started meeting for lunch at a busy Knightsbridge sandwich shop that catered to the local workforce. Our conversation never flagged, and we were both surprised how quickly we were starting to know each other—and *feel* for each other. Just the seeming coincidence of how we met had a meant-to-be quality, too on-purpose to ignore. I said it was a past life thing. Tess wasn't so sure; she was more of a realist. But neither of us could deny the connection. We embraced it.

Of course, I didn't mention my attraction to men. How do you bring *that* up? Perhaps she intuited something or sensed it in my manner. At one point, I got the sense she and Gracie might have wondered. But it hardly seemed to matter or dissuade us whatsoever. We both knew there was something real going on. My "old life" in Earls Court was quickly being replaced with the "real life" I always knew was waiting for me.

~

Christmas began early at Harrods, but with so many Americans living in London, the store was only too happy to include Thanksgiving as a jumpstart to the season. The Food

Halls stocked plenty of cranberries—fresh in the Produce department, canned in Grocery. Frosted Food had them frozen, along with whole turkeys that sold out early. Mr. Taylor might have doubled his order, but he really didn't understand what Thanksgiving was all about. On the Wednesday before actual Thanksgiving Day, traditionally the last Thursday of November, there were so many well-heeled Yanks at Harrods it was almost understandable—though embarrassingly lamentable—when I overheard one American girl ask if the English celebrated Thanksgiving, too?

But one seasonal phenomenon that knew no cultural bounds was winter itself. London was cold, sometime arctic cold, and it was often wet and dreary. Dusk came at four o'clock, so it was dark when I walked out of the employee entrance on Basil Street heading for the dusty-smelling warmth of the Tube. In the heat of summer, it was the last place you'd want to be, but in winter even the Underground was a respite.

With the cold came winter wardrobes, and Harrods' wealthy customers put on a show. I'd never seen so many spectacular fur coats in my life—especially on the Italians. Add the pricey kid gloves and thousand-pound knee-high boots, and there was no question that this was how the other half actually *did* live.

From a fashion perspective, England's masses were a pretty dreary lot. America in general took *casual* to a new low. All of my school clothes growing up came from J.C. Penny's or Sears. In temperate Southern California I had had no exposure to the world of seasonal styles, least of all a vocabulary in designer brands. Levis, Lee and Hang Ten were the extent of my label awareness.

That all changed at Harrods. I began to understand the fuss about fashion, and particularly the difference between fashion and style. It wasn't just about status symbol brands which anyone with money could buy; it was also about beautifully made garments and how they could define one's personal persona. Designer names began to appear on the outside of clothes for the very first time. Christian Dior had a coat entirely embroidered with its ornate CD signature, which I thought verged on crass. Gucci evolved from its simple green and red stripe to announcing "Gucci" on the outside of its handbags. Hermes went from its discrete gold stirrup to putting Hs on everything. Crass or not, the trend caught on—permanently.

I'll never forget one statuesque German woman in her late thirties who came in regularly. One afternoon I saw her walking on the streets of Knightsbridge wearing a billowing overcoat whose deep purple color was so voluptuous, so lux and worn so dramatically that she literally turned heads. In this case no outside label was needed. For those in the know—and I was learning!—purple was Valentino's color that season and it was his to own, tantamount to a signature. On the few women wealthy and confident enough to wear such extravagant luxury *and make it look easy*, the effect could be breathtaking.

But high fashion didn't have to be showy. Harrods clientele were out shopping, not hitting the red carpet. The best-dressed of them were decidedly understated. This was a lesson, too. By contrast, I once saw a gruff, thick-necked man whom I heard speaking Russian, expensively dressed but no less thug-like, leading his plump wife and three plump daughters around the store. They (all the ladies) were dressed head to toe in their new Chanel purchases, except it looked like they were in costume. The clothes were wearing them as truly as the expression was ever meant to mean.

I also learned about style from Gracie. She had it in spades, creating her own *self*-styled look. Living on a shoestring as we all were, she had an eye for one-off items she'd find at tucked-away shops on the Kings Road, or the Portobello flea market, which she often visited on Saturdays. She'd bring home a little jacket, a scarf, blouse or broach, none of them "designer", then put them all together with original flair. Her wardrobe was literally bulging with interesting clothes and I rarely saw her wear the same thing twice. This rubbed off on me and I started wearing scarves, bracelets, sometimes an Italian beret (the French ones are too floppy) to accent my nascent London look.

Harrods had its trendy side, too, with the store-within-the-store called Way In. It had its own elevator, with music to set the stage, going directly from ground level to the fourth floor. (It was in that elevator I first I heard snippets from Joni Mitchell's then-latest "Hissing of Summer Lawns" album, which would become the soundtrack for my time in London.) The Way In was dark and hip and a world away from the staid Ladies and Gentlemen's departments downstairs. It was there I became familiar with the French designer Daniel Hechter, whose style, I decided, suited my own fashion aspirations. There was a particular jacket I pined over, but even with my employee discount it was way out of range.

The discount did make all the difference at sale time, however, and browsing regularly, I often had first pick. Some items came with an added discount if I let the cheeky Aussie tailor's hands linger as he fitted a pair of trousers in the Way In's private dressing room. Over time I would glean from a rolled eye or quiet chuckle that even some straight employees had their limits challenged, deciding how far to let the tailor go, knowing a generous price slashing was literally up for grabs.

~

About ten cold and rainy days before Christmas, I arrived home to see a yellow Jaguar XKE parked in front of our address. The sleek, low, two-seater was rare enough in London, but parked on Wandsworth Bridge Road, never. I glanced at it over my shoulder as I dug for my keys, juggling my green and white Harrods Food Halls shopping bag from one hand to the other. Once inside, I heard the sounds of lively conversation coming from the sitting room. When I entered, Finn and Gracie were having wine with someone I hadn't met. A new face. In fact, it was *The Face*. I couldn't believe my eyes.

"Terry, this is Sebastian," Gracie said as I put my bag on the dining table, barely able to keep my eyes off the visitor. Gracie's sly smile matched Finn's, who was sprawled in his usual spot on the couch. They were both looking at me expectantly, waiting for my reaction.

"Yes, it is," I replied, sounding oddly unsure.

Actually, I was speechless.

Of course, I knew *who* he was. Everyone in London—maybe all of England—would have recognized him if not by name then certainly by his unusually handsome face and truly remarkable opal eyes. He/they were suddenly everywhere: from magazines to ten times life-size on Tube station walls. Sebastian was advertising's "new direction", its first dark-skinned supermodel—though not *too* dark. He was a Londoner of West Indian (Jamaican) extraction. England was finally acknowledging its multicultural demographic (or more accurately their buying power), albeit with an exception so off the charts that the press had coined him *The Face*.

Yes, I knew *who* he was. But...*what was he doing in our sitting room?*

My reaction must have been pretty funny because when I looked back at Gracie and Finn, they both burst out laughing. *Yup, that's him*, they seemed to be saying.

I knew some basic facts because all the fashion mags were doing blurbs. Sebastian was twenty-nine, a Gemini, six foot one and one-half inches tall not including the halo of tight black curls falling low on his forehead and just below his ears. Trim and fit at just over thirteen stone (about 185 lbs.), he had cheekbones that rose high and wide under mocha-colored skin. What made the stories more interesting, indeed surprising—more than just about a pretty face—were the reports of Sebastian's business acumen. Defying stereotypes, he seemed to have clever entrepreneurial fingers in a variety of business pies, the most recent being the launching of his own modeling agency favoring "people of color". He was a trail-blazer and everyone wanted to know more.

But every story, every reaction, started and ended with Sebastian's startling green/aqua eyes. When he smiled—which he was now doing *right at me* with a wide mouthful of pearly white teeth—I was left literally speechless. I'd never been face to face with anyone of such exceptional beauty, and the up-close of it was like nothing I'd experienced.

"Harrods!" were Sebastian's first words. He eyed the bag on the table behind me. "I love that store."

"Terry works there," Gracie said. (Did I detect a note of pride?)

"In the Food Halls," added Finn, jumping up to take the bag into the kitchen. "Let's see what we've got today."

"Just cheese," I said. "Nothing glamorous."

"Sure it is," said Sebastian, extending his hand. "It's Harrods. And you work there. Nice to meet you, Terry."

"You too," I replied, still at a loss for words.

"So, I guess you're wondering…." Gracie began.

"*Yes, I am!*" I exploded, unable to contain the suspense any longer. "You were on the 22 bus I took to get here. I mean, your picture was on the side of it."

"Yeah, that. It's a new campaign."

"And a good one, I guess. It got *my* attention."

"Just bringin' home the bacon," he replied with what could only be false modesty.

His accent was of a Jamaican East Ender, and, like the whole package it was a perfect blend of influences. But those eyes! The more one looked, more was revealed. Amidst the bright Caribbean azure, they were flecked with hazel, green and gold. And no, it wasn't a trick of advertising photography, I realized.

Yet, there he was, settling himself on a chair opposite our ratty couch where I took a seat beside Finn, still staring dumbly.

Finally, Gracie broke the spell to explain things.

"Sebastian bought the building next door to the theater where I work. I knew there was construction going on, but now he's moved in we've been running into each other."

"And Sister here was about to get caught in the rain, so I offered her a lift," said Sebastian.

"Wasn't that nice of him?" Gracie said.

"Right neighborly," Finn called out between the clatter of cups and plates. He was all ears, listening from the kitchen.

"And on the ride over," Gracie continued, "Sebastian was telling me that he's putting a restaurant in the big ground floor space below the new offices upstairs. They've already started work and..." She looked at Sebastian excitedly, letting him finish.

"And Gracie told me about Finn, because I'm looking for an artist to do my portrait for the dining room."

"And guess what the restaurant's going to be called?" Finn shouted out from the kitchen.

"*Sebastian's*?" I ventured. It didn't take a genius.

"No, *Sebastian*, singular." He made a just-so gesture with both hands.

"Isn't that perfect?" Gracie said, sounding almost giddy.

"What else could I call it?" said Sebastian, laughing.

"Think of it, Terry. First dinner, then the theater—right next door!"

"Or a late dinner at *Sebastian* after the theater," Sebastian countered. "Which might be cooler."

Gracie nodded enthusiastically. "Yes, that's it! Late dinners are definitely cooler."

Oh, my God, she was smitten already. I had a feeling Finn was probably smitten, too, especially if there was a job in the offing. Just one look at The Face and you almost felt dreams *can* come true.

Sebastian continued: "And since Gracie's already doing press for the theater, why not combine forces and bring her in to do PR for the restaurant?"

"A mighty force, indeed," said Finn, bringing in a serving plate with three cheeses: my favorite brie, a ripe blue cheese from Scotland and a slice of Italian cheddar.

"Sorry, the crackers are from Tesco," Finn joked. "I guess Harrods doesn't have the frozen kind."

"There's no such thing as frozen crackers!" Gracie laughed. Then to Sebastian: "Don't mind Finn, he's always joking."

Finn darted back to the kitchen and fetched a wine glass for me.

Then apropos of nothing, Gracie suddenly blurted out, "Terry's a photographer!"

Before I could even protest, Sebastian turned, studying me. "Is that so," he said. It wasn't a question.

Finn poured more wine and raised his glass. "I say we make a toast."

"Yes!" Gracie said, "To us!"

We all raised our glasses. None of us could take our eyes off Sebastian.

~

When I wasn't taking my second break of the morning in the kitchen-staff dining room, or keeping our shelves stocked with items sent down the chute from the deep freeze, half my job was ringing up customers. In the days before computers, bar codes and ubiquitous security cameras, we rang up purchases pushing number buttons on either of our department's two bulky cash registers. I learned to add up columns of numbers at a glance and give change the way cashiers these days seem incapable of doing without automatic calculators thinking for them. But there was never a time when our end-of-day numbers balanced—ever. I'm sure these unbalanced accounts rarely happened (or would even be tolerated) anywhere outside the Food Halls. But with its many small items, sometimes bag-loads of them, the weighing of things in cheese and produce…well, mistakes were made…regularly.

My favorite customer was a dear little lady named Dolly. She came in every Friday morning, small, frail, with straggly white hair and watery eyes, to shop for groceries. Dolly was one of many long-retired employees who still shopped at Harrods because the company extended employee discounts to them. Rain or shine, she wore an old blue overcoat, threadbare at the turned-back sleeves, and ankle-high old lady shoes. She told me proudly that she'd worked at Harrods for forty-five years. Even if she had to wait, she'd queue at my counter so we could have a little chat while I rang up her items.

"Don't forget me discount," she'd always say with her delightful Cockney accent, looking up with a twinkle.

Players were for the working class, and if you smoked "classy" Rothmans, therein lay an opportunity to look down upon those who didn't. Someone tried this game on me, a Players smoker at the time, but I didn't catch the slight. By the look on his face (waiting for the thrown pie to land), my complete non-reaction was almost disorienting. When I realized I was meant to have been put in my place, I just laughed.

Another example: I was never entirely sure of the terms "tea" or "tea time". For working-class people, "tea" seemed to mean the evening meal, separate from just having "a cuppa", which one might have any time and was indeed the elixir for all that ailed. But outside the working-class vernacular, having tea seemed to mean doing just that: sharing time over a cup of tea.

I once made overtures to a young man I'd just met who still lived at home. When I suggested we have tea, I realized he thought I was inviting myself over for dinner to meet his family! I knew at that moment we were, dare I say, of different classes. In terms of education and relative financial and cultural backgrounds, we probably were. It was all summed by the use of one word.

Similarly, "toilet" v. "loo" v. "bathroom" seemed to be parsed along cultural lines. I always said, "go to the loo", which undoubtedly rang some kind of class bell. You had to be born into the colloquiums. England thrived on these nuances, the little one-upmanships.

For some, like the old soldiers and an elder statesman I encountered regularly at Harrods, these little power plays were all they had left. The "bright young things" of *my* generation were casual to a glaring fault. We were too familiar, which in old world terms meant we didn't know our place. When corrected, they bristled. I was once sternly reprimanded by Mr. Taylor for being a little too cheeky to one customer, but the lady's imperiousness was really from another time.

Another regular customer I always enjoyed seeing was an elderly lady, tall, lean and elegant, who in winter wore a an Burberry trench coat over a simple Hardy Amies dress

Because besides her entitled discount, she quickly caught on that I always knocked off an extra fifty percent. It was our little secret. At Christmas she snuck me a five-pound note. I tucked it back in the pocket of her coat when she wasn't looking. There were other old pensioners, too; retired Harrodians to whom the posh-speaking top management gave gold watches (they actually did that) after an entire working life in service. The old world was alive and well, I was discovering.

Even after the 1960s cultural sea change, most young working-class men and women still had limited options. And so it had been for all the generations before. Things ran smoothly as long as "upstairs" and "downstairs" knew their place. And nothing signified one's "place" (even job prospects) more than one's accent.

All this was perpetuated, indeed shored up, in England's best prep schools and universities: Eton, Oxford, Cambridge and the like. But there was another place where the English language was also lovingly incubated and that was at Harrods.

It was there I came to appreciate *language*—not to mention the surprising hint of my childhood Kiwi accent re-emerging. I also discovered the different approach to the English versus American *use* of language.

For Americans, it was a way to get from A to B. I'd never considered language as anything else. But the well-spoken British—even the clever Cockney—used their native tongue as a musician does an instrument, *playing* vocabulary for its expression, tone, phasing and above all humor. I was always impressed with Queen Elizabeth's compliment, on the passing of Sir Winston Churchill, that he was, among other things, a master of the English language. In England that mattered. No one can sidle an insult, at least in English, better than an Englishman.

But class distinction exerted itself in other ways, Something as mundane as which cigarettes one smo marked a peg on the social rung. In America, one's b was simply a matter of taste, no better or worse choosing a favorite flavor of ice cream. But in En and Gucci shoes. She came in on a walker, gripping its aluminum rails with dated diamond clusters on her long, manicured fingers.

When she first asked for assistance, I was just on my way up for my morning break and didn't want to be bothered. But clearly the lady needed help. Very soon she started asking for "the American chap" every time she came in. If I was busy at the register, she'd ask Mr. Taylor, who would wave in a replacement so I could help the lady as she browsed the shelves.

To my surprise, we became friendly almost immediately, mainly, I think, because I was refreshingly (for Harrods) unservile. Her sharp, bossy bark, typical of some upper-class ladies, softened to easy banter. I asked how long she'd been shopping at Harrods, and she laughed. "My *parent*s shopped at Harrods! I grew up here! All my school clothes were from the girls' shop upstairs!"

One day I asked about the walker, how fortunate it was that she still managed to get around. "I have help," she said, explaining there was a car and driver outside.

"But I like to be as independent as possible. I was always so active," she said of an era that would vanish with her passing. "We danced and danced between the wars. You would have been so amused."

As Christmas drew near, the number of shoppers grew denser every day. Harrods could actually be a madhouse, especially in the Food Halls, where "staid" was thankfully not the byword it was in most every other department. Sometimes there was such a crush we had to squeeze between customers just to stock the shelves. Entire families would come in to do their Holiday shopping. Once I heard a posh-accented lady shriek over the din to her little four-year-old: "*How dare you sit on the floor!*"

The little guy had just collapsed amidst the mayhem.

~

One day, perhaps two weeks before Christmas, I arrived

home exhausted and found the whole gang in the sitting room with Sebastian in their midst. Finn was in his usual place on the couch. Gracie and Sebastian had brought two chairs from the dining table over to the coffee table and were seated side by side leaning over papers spread out before them. I was almost as surprised to see Sebastian as I was the first time, but now there were no more than some casual "Hi, Terrys", so I just rolled with what seemed to be the suddenly new normal.

Tess was in the kitchen, standing at the sink with her back to the sitting room. I went in to say hello, pressing up behind her. We were playing four hand dishwasher when I heard Gracie ask:

"Why are you cutting celebrity names in favor of people nobody's heard of?"

"Business before pleasure, luv, every time," Sebastian replied cryptically.

"Yes, of course," Gracie demurred.

She was learning on the job, but clearly taking things quite seriously.

Tess, who had been following along before I arrived, turned her head and whispered in my ear: "I don't like him."

This came as a complete surprise, and I leaned around to look at her.

I don't, she mouthed.

She'd already remarked to me in private about the speed with which Gracie and Finn had been brought into Sebastian's orbit. It was true. Suddenly, Gracie was on the phone more than ever, talking quietly—presumably with Sebastian. Several times when I got home, she pointed to the ceiling to indicate that Sebastian was upstairs with Finn. We assumed they'd started work on the portrait. Gracie kept saying it all made sense.

Tess's were the only discouraging words, but going from wariness to "not liking" seemed a leap. I looked at her questioningly. She just nodded. There was nothing more we could say right then.

"I'm making tea for me. Get yourself a wine glass and go sit down," she said. "We'll talk later."

I took a glass from the cupboard and headed back to the

sitting room.

"Good day at the office?" Finn asked as I gestured for him to pull his feet up. I dropped down on the couch beside him.

"Christmas at Harrods," I replied. "You don't want to know."

Sebastian, sitting opposite, poured wine into my glass. "You're on the list," he said.

I wasn't sure what he meant.

"For Sebastian's New Year's Eve party," Gracie said, pointing to what looked like lists of names on the table before them.

"There's a party?" I asked.

"At Sebastian's new restaurant."

Sebastian nodded. "It's still under construction, but that'll be the fun of it."

"We're all guests of the host," Finn said, sounding impressed.

"Great! Thanks, Sebastian."

"My pleasure, mate." He raised his glass in my direction. "Here's to you, Terry. A good year to come."

I marveled again at those remarkable eyes. He was staring at me, and I could barely look away. His gaze was like radar locking in on a target.

"It's going to be so cool," Gracie said, which broke the private moment.

Sebastian continued as if nothing had happened. But let me tell you, something had. When someone as startlingly handsome and famous as he is looks you right in the eye, you feel it.

"And that's the problem, in'it?" Sebastian continued. "Everyone in town wants to come. It's getting too big!"

"Oh, come on," I said with an exaggerated groan. "Isn't that what you want…really?"

Gracie gave me a pointed look.

Sebastian chucked. "Right you are, Terry. And I suppose it *is* my fault. The payoff after managing my career since I was twelve years old."

"How's that?" Finn asked, surprised. "You weren't

modeling at twelve, were you?"

"Actually, I was. That's when it all started."

"Didn't you need a manager at that young age?"

I was pushing back against Sebastian's force field, but Gracie's glare said I was being impertinent.

Sebastian took the high road.

"I'm talking about understanding the business, Terry; learning what's required, how the world ticks. That's gotta come early or the managers, when they *do* come, will just rip you off. No one rips me off," he concluded with chilling finality.

Gracie seemed impressed. "And people think models are..." She stopped in mid-flow.

Sebastian laughed. "You were going to say 'dumb', right?"

Gracie hesitated, scrambling for a save. "Some people might say that," she said carefully.

Sebastian laughed again with that big, toothy smile, his remarkable eyes dancing.

"They do indeed, my luv, but they don't say that about me. I do things different. That's why I liked your idea about Finn doing a portrait for the restaurant. I've got loads of photos, but no one's ever done a painting."

"And we thought Gracie was just a dumb actress," Finn said—tactlessly, I thought.

"Oy!" said Tess, coming in with a mug of tea in hand. "That's my friend you're talking about!" She pulled a third chair over from the dining table and joined the circle.

"Anyway," Gracie said, "you can't compare what I do with what Sebastian does."

"Hold on," Sebastian said. "There's a lot of similarities."

Gracie scoffed. "Like what? I bet you weren't still getting pimples at twenty-one."

"You've got pluck, lass," said Sebastian. "And that's what success takes. That's why I think there's a place for you in my organization."

Then he turned the spotlight my way.

"What about you, Terry? Retail's not the only game in town. I remember Gracie said you're a photographer."

Yes, she had, though I guess I hadn't drawn the whole picture: I'd hardly taken a shot since I'd been in London. There was still film in the camera I shot in Prague.

"Don't get his hopes up," Tess said.

I laughed. "What hopes? I'm only here because my hope ran out!"

"Now, there's where you're wrong, mate," Sebastian said, almost pouncing. "*No matter how dirty the water is, you can always pour clean water into it.* That's what me mum always said. There's always a new door. Finding it is what life's all about."

"He won't work for free."

I looked at Tess. Now she was my manager?

Sebastian darted a cool eye in her direction, but only for an instant. Then he turned back to me. "I'm sure we'll find something," he said, holding my gaze again, giving me a wink.

This time I had to look away. I hoped I hadn't blushed. Tess was sipping her tea; the others, their wine. I hoped they hadn't caught the moment.

But where was all this going?

I had no agenda. Suddenly Sebastian was dangling bait, staring at me as if he knew my weaknesses. If it was a job he was offering, I was ready to listen. If it was something else, I certainly didn't want to advertise my curiosity.

"Anyway," Sebastian continued, "There's room for everyone, that's my motto. I look at life like a giant dance floor. Everyone makes room. The more the merrier."

"Except you want to own the dancehall," said Gracie.

Sebastian laughed, this time a little uncomfortably. "All right, that's probably true. You're catching on fast, Gracie. Are you sure acting is your true calling? I think you underestimate yourself."

She sighed. "My father said any job that isn't giving you berth in six months isn't worth the candle."

But Tess wasn't giving up. "Gracie, you *love* acting."

Now, she was almost insisting.

Gracie turned to her. "Maybe I love a lot of things if it's all the same to you," she said.

They were the strongest words I'd ever heard between them. Even Finn reacted. Tess rolled her eyes.

"I'm going up," she said, rising. Then to me: "You're welcome to join me."

"Actually...," I began.

"Suit yourself," she replied before I said another word. "Have a good night, you lot."

She gave me one last look and left.

Sebastian jumped in, seizing the moment.

"Don't hide your light, Gracie. You too, Terry."

"How about another bottle?" said Finn, getting up and going into the kitchen.

"Experience is like building blocks," Sebastian continued. "But in the early days we don't always know what kind of place we're building."

"I know what you mean," I said. "I was so sure of what I thought I wanted, then the whole house of cards collapsed."

"But what an opportunity!" Sebastian exclaimed. "What did you do?" he asked rhetorically. "What *do* you do when all hope is gone? I'll tell you what: You pick yourself up and keep going! The days unfold. You live and learn. I've been building and rebuilding for twenty years."

"You said you were twelve when you started," said Finn, returning with the wine.

"That's when I started modeling. But I was about nine or ten when I started growing up.

Had to. Me mum got caught up with a sweet talker, and before you know it, I had to fend for myself."

"Oh, that's terrible," said Gracie.

"So, what did *you* do?" asked Finn as he corked the wine and filled all our glasses. "Or maybe I shouldn't ask."

"Actually, you *should* ask, Finn. If you're going to paint my picture, I want the whole story of my life to be there."

"I hope there's a happy ending," said Gracie. I could see the wine was getting to her. "You were only nine years old? Poor little darling."

"I bet you were handsome even then," I said.

"Of course! I've been handsome all my life! It made me who I am, Terry, no different than if I was born blind or disfigured."

"Or had a really big…"

"Finn!" Gracie exclaimed, both shocked and amused.

"Anatomy *is* destiny," Sebastian replied. "I'm the proof!"

"But you can't really call your looks a handicap, can you?"

"It's not what you've got, Terry." He was looking straight at me again. "It's how you use it."

I gulped. Perhaps the wine was getting to me, too, though I noticed Sebastian had hardly touched his first glass.

"Yes, that *is* what they say," I replied slowly.

Sebastian just chuckled.

"So what happened?" Gracie asked.

"Right," said Sebastian, getting back on track. "So, me mum's always been a bit flakey, right?"

"What about your dad?"

"Gracie, not so fast," said Finn.

She was on the edge of her seat.

"Well, Gracie, Dad ducked out early. I don't know why; mum was a very pretty girl. Great eyes—these come from her," he said, pointing to his own eyes. "Maybe that was part of the problem. Men came in and out a lot until this one guy, Don Carlos…but I call him Don Juan…he showed up. Good looking bloke. Lots of flash. Not taste, mind you, but flash—I've learned the difference. And he takes a real shine to me mum. She feels the same, so he sticks around."

"Did *you* like him?" I asked.

"I had no say," Sebastian replied.

"Did he like *you*?" Finn asked, which I thought was a more interesting question.

"Well, that's it, in' it? I was in the way. Just old enough so I didn't need anyone to wipe me bum or cook when I was hungry. Don Juan just sort of took over, and apart from taking us to some nice restaurants to show off, I was left out."

"Didn't your mum…?" Gracie began.

Sebastian held up his hand. "Think what you'd do, Gracie. Single, still attractive. Everyone's got a right to have fun, right?"

"But you were just a baby!" Gracie said, getting misty-eyed.

"Now's where the good looks came in, right?"

Sebastian smiled. "Yes, good looks, Terry, and the rest," he said, tapping his forehead.

"I'm not following," said Gracie.

"Brains, luv," said Finn.

"And with all the built-ins from me mum *and* me dad, 'cause it turns out I got the best of both worlds, if you follow me…"

There was a pause until the penny dropped.

"Oh, now!" Gracie said. "That's not right."

"Sounds pretty right to me," said Finn. "All blessings welcome in that department."

I chuckled, but said nothing.

Sebastian continued: "Before long I was cooking for myself, and finding my own way after school, on weekends."

"You must have been so lonely."

"No, Gracie, London's not a lonely place, no matter what you've heard. It was after school and weekends when I learned the biggest lesson of my life."

"What was that?" Gracie asked, breathless.

"Yes," said Finn. "Secrets of the universe, *please!*"

Sebastian paused, looking at each of us in turn. He could spin a tale, no denying that.

"Well?" I said, prompting.

"No mystery. The lesson was that everybody likes a pretty face."

We all sat silently for a long moment. There were layers to this. I looked at Finn. He was processing too. Then it occurred to me that what Sebastian was saying came from the object of desire, the pretty face himself. His view looking out was very different from the rest of us looking in…or at.

"People react to beauty. It's almost a natural response to…"

"…to *stare*," I said, finishing Sebastian's thought.

"Right!" he said, pointing at me like I'd won a prize.

"Even when you're nine years old?"

"Yes, even then, Gracie. The eyes haven't changed. People always stared, and I began to catch on. Then by eleven, twelve—that in-between age. Very brief, very pretty, and…I got it."

"The end of childhood," I said, remembering the phrase I'd written in my diary at that very age.

"But also the dawn, Terry. The dawn of…"

"…*adolescence*," Finn said with a groan.

"Sounds frightening," said Gracie, taking another gulp of wine.

I poured a splash more into her glass.

"No," Sebastian continued. "I discovered the dawn of my power. The power of beauty—sorry, I have to say it. And I began to approach my looks as a *business*."

He took a moment to let that sink in.

"Sure, the doors opened, but what to do when you're in the room? You can't just stand there and stare back just because they're staring at you. You have to make something happen!"

He let that sink in, too. And I began to see there was little vanity in him. He *was* all about business—from the very start, by the sound of it.

"Then at school—because they *did* teach me a thing or two—I discovered the ancient Greeks and Romans, the Renaissance. All the portraits and statues."

"They practically made a religion of beauty," said Finn.

"Exactly what I thought! Especially adolescent beauty and I realized I was right in the pocket."

"A fucking Greek god," Finn said, not half joking.

"I saw those faces, the adoration… and…"

"And what?" I said, now totally drawn in with the others.

Sebastian sat back, taking a sip of his wine. "I put two and two together, is what."

"Started working the looks," Finn said with an evil chuckle.

"The *appeal*," I countered.

"Yes, Terry! That's a better word! I worked the *appeal*. First to win me mum back, but that didn't work. She only had eyes for…"

"…Don Juan," said Gracie, downcast.

"Right. So I began studying *his* appeal. Like I said, he was a good-looking guy, but there was more…hard to put your finger on, especially as a kid. Then I realized it was the confidence. He was simply at ease with who he was, even if he did dress like a pimp. Still, what can you do when you're only twelve years old?"

"What did you do?" I asked.

"I tried a new angle: cooking."

"The restaurant!" Gracie shouted.

Sebastian laughed again. "You're way ahead of me, smart girl," he said. "Yeah, I had a knack for it; tried to, you know…*chef* my way back to mum's attention."

"How'd that go?"

I truly hoped Finn was taking notes.

"Well, I learned about food, read some books, tried my hand. Mainly I dreamed about owning me own restaurant one day. But as a kid, who can compete with the nice places Don Juan was taking us out to?"

"Of course not," Gracie concurred, crestfallen.

"Then one day I let a local photographer take some pictures of me. He sent them to an agency. I thought it was a lark. But they called back. Then they kept calling. I still hadn't put all of it together, but I caught on quick, didn't I?"

"*Money!*" said Gracie like she'd found a treasure.

"Money and good advice."

"From Don Juan?" I asked.

"No, no!" Gracie said, suddenly excited. "The photographer!"

"Right again!" said Sebastian. "Girlfriend, you *are* catching on quick."

Gracie smiled, thrilled.

"So, that photographer, *he* knew the game. Got me a few jobs modeling catalogues. Boring work showing off trousers and jumpers for Marks and Sparks, but I was the first dark-skinned kid they ever used. There I was in print! Stamp of approval. Then, when I was sixteen, the photographer, who was by then acting as my manager, he put the moves on me."

"Oh, shit," I said, almost involuntarily.

"You mean he…" Gracie let the words trail off.

"That's exactly what I mean."

"*Now*, what did you do?" Finn asked.

"Do?" Sebastian asked as if the answer was obvious. "I did smart. Looked at the big picture. Played like a Japanese schoolgirl."

Gracie laughed out loud. "What does *that* mean?"

"You know: first base will get you this much. Second base will get you a little more. But home plate was…"

"*Out of bounds!*" shouted Finn and I in unison.

"Exactly right," Sebastian said, his tone reeking with mock virtue. "I did have standards. Still do actually, though the goalposts have moved somewhat. Besides, I was scared shitless!"

"You were a tease."

Sebastian smiled coyly. "Not so, Terry; I was a survivor…like me mum."

"And an *en-tre-pren-eur*," Finn said with a French accent.

"Well, that's a big word considering I was basically by myself."

"You diversified!" said Gracie.

"Let's say I spread it around a little. But only to *particularly* useful parties. No need to draw a picture. I wasn't interested in sex. I just needed to open doors. Enough to straddle the next hurdle."

"No pun intended," said Finn.

Sebastian looked around. "Oh, you are a cheeky lot," he said. "But we all use what we've got, don't we? I was still barely seventeen. Still came home to me mum every night. But I was making plans. I wanted bookings like the top boys. Knew I could do the job given the chance. I had the walk, the stare—kind of a cross between fuck you and…"

"…Fuck ME!" I shouted too loudly, the wine having taken hold.

The room went momentarily silent.

Then Finn said "If we must," ever so politely.

Christ, I totally walked into that one.

I actually hated the expression! I'd never heard it before I came to England. I'd never said it out loud. My wine-buzzed enthusiasm was more to blame than any actual leanings in that regard. But Finn clocked it. And Sebastian. He was always looking for an *in*. This may have been the moment Sebastian knew he had me pinned. Still, I was glad Tess wasn't around.

Sebastian continued: "I learned who the good stylists were, the best photographers. Did my homework because, like I said, it's not all about looks. You have to be smart. Hopped from one agency to another until they got me the jobs I wanted, the big brand accounts. I finally got to shoot for Bailey, Scavullo and the rest. When I was in the right magazines, the paychecks started to snowball."

"So there *was* a happy ending," said Gracie. She sounded relieved.

"No, Gracie, that was just the *beginning*! With money, I could truly diversify. Meet business people who were after the same things I was. 'Course, there were ups and downs. But I gained more in experience than I ever did losing money. I started investing. That's where the real money is."

"Like the restaurant!" said Gracie.

"Like that whole big building," Sebastian replied. "And now there's the modeling agency. It's called The Face."

"Fucking perfect," said Finn with genuine admiration.

Sebastian looked at his watch.

"Christ. Speaking of business, I have to get going."

"Oh, no!" Gracie said.

Sebastian chuckled. "Come up to the office tomorrow lunchtime, Gracie. You can meet Dee, my assistant; we'll finalize the guest list there."

Then he turned to me: "And you, Terry...we'll talk later."

"Right," I said, like I knew what he was talking about. But if Sebastian wanted to talk, I was all in.

~

Tess's evening hours could be irregular, so meeting for

lunch in Knightsbridge was our good second option. We loved being together, talking together. She had a settled quality, comfortable as an observer, a very good listener, all qualities suited for the career path she was following. And naturally we shared stories about our growing up.

Particularly impressive to me was the fact that Tess spoke perfect French. From the time she was ten years old, she'd spent every summer with her best friend, Blanche Haddock, whose family lived across the road in North London's tony Hampstead neighborhood, but also had a house in the west of France. In just a few summers Tess learned to speak French without an accent—even the French said so! In her late teens she'd worked several summers as an au pair in Paris, hired by some wealthy families to take care of their very young children. But she soon discovered that cleaning up the free-flowing fluids of babies was not her calling, deciding then and there she could be of more use as a therapist than a mother.

More interesting, she said, was a view into the world of the very rich. In one great Haussmannian apartment she caught a glimpse of the elderly Charles Lindbergh, who was a guest of one family for whom she worked. Tess was never introduced, but she saw him several times in an adjacent room standing by the window, a ghost of history, melancholy as the blue light of dusk.

Every story of Tess's growing up included Blanche and the Haddock family. By all accounts they were a highly creative lot (Blanche herself was a dancer), uniquely English in their eccentricities, sounding very reminiscent of the colorful Durrell family. Perhaps it was no surprise that Tess, an avid reader, knew both Lawrence and Gerald Durrell's books, intense and humorous respectively, both descriptions fitting Tess herself.

With Christmas just around the corner, we were making plans for me to come up to Hampstead and finally meet Tess's parents, Mr. & Mrs. Greenwald, and brother Gerald. The visit would naturally include popping over to meet Blanche and her family. I looked forward to all of it.

After lunch in Knightsbridge we might also stroll back

to Harrods so Tess could do a little grocery shopping in the Food Halls. As her cashier, I'd always deduct my employee discount and a little more. With those perks and a bottle of good plonk from the case Sebastian dropped off—perks of *his* job thanks to ad deals with a French wine label—I can truly say I was never so poor or lived so well as when I lived in London.

~

Two days before Christmas, Finn and Gracie had already left to be with their respective families in Toronto and Wales. Tess was up in Hampstead staying with her parents, so I had the flat to myself. Arriving home exhausted from work I discovered my key didn't turn in the front door lock. Try as I might it wouldn't budge. It was dark and cold as I sat on the doorstep wondering what to do. Panic was beginning to set it, when it finally occurred to me to go round the block, up the alley and try the back door. I'd never explored the neighborhood, let alone spent time in what we laughingly called our garden. But round the block I went hoping to God my key worked the back door lock.

The alley was lined on both sides with brick walls and wooden gates. The backs of the row houses all looked the same, so I had an eye out for my uncurtained window with bookshelves I knew would be visible. When I found our gate it was ajar. Pushing it open I saw the back door wide open. This definitely wasn't right. Stepping inside I saw immediately that the two kitchen drawers were pulled out. In the sitting room there was a blank space where the television should be.

We'd been robbed!

I went straight to the front door and found it had been dead-bolted from the inside, which was why my key didn't work. Turning back to the stairs, I was suddenly terrified.

"Hello!" I called out tentatively.

There was no reply but for a chilling silence, as if I were in not just an empty house but a dangerous one. I made my way up cautiously. The first landing was the bathroom and toilet. Nothing to see there. Then, up to my room. When I opened the door, I saw that it had been completely gone over. The wardrobe doors were wide open and all the drawers in my bureau were pulled out, clothes scattered on the floor. I knew in that instant that the robbers had likely found their prize: the cash I'd tucked in with my t-shirts—money to pay the rent—and my camera at the bottom of the wardrobe behind my shoes. Sure enough cash and camera were gone.

I went up another two flights to Tess and Gracie's room. I'd only been in there a few times, never alone, so I felt like I was compounding the very evident violation. All their drawers and two wardrobes had been ransacked, too. There was no telling what was missing. Then two more short flights to Finn's floor. I'd never ventured (or been invited) up so far.

I knocked gently—a little ridiculous under the circumstances, but my heart was pounding. Then I opened the door and looked inside.

At first it was difficult to see anything. The long wall of street-facing windows opposite the door were covered with floor-length curtains—expensive, deep burgundy-colored velvet ones—to keep the room completely dark. I felt for a light switch. When I found it, my eyes were momentarily blinded by two very bright spotlights clamped to the edge of a worktable in the center of the room. They were directed toward the wall to my left, which was entirely covered in faces!

I was looking at a huge collage of close-ups: striking men and women's faces, hundreds of them, all pages cut cleanly from magazines, sized uniformly, adhered directly to the wall. It was careful, clean and carried a punch, extending from floor to ceiling, side to corner side. When I stepped further in and faced the wall directly I felt like the target of startlingly focused energy. All the eyes were looking at me!

Glancing around, though, and to my surprise, I saw no disruption at all. At the far end of the room was a bulky wardrobe similar to mine; it was center-placed to allow a small alcove for Finn's bed in the darkest corner. But the wardrobe itself was closed and seemingly undisturbed. Near the curtained window was a tall easel. There was a canvas on it facing away from me. Beside it was a small table with various jars, brushes, pencils and tubes of paint. I was most curious about what might be on the canvas and stepped around to have a look. At about 3 x 5 feet, vertically aligned, it immediately suggested Manor House proportions…pretty ambitious. But there wasn't much to see. The surface was gessoed white; there were numerous pencil lines suggesting a three-quarter length portrait. Whether this was for Francesca or Sebastian, I just couldn't tell. Nothing said there was work actually underway.

By contrast, as my eyes were drawn again to the giant collage, I could tell that there had been careful, almost obsessive energy spent to make all the edges align so cleanly. And so many faces! Hundreds! More than orderly or even obsessive, the wall had the feeling of honoring—a wall of wonders. Clearly, Finn was enthralled with beauty.

But why was the room so tidy? Had the thieves not made it up this far? Perhaps the robbers opened the door and felt what I felt: a force field radiating so strongly that even thieving junkies (or whomever they were), were disinclined to push through. Most certainly, I felt I was in a private sanctum I had no permission to be violating. I was an intruder here no less than the robbers downstairs.

And I was fascinated!

I stepped closer. The images were mostly models, stunning males and females, all in closeup. Finn's prime source material was obviously fashion magazines—the expensive ones. But there were also some striking accents: shots of old wrinkled faces; heads of Greek and Roman sculptures like the ones Sebastian had been talking about that inspired him as a young teenager. There was Michelangelo's David; an ash-black African, his face painted with tribal decorations; several early Renaissance Madonnas with golden halos; and children staring back with their wide, wide open stares. Color splashes included a glowing moon, a monk in orange robes, a man on fire, and glistening coral that popped out like the colors in Sebastian's eyes. There were no celebrities; only two of Sebastian himself, neither prominent nor suggesting favor. Maybe these were included before Sebastian came into our lives. There was no way of telling.

But the word Finn used came immediately to mind: "Wondrous."

Here was his wonder world. Perfect youth chased by mortality; beauty a vain promise where somewhere time was laughing. Clearly no single image could capture the wonder he felt. All the stars in heaven weren't enough.

Tears welled in my eyes as I began to understand Finn for the first time. He postured with glib bravado: the petty scammer, pub crawler, beggar at this father's table. All of it was his defense, cheap currency in the face of overwhelming wonder.

I went downstairs and called the cops. When they arrived with checkered caps and notepads, they didn't tell me anything I didn't already know. It was Christmas. Home robberies happened every year at this time. They'd send someone to dust for fingerprints, but don't hold your breath.

I also called Colin, who came over just as the police were leaving. It was all pretty depressing. The sense of violation turned to quiet rage. Tess felt the same when she called from her parents' house later that night and I reported the bad news. I had no number for Finn. There was no reaching Gracie until she got back from Wales. All I could do was hunker down and spend Christmas alone in the spooky flat.

Christmas Day was a huge relief: I could sleep in! I'd never worked in an environment of such sustained clamor as the Christmas season at Harrods. I was actually exhausted and slept till nearly noon, having made order of my room once Colin and the police had gone. I called home to wish my parents Merry Christmas and ask for money to cover my stolen rent. Chatted again with Tess when she called. Mostly, I was glad for the quiet time.

My Christmas present to myself was the purchase of an inexpensive record player so I could finally play the two records I'd bought at the Way In weeks ago but had not yet played. They were Joni Mitchell's latest, "Hissing of Summer Lawns" and John Cale's "Paris 1919". That one I first heard when I was living with Carlos and Burt. Both albums became the musical background for my time in London. (There were two others I acquired early on from Carlos's Victoria Station record shop: Roy Harper's "Commune", and Sandy Denny's "Like an Old Fashion Waltz" with its heart-wrenching song "No End", the story of an artist's lost love. It still gets me every time. I'd gotten over "Tubular Bells" after it was played to death at Earls Court.)

Boxing Day is a very sensible post-Christmas Day wind-down that, alas, commerce dictates we *don't* celebrate in the States because a two-consecutive-day pause in sales (Christmas Day being the obligatory *one* day) is apparently all that insatiable greed can spare. Boxing Day was also to be the day I'd finally present myself to Tess's parents, Mr. & Mrs. Greenwald, and meet her older brother Gerald.

Tess had already fleshed out Gerald's "psychodynamics" (a new world for me), saying he was a nice guy, very bright and amusing when he wanted to be. But he had a fraught relationship with their parents. Mr. Greenwald was a work-at-home accountant who had held strict ideas about how boys should be raised. By the time Tess came along five years later, things had loosened up considerably, and the baby sister was given a great deal more latitude than her brother. Even as a boy, Gerald clocked the different rules—and the unfairness as he saw it—and began to hold a grudge. In fact, by the sound if it, he was on the way to spending the rest of his life exacting amends.

During his school years Gerald came home with perfect marks, then withdrew to his room more or less eschewing his parents until dinner time where, according to Tess, the conversation was just spare niceties if they talked at all.

As for dinner, I was warned that it would be a fixed menu depending on the day. Sunday was always a roast joint served mid-afternoon. Monday was leftovers from Sunday.

Tuesday baked chicken, Wednesday pasta, Thursday meat pie, Friday baked salmon. Saturday was kidney stew. Vegetables were English style: boiled to a paste. And Gerald *always* declined dessert. Try as his parents might to entice him with something new or a variation on their ridged routine, Gerald responded with polite declines. That they continued to try was, according Tess, part of the game and its own kind of sad masochism. Gerald's entire life was a show of little retributions, depriving himself of pleasure to remind his parents of the perceived injustices he had suffered as a child.

Then there were the Haddocks just across the road. By Tess's telling they were the mirror opposite of her own family providing the warmth and spontaneity the Greenwalds did not. She said she'd be an entirely different person had not Blanche and *her* family been a literal home away from home. Aside from Tess, the two families had almost no interaction whatsoever.

All this would become clear when I finally made my way to Hampstead. But first I had to get there. Tess said the bus was more direct than taking the Tube, so bearing Harrods' jam for gifts, I found the right stop and waited. On quiet Boxing Day the streets were nearly deserted, and the bus was, too, when it arrived. I took a seat on the upper deck. There was only one couple sitting up front above the driver, where the view forward was unobstructed. I chose a seat on the opposite side of the aisle and several rows back so as not to intrude.

After a few stops the couple got off, and I heard footsteps of someone new coming up. I looked around and locked eyes with a guy as he passed me heading for the now-vacant front seats. He was about my age with a handsome look I pinned as Middle Eastern. Soon, the fact that we were alone became electric when he turned back several times to look at me. Then he slid away from the side window extending one leg into the aisle. I couldn't see much, but from his movements I knew he was rubbing himself—and making a point of letting me know. Before long he turned completely sideways to reveal his open trousers and a stiff, circumcised cock. A real show-off, God bless him, and he waved it at me for the next ten minutes, allowing as much of an eyeful as possible. I had a full erection too, though I kept it in my pants. We never changed seats, and he only got a peek of my bulging trousers when he headed back down the aisle to catch his stop.

Then, as it happened, the bus remained in place for several minutes. I watched my obliging friend cross the road and approach a waiting car, where four girls got out to greet him, two wearing Islamic headscarves. They chatted for a while, laughing and hugging. When the bus finally geared up, and as we pulled into the road, the young man looked casually back over his shoulder. He didn't wave or even smile—but he might as well have.

Tess was waiting near the bus stop in her parents' car, a very sensible economy vehicle about five years old. It was strange seeing Tess behind the wheel, common enough in America, but very uncommon for most young Londoners. We laughed about it, and her very careful driving, all the way back to the family home, not five minutes away.

Row houses, common in London, were not common in Hampstead. But this was an updated (and up-scaled) nineteen fifties version on a pleasant woodsy street. A gated entrance to Hampstead Heath itself was at the end of the block, so the neighborhood was altogether desirable. Mr. Greenwald opened the front door as we pulled up. He was a studious-looking man, lean, mostly bald, with a ready smile. I had the sense that this was a big day for everyone. I was Tess's first real boyfriend so of course they were curious. We shook hands on the doorstep, a warm greeting, as I was welcomed inside.

I was immediately struck by the spare, tidy whiteness of everything. As non-observant Jews, there were no signs of Christmas per se, but the hallway was decorated with some leafy, seasonal adornments. Vines of artificial holly with red buds brightened the arch leading to the dining room just left of the entry hall. I saw five places all set out for lunch. Stairs leading to the second floor were straight ahead.

Mr. Greenwald called to his wife as we followed him straight back to the sitting room where wide windows gave view to a wintery rear garden. There were small, unremarkable pictures on the walls. My entire first impression was of a very careful home, functional and sufficient. I wondered how much influence Gerald had on the choices made. Slow I was to grasp that my very presence was tantamount to breaking every egg, the family walked on constantly to keep Gerald placated.

Mrs. Greenwald came in wiping hands nervously on her apron. She was stout, conservative, wearing a kitchen apron over her white blouse and straight, navy blue wool skirt that hung nearly her ankles. She had a sing-song voice full of English pleasantries, but there, too, was Tess's perfect skin and wide cheekbones. There was no mistaking the family resemblance, and I remarked with a compliment immediately. Both Tess and her mother blushed. Mr. Greenwald beamed. I liked both of them. There was no reason not to.

Mrs. Greenwald returned to the kitchen, and when dinner was called, I heard footsteps on the stairs. Gerald came down as we were entering the dining room. I wasn't sure what to expect: someone sullen, perhaps. Certainly not the wiry young man, a few years older than me, who loped forward to shake my hand. Mr. Greenwald probably had the same physique and premature balding when he was Gerald's age. The toothy smile was the same. He looked nothing like Tess.

We all sat down, Mr. Greenwald at one end with his back to the front window, Gerald opposite, co-head of the table. Mrs. Greenwald was opposite Tess and me.

I remembered what Tess had said: "We don't talk at meals." It seemed beyond possible. But it was just as foretold—including the roast chicken, this being Tuesday. And because it was a special occasion (that would be me), Mr. Greenwald offered wine. Gerald declined with a quick shake of his head, opting for water. I tried making small talk, probably something about Harrods. But after some polite, "oh, yeses" and an obligatory chuckle, the conversation fell flat. I was puzzled. These were smart, educated people! Gerald was already a full-fledged accountant, though working independently from his father at an accounting firm. Surely they had opinions, thoughts, something to say about...I don't know...economic affairs? Even the latest royal family gossip? Instead, we ate in silence.

I would soon see that behind a politely amusing and intelligent exoskeleton, Gerald was very tightly wound. When he wasn't smiling his mouth set in a thin, humorless line. His gaze was furtive; I felt he was highly suspicious of...not just of me but my very presence as an outsider.

When it came time for dessert—a cream-filled trifle Mrs. Greenwald had made specially—Gerald simply nodded another impatient *No* when it was offered.

"There's just no pleasing him," Mr. Greenwald joked feebly for my benefit. Even knowing that Gerald would rebuff their constant efforts to please him (in this case the wine, the trifle), the effort *and his parents' show of disappointment when he declined* was in fact the atonement—almost a ritual he required to somehow square an unsquarable circle.

Tess had long come to take it all in stride until, several years earlier, she said, when Gerald surprised everyone by accepting his sister's invitation to take a week's summer holiday joining her in France with the Haddocks. Tess said she was struck speechless when, away from home, Gerald indulged in sauces, spices, all the wines, the bluest cheese, cakes, tarts and ice cream, in short everything he wanted— that he *really* wanted, Tess realized—but punished his parents by willfully abstaining.

When our late lunch was over and it was already dark, Tess said what I guessed was a familiar *"We're going over,"* and we gathered our coats and headed across the road. The Haddocks' was a large two-story house with vines covering its block brick facade and lights glowing warmly in all the criss-cross Tudor-style windows. Tess was already smiling as she rang the doorbell.

"There you are!" said the young woman who opened the

door. "Merry Christmas!"

I knew from a photo that this was Blanche. She was my height, tall for a girl, with a dancer's body, lean and straight. She smiled with genuine pleasure, almost laughing when I was introduced.

"I've heard so much about you," she said.

"Me too," I replied.

As we stepped into the entry hall, I felt a wave of not only Holiday ambience, but relief. It must have been the same feeling Tess felt growing up, coming from the stark, scrubbed ambience of her biological family into the warm bosom of *this* one with whom she had miraculously found refuge for half her life.

The house was flush with Holiday smells: a woodburning fire, baking from the kitchen I spied beyond the angled staircase. We'd hardly stepped in when an older lady came rushing forward, apron on, hair a wild mass of kinky, grey streaks held back with a hair band.

"You're Terry," she said as if we'd met before, but perhaps she'd forgotten. "I'm Julie. I won't shake your hand," she said, waving her flour-covered fingers. "I'm about to put a tart in the oven. Not *that* kind of tart, of course, my tart days are over, alas."

"Mummy!" Blanche cried.

Julie chuckled, leaning toward me in mock confidence. "I'm a constant embarrassment."

"I am, too," I whispered. "And yes, I'm Terry, the much heralded."

"Oh, you are indeed!" Julie said, exploding with delight. "We've all been dying to meet you! But I have to...the tart...."

She waved her fingers again, then turned abruptly and scurried back to the kitchen.

"That was my mum," Blanche said.

"She's fun."

"That's the *problem*," Blanche replied as she steered us into the large living room. "We're all *too* much fun."

I looked at Tess. She was still beaming, proud to share if not her real family then her soul one.

The fireplace was centered on the long wall opposite. To the left, framed in the tall front window, was a medium-size grand piano. In front of it, resting sideways on the floor, was a cello. Tess had already informed me that Julie played second cello in the local North London Community Orchestra. I wondered who played the piano. At the other end of the big room was a tall Christmas tree, magnificently decorated in silver and red balls with tiny lights hidden in its branches.

An older, professorial man rose to greet me from the pair of facing couches on each side of the fireplace.

"I'm George," he said, offering his hand.

"Terry, this is my father," Blanche said.

"Just call me George; pleasure to meet you at last."

I knew his story, too. Mr. Haddock was a professor at the London School of Economics; a noted scholar with several books on economic history to his credit. He and Julie were long divorced but he lived nearby and was part of the family for all significant occasions. He had a rumpled Beat Generation air about him. Both he and Julie would have caught the sixties in their forties, but no doubt kept pace.

Then Blanche turned to the other seating area near the Christmas tree.

"Come on guys, come and meet Terry," she said.

There were two women and a young man whom I hadn't seen when I first glance around the room. They were all reading quietly at a small round table in the corner furthest to my right. Jo, for Josephine, stood up as we approached. This was Blanche's older sister, the actress I'd heard about. She was thirty, tall, finely boned, with clear, bright eyes, who co-starred in a popular television drama I'd never seen. She was holding a script, presumably learning lines.

Then Blanche's brother Timothy stood to shake hands, and if I thought I was starting to feel comfortable amongst this interesting family, I was suddenly put entirely off balance. I already knew Timothy was a year older than me, down from Oxford for the holidays. But no one had said anything about how handsome he was... how *adorable*.

He had a smaller, utterly huggable frame, crowned by a

tussle of sandy blonde hair. Both cheeks had ruddy smudges—a particularly appealing asset—and he was beautifully spoken with a low tenor tone. Even more than looks, however, Timothy radiated a gracious *charm,* which is another word for magic. He had a quiet glow to which I'm sure *everyone* responded. My guess was his actress sister emanated a similar kind of charisma when she was working. But Timothy's was happening here and now, and rather than stare, I had to look away. It was as if fate had purposely challenged me, naked in front of everyone, to pretend I *wasn't* rattled by one of the most truly attractive, desirable young men I'd ever encountered.

Third at the table was a tall, lean beauty (taller than me) who wobbled a bit when she stood to shake my hand. Timothy joked that she'd tripped on one of her theorems, which was why she broke her ankle and her right foot was in a cast. She was introduced as Timothy's girlfriend, Andrea. My first guess was that she might have been a fashion model, but in fact she was studying "high maths", also at Oxford, where Timothy was "reading" philosophy. It was almost overwhelming how brainy and creative they all were!

We gathered on the central couches—minus Jo, who excused herself to do "homework" upstairs. Andrea asked me about life in Los Angeles, which, for completely ungrounded reasons, seemed to have an air of glamour for them. Timothy wondered why on earth I was in dreary old London? He said I couldn't possibly have come all this way for the weather—*not by choice*. When I said it was by accident and left it at that they all nodded as if it was the only rational explanation. Blanche mentioned what Tess had surely told her, that I worked at Harrods. This garnered the usual pricked ears and seemed to bestow upon me a certain cache. No need to mention Frosted Food.

A little later George and Timothy sat down side by side at the piano. I looked at Tess questioningly, and she just nodded as if to say *Wait for it.* Then, after setting up the sheet music, they began to play Bach's *Jesu Joy of Man's Desiring* for four hands. It is an exquisite jewel of a piece, barely four minutes long, whose reoccurring theme is urged on by a gently propulsive cadence played by George in the treble part, while Timothy provided balance on the lower keys. As he played, his eyes darted from the page to the keyboard, studious and completely in the moment. Watching him, I was transfixed. Tears filled my eyes. I had never met anyone who emanated such rare outer and *inner* radiance—so much more wholesome and believable than the professional beauty embodied in the likes of Sebastian. As accomplished amateur musicians, father and son didn't miss a note. Most certainly they caught the quietly joyous spirit of the music but also the enduring warmth of the Christ Holiday resplendent all around us.

And, too, the honor of witnessing one of Bach's great musical gifts not as a disembodied recording or even an arms-length performance from the concert stage, but right there in sublime intimacy. I glanced around the room. Everyone seemed spellbound, including Angela, who sat with eyes closed by the fire, clutching a cup of warm cider with both hands. I looked at Tess. She saw the tears in my eyes. How could she know my heart was almost breaking over Timothy?

After the concluding notes, a breath of silence filled the room until Julie, who had been watching from the archway, sighed an audible sigh.

"Dessert in the dining room, everyone," she said quietly.

At that point, we all came into the present. George and Timothy rose from the piano, and we all clapped approvingly.

"Now," George said brightly. "Time for some *real* music!" He went to the hi-fi console and restarted the Bill Evans that had been playing quietly in the background since I arrived.

We all migrated across the wide hallway to the dining room where the centerpiece was an enormous fruit tart, which everyone seemed to have had a hand in preparing. An almost comically oversized parfait glass was filled to the brim with fresh, Grand Marnier-flavored whipped cream. We were encouraged to dollop without restraint. Back in the living room, plates on knees, we chatted, laughing, drinking champagne—the very good kind that doesn't make you drunk, just more delightful.

I realized, as Tess had said herself, that it was nothing short of providence she'd had this alternate family as part of her growing up. I marveled, too, that, minus the accents and British eccentricities, I seemed to fit right in—at least I hoped I did.

As the evening progressed, Tess and I sat closer and closer on the couch. I think we both knew that night we were in for the long haul.

~

It was back to work on the twenty-seventh, an early start to Harrods' sale days that would extend the chaos well into January. In other words, there was no relief in sight *except* Sebastian's New Year's Eve party. The build-up had its own exciting momentum. None of us could believe our luck. We'd all seen the guest list and knew it would be one of London's coolest events of the season. That we were included meant that it would be the event of *our* season, too. Gracie said there'd be paparazzi. The wait staff would be models from Sebastian's new agency.

"It all makes sense!" Gracie said again, which was her way of pinching herself to make sure the sudden burst of glamour and opportunities were really real. There was even an ironic twist: Even that which was serving Gracie not at all as an actress was aiding her newfound direction. Tess told me that the one thing sustaining Gracie's theater dreams—the ones that *weren't* giving her berth—was her near photographic memory. She could learn pages of dialogue in triple-quick time and used it as a selling point to every director she auditioned for. Sebastian had caught on to this right away as they were going over the ever-changing guest list: useful skills he was ready to put into service!

All week Gracie would come home, dropping names of the people who had sent RSVPs. She seemed to be taking the initiative, managing more and more of Sebastian's PR affairs. Mention of his name, not to mention the actual face-time drop-ins, became a curiosity we almost got used to. But mostly, Sebastian spent his time upstairs with Finn. My queries in that regard were firmly discouraged.

"But the portrait's going to be big," Gracie said excitedly.

After seeing the wall-size collage in his studio, I wasn't surprised. Then I wondered how they'd even get a canvas that big out the door, let alone around the narrow turn of the stairs. I decided it wasn't my problem.

Meanwhile, there was no relief at Harrods. To be sure, most of the post-Christmas/pre-New Year crowds *weren't* coming for Frosted Food, but they kept coming just the same. The Food Halls were always an attraction, and by the time I came home from work, all I wanted to do was shower off the kinetic overload. One day I stepped out of the bathroom, hair still wet, just a towel around my waist, when Finn bounded up the stairs past me followed by Sebastian.

"OH!" I exclaimed, immediately followed by the English sorry-for-everything "Sorry."

My surprise, combined with an instinctual reaction to cover myself, must have made a comical picture because they both laughed.

"Just heading up," Finn said, not slowing his pace. But Sebastian lingered for a moment. He gave me a playful up and down, then leaned in close.

"You need something to wear," he whispered, brushing my nipple with the back of his fingers.

He didn't wait for my response, but followed Finn up. I was left standing with a slightly distracted sense of amazement. One of the most electrifying "New Faces" in England was suddenly making himself at home—*quite* at home, I'd say—in our flat! Would wonders never cease! I waited until I heard Finn's door close before continuing to my own room. The weird fact was that we were all suddenly rubbing shoulders (and more!) with someone so famous we *all* still had to pinch ourselves. That said, the others still had more direct dealings than I did. But there was no ignoring the feeling of specialness staring face-to-face—*having your nipple touched*—by one of the most famously beautiful people in the world.

Gracie kept saying how it all "made sense". I guess she thought it also made sense when she introduced Sebastian to Colin. It was only a matter of time before their paths would cross. And they clearly had mutual interests in real estate and property development. Once, when I was in the kitchen making tea, I heard Colin chatting with Gracie in the sitting room about something they must have been discussing earlier with Sebastian. I was barely paying attention when I heard Gracie catch herself. There was a pause, as if she realized she was talking out of turn. Then Colin continued, explaining things Gracie said she didn't understand, and he always obliged. But after that little moment I noticed Gracie was more careful with her words, though never short of questions.

~

Of course, I talked all this out with Tess. (Didn't mention the nipple business.) I wondered if there was a place for me in all this benefactory.

"Leaves from the money tree fall on those standing under it," I said.

She rolled her eyes at my little homily but was of two minds as to my point.

"Why don't you like him?" I asked.

She couldn't quite say.

Yes, she agreed, it all looked good from the outside. But the swiftness of things bothered her. Gracie was changing before her eyes, she said, becoming more purposeful and at the same time more distant, less chatty.

How is that a bad thing? She's growing up. Finn was always hungry, which made him a too-easy a mark.

Artists require patrons!

Based on what I told her about the barely started canvas I'd seen, we both wondered if Finn would ever finish the even larger commission for Sebastian. But Gracie had it on Sebastian's good authority that *his* portrait was indeed underway. None of us really knew for certain. Not only was Finn's room off limits, but so was any mention of *whatever* he was doing, in or outside the flat.

He knew I'd been up there after the break-in, but even mentioning that seemed awkward, as if I'd seen something I wasn't meant to. He did, however, have good manners enough to modulate his umbrage, knowing the girls' room and mine had been totally upturned and for some reason his had not. The mystery surrounding Finn was only increasing.

As for the TV in the sitting room, it was hardly missed. It had never been part of anyone's life the way television was in America. Sometimes TV shows were all Americans talked about, one common denominator in a country of vast cultural diversity. My knowledge of British television came more from US airings of "Upstairs Downstairs" and "Monty Python"—and my time with the Langers watching their new color TV. Our grudge was more about the violation. Mostly, Finn said that he hoped the bastards who broke in would burn in fucking hell.

~

Trendy if not rich, we all had special clothes for the New Year's Eve party. I knew Gracie would mix and match, concocting her own stylish look. I had my frisky tailor at the Way In to thank for a very fitted shirt and last season's Kenzo trousers I found on the sale rack. The only jacket I had was so American in style I hadn't worn it—had no occasion to—since I arrived in London. I rationalized that its red weave would fit the festive occasion. But Sebastian was right: I needed some new clothes.

I imagined Finn would dress down but cool as usual, probably with a hat for flair. He was an attractive guy when he made an effort. Tess decided to use some of the Christmas (ne, *Holiday*) money from her parents to buy a new dress. It was going to be a surprise, and I heard much muffled laugher behind closed doors as she and Gracie played dress-up in their room.

Sebastian had paid—he called it a late Christmas present—for a professional make-up artist to come over and do the girls' faces—a subtle but startling transformation Tess later described as a magic veil that made her more glamorous than she'd ever seen herself. Sebastian (with Gracie's help) also organized a private car to take us to the new *Sebastian* restaurant-to-be, which was indeed right next to the theater where Gracie worked. They were already devising a marketing strategy that supported both businesses. I had no doubt that success was guaranteed.

A crowd was gathering on the sidewalk when we arrived just before ten o'clock. The promised paparazzi were there taking pictures as the cars lined up and dropped off their exclusive passengers. We couldn't believe we were part of it. Finn stepped out first, offering his hand to assist Gracie. She was dressed in a quirky mix of hippie chic and 1930s glamour (including a man's hat), that well predated Diane Keaton's style in 'Annie Hall'—all of it, sans expensive labels. Then I stepped out with Tess. Her new, cream-colored dress scooped low for a bosomy décolletage that had made her blush when I admired her in it for the first time. She looked spectacular, but even glammed up, she never saw herself as sexy.

The photographers loved us for a moment until they realized we weren't famous. Then the flutter of flashes dwindled to a few polite bursts just in case a fashion editor knew more than they did, and they'd unwittingly caught a first look at the next up-and-comer. Of we four, I knew Finn would be that person once his portrait of Sebastian debuted as the restaurant's signature.

Inside, there was no hiding the unfinished walls and concrete floor, but as Sebastian had suggested, it added its own sense of fun. Once invitations were presented in the reception area, the space opened into the large future dining room. Balloons blanketed the ceiling to distract from the raw surfaces overhead. Music came from a DJ in an alcove of newly installed beams and wooden studs. Across the room was a blank, floating wall, which I surmised was the future home for Finn's portrait. The dimensions were large but not near the wall size of Finn's studio. Its placement, however, meant it would dominate the room.

As the party revved up the beautiful people swirled

around us. The roving waiter/models serving round after round of champagne and finger food were stunning.

"Why do I never see them on the bus?" I wondered.

"They travel on the Model Line," Finn said. "Hidden tunnels. Not for the likes of us."

In the mix, too, was a slightly older contingent. The men all wore expensive suits and ties, but they weren't the svelte or stylish kind. Their wives (or too-young dates) were in expensive party dresses and bouffant hairdos fresh from the salon. But they didn't have flair, either. I surmised that these were the "business" part of "before pleasure" on the guest list Gracie had been questioning—where the money met the road, I thought. I noticed Sebastian spent more time with this group than he did out on the dance floor mixing with the trendies.

As drinks flowed, the DJ spun everyone into a frenzy with classic R&B and the latest disco hits. It was my first time dancing with Tess, and I found it uncanny how our moves seemed to compliment each other. Mine had *steps*; I raised my arms, made full turns. Tess danced with a more guttural sensuality. Best of all, though, was dancing close. There was an ease to our pairing and, once again, the feeling of a very familiar connection. In the future decade of our off and on relationship, music and dancing would always be our most common ground.

Party hats appeared, and little horns to toot. Then the raucous countdown to midnight. I held Tess tightly. Her breasts, never so revealed, were larger than she ever dressed to let on. Perhaps I was giving her permission to find herself as a woman just as she was encouraging me to express myself through fashion.

Five! Four! Three! Two! ONE!

Cheers rose. Confetti rained down. Tess and I kissed, a proper lusty kiss. I felt her nipples hard against my chest. I know she felt my cock. Wasn't that the point?

Back at the flat we said an awkward good night on the landing, neither knowing quite how broach that last inevitable step. But that New Year marked our personal breakthrough to the grown-up realms of intimacy. I was undressing alone when Tess knocked softly. I opened the door. It was time.

~

About two weeks later I came home from work and heard laughter in the sitting room. I recognized Sebastian's strong voice and Gracie's familiar giggle.

"Terry!" they cried in unison when I walked in.

"Just the man we've been waiting for," said Sebastian.

After New Year's Eve, I hadn't seen him at all—besides in the magazines Gracie started to leave pointedly open on the coffee table featuring him in ads and fashion spreads. Now, they were motioning me in like family.

I put my Harrods shopping bag on the dining table. Then Gracie held out what at first glance looked like a small purse. When she touched a button on the side, it kind of unfolded in my hand and came to attention as a brand new SX-70 Polaroid camera.

"What's this?" I asked.

"It's for you," Gracie replied.

"I need pictures," Sebastian said.

I looked at him, surprised. "*You* need pictures? You must be joking."

"Oh, yes, I do."

"Sebastian, please. Of anyone I will ever meet *in my entire life,* you are the last person who needs pictures."

"Not like that, Terry," said Gracie, laughing. "He means…" she groped for the right word.

"I mean, a little bird reminded me you're a photographer," said Sebastian.

I looked at Gracie. "A little bird?"

Sebastian stepped forward, putting his arm around my shoulder.

"I'd like you to help out…Andy Warhol style."

Oh, brother. If this was flattery, it was way out of proportion. Of course I knew about Warhol, the whole hip New York scene, the Polaroid portraits. But I still wasn't making the connection.

"Like *Interview* magazine," Gracie said.

"Not paparazzi," Sebastian added. "More personal stuff...when we go out."

"I don't go out, Sebastian."

"All that's about to change, mate," he said.

"We want a new look," Gracie said. "And Sebastian thinks..."

"...Polaroids are cool," he said, finishing the thought.

"Yes, they are, but what's that got to do with me?"

"You can do it, Terry," he replied. "I know you have it in you."

"Have what? Do what?"

"We'd like you on the payroll," said Gracie.

We? There was obviously more going on behind the scenes than I realized. But I still wasn't getting it.

"I already have a job, Sebastian! I work at Harrods."

"Now you have two jobs! You can hang out with me...and I'll pay you," he added, pointing to the camera.

"As a photographer?"

"As my *personal* photographer," Sebastian replied.

"You should do it, Terry. I told Sebastian you work too hard."

I laughed. Yes, I came home tired, but I felt lucky, too. There were a million no-name shops selling frozen food, but at least I was doing it at Harrods. Yes, the perks were pretty good, but I had to admit the routine *was* getting to me. Amidst the throngs I was able to spot the employees from the customers not by their faces, but by the unexcited pall. I hoped I wasn't getting that same look, especially wearing the same old clothes under my white, four-button smock. Whatever dreams I had as a budding...what? Filmmaker? *That dream was looking at sunset.* Photographer? *Before my camera was stolen it only brought painful associations.* Writer? *Very early days...*

The truth was, I didn't know where I was going, so it only took a minute to recognize the opportunity Sebastian was offering.

I turned the camera in my hands. It was compact, lightweight, super modern. Expensive, too, I knew, at nearly £200, and the film packs weren't cheap either. This was no small commitment on Sebastian's part.

"Now, you're feeling it," Sebastian said softly, as both he and Gracie saw the dawn light (or was it the night lights?) breaking in my eyes.

"And there's one more thing," said Gracie.

"Oh, right! Blimey, I almost forgot."

Sebastian stepped across the room and picked up a coat bag lying flat on the couch.

"What's this?"

"I told Sebastian you didn't have a good jacket."

"And now you do," Sebastian said. He handed me the bag, familiar green in color, with Harrods' logo printed on the front.

This was coming completely out of the blue. I certainly didn't know Sebastian well enough to be expecting *clothes*. But I wasn't going to say no, either. While he held up the protruding hook, I unzipped the bag. Inside was a jacket I recognized immediately.

"It's *the* Daniel Hechter! How did you know?"

"Trust me, Terry," was Sebastian's reply.

"Try it on," said Gracie excitedly.

I eased the beautiful jacket off the hanger. It was deep burgundy velour, a soft cotton and silk blend with just a hint of sheen. The cut was slightly looser ("deconstructed" was the word Sebastian used) than the more fitted look in vogue; the cuffs and narrow lapels edged with a very thin line of black brocade. It had casual flair, but was just formal enough to step up if an occasion warranted. I'd been eyeing it at the Way In since before Christmas; even tried it on once, but its nearly three hundred pound price tag put it totally out of reach. I might have earned discounts for *small* favors, but I wasn't about to give away the store (or get fired!) for the bargain cost of the Aussie tailor's Russian hands and Roman fingers.

Sebastian tossed the bag aside and held the jacket open. I felt the smooth satin lining as my hands slid down the sleeves. The fit was perfect on my shoulders, under my arms. The rich color suited my skin, my dark brown hair.

"Perfect," purred Sebastian as he turned me around.

"Smashing," said Gracie.

Then it was Sebastian the stylist adjusting lapels, patting my shoulders, shaking out the sleeves, squeezing my upper arms. He looked me in the eyes, smiling. I looked back into the face of unadulterated beauty. I might have kissed him impulsively if Gracie weren't standing right there. Maybe Sebastian knew it. That was his power.

"We need a picture!" Gracie exclaimed suddenly, breaking the moment...probably just in time.

She took the camera I'd put on the coffee table and held it up. The flash popped before I was ready. I was still looking at Sebastian, but he was turned to face the camera. Our heads were close. When the frame popped out, I took it immediately.

"Thank you," I said to Sebastian.

"So, how about we start tonight?"

"Oh, yes," Gracie said. "You've got that book thing."

"Exactly," said Sebastian, and handed me the camera.

"A book thing?"

"And now you've got something to wear. I'll be out front at eight o'clock."

"Okay," I said, my head spinning at the speed of things as Sebastian patted my shoulder again and turned to the door.

"Have to go. Be ready at eight."

I thanked him again, distractedly, still trying to imagine what being a "personal photographer" entailed. He gave us a quick thumbs-up and was gone.

After he left, Gracie and I looked at the Polaroid she's taken, which was now fully developed.

"Smashing," she said again. "Quite a team, I'd say."

Of all the countless pictures I would take of Sebastian, this would be one of the very few of him and me together. I always thought that was strange.

Just before eight I came downstairs, freshly showered and shaved, new camera swinging on its long strap over my shoulder, all ready for my first night on the job. Tess and Gracie were in the sitting room, and I went in to say goodbye.

"How do I look?" I asked.

Tess smiled admiringly.

Gracie took a long look, then said, "No, no, no."

I looked back at her aghast.

"What's the matter?"

"That's not right, Terry," she said, almost scolding. "What's in your pockets?"

I looked down. Two extra boxes of Polaroid film were in the left and right front pockets of my new jacket. You could see the pointed outline.

"It won't do, Terry," she said seriously. "Take the camera off the shoulder strap." Then: "Wait here." And she flew upstairs.

I looked at Tess, who seemed as surprised as me.

By the time I had dutifully unclasped each end of the camera's only accessory, Gracie was back holding a small shoulder bag with a long narrow strap. It was Tibetan-style, made with thin, colorful, double-layer fabric.

"Put everything in there," she said. "And wear it *under*."

So I took my jacket off, put the folded-down camera and boxes of film inside the bag (a perfect fit) and slung the shoulder strap across my chest. When I put the jacket back on the bag disappeared.

"See?" Gracie said. "Now, you're not obvious *or* ruining the line of your beautiful clothes. The cross strap looks cool, too."

I looked at Tess. She smiled and nodded. Gracie was a natural stylist. We should have seen it coming. Finally scrubbed and polished, I was like a kid ready for his first day at school. But Gracie wasn't done. She had her eyes on my shoes. Tess and I looked down...

"One step at a time," I said by way of apology.

Sebastian's yellow Jag pulled up at exactly eight o'clock. A few minutes later I was experiencing the unusual luxury of not just traveling in a car (rare enough for a working guy in London), but an XKE. As we zipped down the King's Road I laughed out loud when we passed my 22 bus with Sebastian's face on the side: a Mary Quant ad for make-up—for men.

"I don't wear it," Sebastian said. "It'll never catch on." (He was right!)

But it was all so exciting, I had to take a picture. I reached down for my new camera bag, discreet beneath my jacket, and Sebastian commented immediately.

"Smart," he said. "And you won't ruin the line of your jacket."

"That's what Gracie said. It was her idea," I confessed.

He nodded, no doubt considering even greater possibilities for his new publicist.

I popped open the camera knowing we were a bit too close of quarters. But there was something classic about the whole moment—one of those "carefree model behind the wheel" shots. Sebastian turned to me and smiled—almost as dazzling as the flash. The frame slid out with its distinctive whine. When the picture fully developed, Sebastian studied the result, holding it above the wheel with his steering hand.

"Nice as a graphic," he said, because it *wasn't* a good photo in the expected sense. His mocha skin was blasted out to nearly white. But the eyes, hair and lips were almost perfectly exposed.

"You're too close for the flash," he said, handing the frame back to me. "But you knew that."

"I couldn't resist."

He smiled at me again, but this time it was not his switched-on professional smile, but a softer one.

"Pace yourself," he said as if cautioning an eager lover.

I sunk into embarrassed silence.

He'd probably seen that eagerness all his life. People became instantly smitten—just as I was, truth be told—and ached to be close to him. He was impossible to simply pass by. The looks, the energy was just too arresting.

After a few moments Sebastian was all business, offering the first bit of technical advice which, over the months, he would occasionally impart if he thought my photography skills needed improvement.

"One thing about my dark skin, Terry," he said, "it absorbs more light than white skin. White backgrounds fool the autoexposure and the aperture closes down. Black people are often underexposed. You can compensate with a regular camera, but not with a Polaroid. I'm mid-tone dark, so you'll have to find the perfect distance. Learn to read the light."

"So, wait…" I said, considering all this. "Cameras and film are calibrated for white people's skin?"

Sebastian chuckled. "Like a lot of things, Terry. You learn to compensate."

"Jeez…" I said, followed by a quiet, collective apology. "Sorry."

"That's all right, mate, we all work with what we have."

SPRING

Besides the exciting new routine working with Sebastian, the biggest change to life at the flat was Tess's moving out.

The way things were going, it was almost inevitable.

Gracie's PR work for the theater had diminished as quickly as the increasing work she was taking on with Sebastian. (It wouldn't have surprised me if he bought the theater out right one day just to maximize profits; when I mused out loud about this, Gracie said neither yes nor no.) As for her future in the out-of-work actor business, the writing was on the wall.

Tess still held the romantic notion that Gracie should stay the creative course. Her big break would come, she said, by sticking at it. No one was amused when I made the joke about the guy not wanting to abandon his job cleaning up elephant shit at the circus: *What, and give up show business?* It was pretty clear Gracie's circus days were over.

Sebastian also started making more regular personal appearances. Mostly, he holed up out of sight with Finn, but if Gracie was around, they'd huddle in the sitting room. I'd become part of the PR team, too, but only worked the night shift. My days still belonged to Harrods.

With the New Year's Eve party behind us, *Sebastian* the restaurant was the next big buzz. Naturally, there were delays. Union workers could be stubborn. Colin had similar gripes as he dealt with the workers on his own properties. Meanwhile, according to Gracie, the nearly completed offices above the restaurant were already bustling with Sebastian's burgeoning enterprises—*plural*.

"He's got all sorts of things going on up there," Gracie said. "And guess what? I saw my name in his Rolodex!"

Depending on *whose* Rolodex, before cellphones and speed dials, this was a true sign one had *arrived*. Then came the over-the-top perk—basically the last straw for Tess: Sebastian had a small desk and phone installed in their room so Gracie could be reached day and night. Sebastian was paying for everything, of course, but it was all pushing Tess's tolerance to the limit.

As it was, Gracie's eclectic wardrobe was grievously overstepping her half of she and Tess's shared space. Indeed, with better money coming in, I'd already noticed a troubling shift in Gracie's overall fashion leanings. Her very original thrift shop creativity was slipping into a period of what I can only describe as *pre-couture*. On one hand, I could relate. It was a slippery slope I didn't know existed until I started working at Harrods. Now we were *both* looking at labels!

Tess started calling it the Lothario Syndrome. I didn't know if that was a clinical term, but I got the gist.

"He's commandeered Gracie," she said. "And Finn. I think that huge painting is starting to take over his life!"

She left the rest unsaid, but the obvious potentials were gathering in my gaze, too. It was hard to ignore what Sebastian was offering, which boiled down to modern culture's crown jewels: money and fame...or at least proximity to them. If I started to heed Tess's discomfort, Sebastian picked up on it right away. All he had to do was set a date for another night on the town, and my surrender was reaffirmed.

Granted, along the way I was becoming an ever-better photographer. Gracie said they were starting to submit my Polaroids—with that Warhol Polaroid look Sebastian was after—to magazines. There'd be more money coming, I was promised, besides the twenty quid I got, which Gracie would hand to me in a check from Sebastian Ltd. a day or so after every night we went out. And all the while, Sebastian's business star—the model agency and "everything else" as Gracie put it—was in ascension, and she was becoming increasingly involved.

At first, the crowding out spilled happily down from Tess and Gracie's room to my own. We exchanged our mattress for Tess's slightly larger one, which gave us both more sleeping room and equally more play room. Because after that first New Year's night we both discovered the joys of sex. Neither of us could get enough!

Tess had a body made for pleasure: soft and curvaceous with ample breasts and inner thighs as silky as any human flesh I've ever known. There was something wonderfully comfortable about the way we fitted—just like our dancing. We always moved together well. As far as we went sexually, it *was* a perfect fit.

And I have to say, there was something relaxingly normal about it, too. Vaginas are *designed* for penises. Properly primed, the female muscle's long grip embraces the entire shaft, not like the sphincter with only its tight entryway. That's not *necessarily* to say that anal sex isn't normal; it certainly has never been exclusive to homosexuals. But in the gay world o*ne works with what one has*, to quote Sebastian.

I was never that keen on anal sex myself; or more accurately, the places where I engaged in sex with men were never conducive to the act—at least in the horizontal position. Besides, there was always the matter of cleanliness, which is never guaranteed in spontaneous circumstances.

"Put it in me," Tess whispered as we embraced. Yes! That's the woman's satisfaction…at least part of it. And I was happy to oblige. At its best there's nothing passive about the receptive role. But alas, with Tess I was never an adventurous lover.

Hindsight paints a selfish picture. Yes, the sex with Tess was always satisfying—*for me*. As far as it went for Tess, too, according to her. She once said, "You're the best," after one of many good romps. But in foreplay, I was never inclined to explore the lower regions with any more than my fingers—not even to go down and have a look around. It was only later I realized I never brought Tess to orgasm. Some men crave taking a woman to sexual abandon. I found the idea a little unsettling. Did I even know what was required? No, I did not. To admit that now makes me terribly ashamed.

Then, on the last day of January, Tess called me at work.

She sounded excited and wanted to meet for lunch. The news was twofold: Blanche had just been accepted into a noted dance company, something she'd been working toward for several years. Now she could finally afford to move out of the house in Hampstead. "Too many big personalities," was the way she explained it.

More to the point, through family connections, there was a two-bedroom flat available in Hotting Hill Gate, an exceptional deal, and Blanche asked Tess to move in with her. The rent would mean little more than what she was paying to Colin, and considering life with Gracie, there seemed every reason to jump.

~

I'll always be grateful to Sebastian for seeing before I did my potential as a professional photographer. If I wasn't ready to call it destiny, I had to agree with Gracie that the way things were working out for all of us did seem to make some kind of crazy sense.

With my new Polaroid, sporting my new Daniel Hechter jacket, arriving with Sebastian in his XKE, I felt like a pretty cool cat. And I was getting the shots! But there was more to it than photography. I learned how to socialize, how to mix, which I'd never done before. Just the way one entered a room could be an indication of belonging. Once I lost Sebastian in a crowd and stood there looking around. But to others I just looked lost or worse: like I *didn't* belong. Sebastian came to my rescue, so I was automatically redeemed, but the protocol was clear: "Watch from the edge."

Giving directions to photo subjects could also be a delicate matter. On one occasion, at a posh reception for Andre Previn, conductor of the London Symphony, I was taken aside by the host and scolded for telling her very important friends to "stand up straight". (They'd been leaning in sideways as if my frame wasn't wide enough.) Another time when I asked a small circle to "just look this way", they instantly rearranged themselves, lining up shoulder-to-shoulder, ruining the spontaneous moment. I became impatient, saying, "No, no, no," and ended up not taking the shot at all. I heard about that later, too.

None of these occasions were heavy drinking affairs. Sebastian hardly drank at all. I would never see him intoxicated. Following his lead, I hardly drank either. We were both there to work. He said that being prompt for appointments and keeping one's wits was crucial. "There are sharks on every corner," he said more than once.

Our destination that very first night was a trendy restaurant where an up-and-coming photographer was celebrating the publication of his first book.

"I want portraits, not paparazzi," Sebastian reminded me as we walked from the car to the restaurant where a few photographers were gathered on the sidewalk. Seeing Sebastian they pounced, grabbing what shots they could, flashes exploding. He slowed but didn't stop, and I followed him straight in, my own camera discreet under my jacket.

The room was long and narrow, brightly lit with a bar at the far end serving complimentary drinks. The restaurant's tables had been cleared for schmoozing. Framed prints lined the walls, and Sebastian was in the largest one, lying nearly naked on a rocky beach. The masculine contours of his body blended with the glistening curves of the stones. He was certainly more famous than the photographer they were celebrating, and everyone came by to have a word. I had no idea who was who, but quickly caught on that putting names to faces was also part of my job.

In the crowded mix there were also several stunning female models. I recognized them from the photos, caught in a frozen wave or posed standing tall, gazes fixed on the distance like Easter Island statues. But here, in person, they smiled exaggerated smiles and laughed with their heads back. One had a rose in her teeth from the huge bouquet on the bar. All that was missing was the lampshade crown.

Sebastian knew everyone's secret desire was to have sex with him because…well, everything always boiled down to sex. Or the dream of it. People whispered that he swung both ways and it may have been true. But I was in a unique position to glean (slowly) the nuances of his sexuality and decided even that was all about business. Sebastian was simply opportunistic in his attractions; strategic in the way of predatory animals who know instinctively where to place themselves, how to entice, how to corner. In that regard we were a pack of two on the prowl. No "significant others" ever appeared on the sidelines or came up in conversation.

Yet he was always mildly flirtatious. I never felt he was serious about actually getting *me* into bed, but he dangled promise, tested limits. I was determined not to be a conquest. Besides, I didn't want to mess up a good thing. I think Sebastian appreciated that I *wasn't* easily swayed. But he was always throwing out a line to see if I'd bite. Then I realized he did that with everyone.

Shooting Polaroids is not the same as shooting with a standard film camera. First, the film is limited: only ten shots to a pack. It kept me from flashing at every random impulse, which was exactly what Sebastian *didn't* want. He wanted considered moments along with that Polaroid feel. Having worked with all the top photographers as well as the best magazine and fashion-house stylists, he was not just a connoisseur of photography as a process, but had become a collector as well. It was through Sebastian I learned the language of fine art photography and about artists like Duane Michales, Herbert List, Alfred Stieglitz and Diane Arbus. I already knew the great fashion photographers from magazines.

One reads about the swell functions, celebrity parties, the "beautiful people". Ninety-nine percent only know that world from a distance. Suddenly I was in its center. Our outings became a weekly—often twice weekly—thing. I began to spot the same people at the different clubs, openings and private receptions. Sebastian was invited to all of them. I accompanied him so often I was kind of accepted as his de facto plus one. When I didn't have a name, it was *You're Sebastian's photographer!* Even that was pretty cool. But my job was to craft his image. As such, my eyes were always on him, ready for a quick glance to indicate that he wanted a shot with some particular person or small group.

To my surprise, Sebastian wanted fewer shots with famous people or the glamorous types who sweetened the social mix, favoring a more savory ingredient. These people, always men, were not exactly UNsavory, they just seemed a little out of place. I'd seen them at the New Year's Eve party, too. Now I was taking their picture—and slowly *getting* the picture.

Rule number one was to never give away the shots. I quickly learned a deft slight-of-hand: as every frame slid out of the camera, I spirited it straight into the pocket of my jacket where it developed sight unseen. When people protested, Sebastian would say, "It's for my archives," which usually ended the matter. Mostly, they just wanted to be seen with him; *that* was the favor he was giving out.

It was portraiture on the fly; an instant of trust between photographer and subject that is purely intuitive. In my photos everyone was always looking at the lens. I was photographing people, not bodies; not looking at them but for them.

But context is everything. I was often the only photographer in an exclusive setting. In *that* context, a person who normally shies from the paparazzi (usually resulting in a pained, unflattering photo) would relent in deference to the host, who obviously granted permission for me to be there in the first place. People who might not "smile for the camera" actually did for me. Only once did a very famous American actor bark rudely "Don't take my fucking picture!"—just as I took the picture. It became a moment published for posterity. What a jerk. I never watched any of his movies after that.

I also learned how to *read the light* as Sebastian had said, and create different looks. Balancing my flash with a room's ambient light—or lack of it—I could create an image that was stark and bright or make Sebastian's caramel skin dark and fierce so those famous blue-green eyes sparked like sun-points on water. I also had a knack for quick and clever framing, catching the unguarded moment then retreating without holding up the social flow. It was an art just not getting in the way.

And one more thing: a crucial piece of advice I read somewhere from photographer Robert Capa: *If your pictures aren't good enough, you're not close enough.* This I took very much to heart, and it didn't make everyone comfortable. I once photographed Sebastian with Joan Collins. "You're so close," she said as I stepped in for the money shot. But Capa was right. The shot was better than good and published in *Tattler* as a full-frame Polaroid (Andy Warhol style!) a week later.

We worked as a team, but, again, it always seemed to be a high-wire act teetering between professionalism and flirtation. Sometimes when he smiled at the camera I felt his startling aqua eyes were aiming right through the lens and looking directly at me. Mini seductions as quick as the flash. Or maybe it was the nature of the job. Everyone was looking for a piece of him but also hoping to be taken. Sebastian was never *not* in the power position. I had a task that kept me focused, but sometimes a look, a conspiratorial wink as we worked a room...sometimes I just melted.

That professional arm's-length bent considerably when, at the end of the night, we were back in his XKE, literally shoulder-to-shoulder as we flipped through a short stack of now fully developed images. We were both seeing them for the first time, and I was close enough to smell Sebastian's breath, his body scent, to study the contour of his trousers.

"I knew you had a knack for this," he told me at the end of that first night out.

How he knew I'll never know, but yes, it seemed I did. "You have a knack for flattering people." Indeed, among the good shots, I caught everyone's nice side. One night, according to Sebastian, I even out-did myself: I made a group of lawyers look compassionate! Turns out they were *his* lawyers, and Sebastian chuckled about it all the way back to Wandsworth Bridge Road, where he dropped me off as usual.

It became a personal challenge to never shoot more than

three film packs (thirty frames) a night. I never carried more. This forced me to be selective. It also made the reviewing process quick work. Sebastian was a ruthless editor, shuffling through frames at lightning speed. He'd instantly toss the least flattering shots between his legs onto the floor of the car. I'd never see them again. Out of a single night's work there were always four or five shots that stuck out.

"Give those to Gracie," he said, which I did either later that night if she was still up, or the following morning.

She told me that Sebastian personally destroyed the outtakes with a hinged-arm paper cutter so no unflattering shots of him would ever end up in print. The good magazines never ran unflattering photos, which was some comfort. But Murdoch's rags loved to get their hands on anything that tore people down. As for the rest of the image-making process…well, I had yet to learn how things worked behind the scenes. I hadn't been up to the office. Didn't yet know I wouldn't get photo credit. And I hadn't met Dee.

So, my proximity to Sebastian Ltd. did not always come with information. For a socially gregarious guy, Sebastian played most things very close to the chest. At first I gleaned more by catching up with Gracie as I wondered who some of the no-name people were Sebastian seemed to favor. She claimed ignorance, and I had no reason to doubt her; we were both new to the scene. But then she became cagey and uncharacteristically tight-lipped. She was learning more than she was telling, and with that came a distancing from me and Finn and Tess, whom she was losing quicker than any of us.

~

Tess and I saw each other as much as we could considering her own sometime-erratic schedule as a social worker-in-training. But no matter where—over lunch in Knightsbridge or at her new flat in Notting Hill—Sebastian's name always came up. When my photos started appearing in magazines she began to feel excluded. I recognized that it was hard to compete with The Face, so I tried to cast my experience in a light she'd understand. We, Sebastian and I, were actually doing our own kind of social work, I said. It was *our* job to party for all those sorry sods who would *never* be on a guest list or hang with the in-crowd. But through us—through my photographs—they could be cool vicariously! We were doing it *for them*!

Tess just laughed at my strained reach for parity.

~

I was eventually invited up to see Sebastian's new offices. I couldn't wait. From everything I'd heard, I had the impression of a building ready to burst open like the Ten of Pentacles in a dazzle of monied stars. Indeed, seen in daylight, the long, two-story building was impressive. It was certainly much more finished than I remembered from New Year's Eve. There were new windows across the ground floor, albeit papered over to hide the construction still going on inside. Entrance to the upstairs offices was a single door at the far left end set into a small vestibule. The door was painted Chinese red with a simple polished brass 'S' at eye level. There was an intercom by the door and a bulky camera overhead. I pressed the buzzer and after about thirty seconds I heard a voice say *Come up*. A lock clicked, and when I pushed the door open, I was facing a plain stairway leading to the first floor. The walls were bare. I could smell fresh paint. Gracie was at the top and waved me up. Sebastian wasn't there, she said, so she'd show me around.

The space was bisected by a long central corridor with a line of closed doors on the left—the rear side of the building. What might have once been a similar line of small offices on the right was now an open plan extending to the far end wall. Wide front windows overlooked the street filling the space with light.

"Most of this is The Face Agency," Gracie said with a wave of her arm.

Indeed, more than half the floor was occupied by low-partitioned spaces with desks for the booking agents. I saw three stylish young women busy on the phone. At the far end was a seating area with colorful, pop '60s furniture—

windows at both corner angles. Lounging there were several striking young models, all "of color", light and very dark, male and female, sprawled awkwardly on the chairs and couches that barely fit their lanky frames. The girls were young and coltish, chatting and giggling as girls do. It was different with the guys. They were at once masculine and gamine. Their slightly exaggerated bonhomie disguised a sexual ambiguity. Yet how beautiful they were! How could they not admire *each other* like Narcissus in the mirror?

As for the rest of the floor space, that which was not devoted to the modeling agency was devoted to all things Sebastian himself.

"I'm in the Sebastian Limited section," Gracie said. "Dee and I do all the press and PR stuff."

She pointed to a smaller quadrant of the floor-space across the room where a heavyset figure of indeterminate gender was leaning over a worktable. I assumed this was the Dee character I'd heard about. Gracie filled me in as we approached.

Dee was the quiet power behind the scene—literally quiet because she was a deaf mute. Clearly of West Indian descent, she was a childhood friend from Sebastian's old South London neighborhood. Finding employment difficult because of her hearing impairment and an inability to speak clearly, Sebastian had hired her five years earlier as the first-ever person on his payroll. She was devoted to him and, by virtue of her near-family status, was the one person you weren't allowed to cross.

Like her appearance, even Dee's name was in the middle, somewhere between Danielle and Daniel. But whatever her gender, she went by the feminine Dee. She was a good forty pounds overweight with a short bowl haircut. Gracie said she made her own clothes, and it didn't surprise me. On this day she was wearing wide trousers and a very long shirt that might be a dress. Everything was in black knotty silk; body-concealing; part Asian, part African, part West Indies, re-fashioned through the eyes of her own very personal style.

Dee was the keeper of the keys. I was astonished at the

organization. Against one wall were cabinets with rows of custom-size drawers. These were for the Polaroids and color slides, every drawer labeled with names and dates. Two other cabinets had many wide, narrow drawers for photo prints and magazine tear-sheets. There were two large work surfaces with more wide drawers underneath. Dee, I learned, had a major say delegating what shots went to which publications. Sebastian was in such demand they could actually pick and choose their outlets. He used the press to his advantage, and they paid him for the privilege!

As for my Polaroids, I saw some recent ones laid out on the big work table. I knew Sebastian had already destroyed the "dead" ones. The second best would be rated, then either filed away or destroyed. Two decades before digital *anything*, Dee would take the final selections and photograph those (the entire Polaroid frame so it was identifiable *as* a Polaroid) with a 4x5 copy camera set up in the corner. It was those large negs of the originals that would be processed and proofed at the most reputable photo lab in London—one that didn't bootleg images—then sent to the magazines upon request. The one-of-a-kind frames remained in Dee's tightly guarded archive.

What I hadn't seen coming was that instead of a photo by-line, my work would be credited as "Courtesy of Sebastian Ltd." When I protested, Dee just gave me a look. I was in no position to bargain. The trade-off came by way of usage fees paid by the fashion and tabloid press or upscale society magazines like *Tattler, Country Life* and *The Lady*. If it was a music scene, *New Musical Express* and *Sounds* were always eager for something up to the minute. I split 50/50 with Sebastian Ltd. After a while I started earning such good pocket money I even contemplated leaving my job at Harrods. But I couldn't predict when Sebastian was going to call. Sometimes it was once, twice, maybe three times a week, then nothing for ten days.

Tess was always of two minds. She tried to share the excitement about my night-owl escapades, the extra money, stories of hobnobbing with the glamorous set, but it all came to her secondhand. "That's my photo!" I'd say excitedly even though my name wasn't present. She knew I wasn't lying. But like everything to do with me, she had to go on trust. I kept telling her *It's just business.* Yes, Sebastian was flirtatious, but that was his way with everyone. This was *work*. We both wanted to believe it.

At first, with *two* jobs keeping me busy, my *other* urges didn't get in the way. But once Tess was happily ensconced in Notting Hill and we were seeing less of each other day-to-day, I had occasional time to allow for male company. That meant hanging with the tribe at the Coleherne, sometimes finishing the night at Catacombs. If sexual activity occurred, it was the stand-and-deliver kind, an activity so entrenched in England it actually had a name: cottaging. I never went to actual bed with anyone, nor was there a shred of romantic distraction. The sex was a guy thing. Emotionally, there was only Tess.

~

We have built grand expectations around the idea of fidelity. There's an agreement partners make and to those who can keep those promises, more power to them. The world is a better place for the true-blue consistency of faithful relationships.

Then there's the way it is.

I pity the little girls raised with dreams of a princess wedding and "happily ever after" only to confront, once married, the hunting nature of male sexuality—a plot-line not in the storybook. Or conversely, the boy raised with all the macho expectations *assumed*, encouraged to "sow some wild oats", then hit a brick wall when he has to stop fucking around. The contradictions can be crazy-making.

To alleviate this dilemma (and with enough world travel under my belt to certify my conclusions), cultures have evolved entire settings to accommodate the male…how to say…egalitarian sexual nature: onsens and Geishas in Japan, hammams in the Islamic world, saunas in Nordic countries. And unambiguous gay bathhouses for same-sex recreation.

In male-male partnerships, extracurricular sex can sometimes (but certainly not always) be an accepted outlet, something akin to work versus play where the twains never meet. Obviously, infidelity is not uncommon in the heterosexual context, either. Having a mistress was (may still be!) a matter of custom among the French (and titled Brits). Maintaining harems of concubines was the way of things for centuries in a variety of cultures. These days, with prenups and NDAs, it can be more complicated. But the general assumption has always been that the wife at home should just quietly go along. Gay people, too, had to quietly "go along" as second class global citizens, if seen, then preferably not heard.

That all changed during the most eventful year of 1969. It was the year I graduated from high school; the year the first man walked on the moon. It was the summer of Woodstock. And the summer of Stonewall. Far greater than a neighborhood rebellion, Stonewall lit a fire of liberation overdue to be set. *Enough is enough of indiscriminate harassment!* By the end of that year there were "gay pride" marches all over the world—a first—proclaiming out loud what people have always really known: *"We are everywhere...always have been!"*

Yes, even *your* kids could be gay! Gulp.

On my first day at Los Angeles City College, pushing the envelope, I wore a small button that said Gay Power. All that was *very* new.

~

I remember the moment of my earliest awakenings when I noticed the veins in the arms of a teenage neighbor. I watched a handsome lifeguard getting dressed in the big open-air men's changing area at our local public swimming pool. I wasn't aroused, but there was something more than curiosity; it was *attraction*. My feelings had no name. I was only ten years old.

By twelve, I was noticing other boys, especially in the shower in gym class. I began to have fantasies. I hadn't even started masturbating. I had girlfriends; was still years away from losing my virginity at eighteen—as brief a moment as *that* was. I had *no* idea what I was doing. I didn't know much more when I first had sex with a guy at nineteen.

But I was never conflicted about my sexuality. Never denied my attraction to either sex. Had no "coming out" issues at all. Liking girls, liking boys…it all felt natural. Nor was there pressure at home to "be a man"….well, except that one time when I was thirteen, waxing wonder over Twiggy, and my father said, "Leave Twiggy for the girls." Okay, so they were probably catching on, but for me, Twiggy was part of the whole sixties cultural explosion, which I felt viscerally early on, and excited me no end!

Fortunately, both my brother Walt and I were raised in a very open-minded atmosphere. We weren't force fed any strict religious edicts. My mother was raised by bitter nuns and swore she'd never pass *any* religious dogma onto her kids. My father was raised as a non-practicing C of E. New Zealand was never big on Bible Bangers. Not so in America! Religion—church-going—seemed to be everywhere. Walt and I did get the basic Bible stories from a brief interlude with the Mormon Church until my parents felt there was something just a bit weird about their family-oriented conservatism. As a consequence, Walt and I were free to follow our own paths, both religious and political, and it turned out that as different as we were in so many ways, both of us were very spiritually minded.

It was curious, however, the way our spiritual paths went in such opposite directions.

I took a more spiritualist way including a brief interlude with the B'hai faith (so warm and loving; they introduced me to Kahlil Gibran and "The Prophet") until I learned they didn't believe in reincarnation. *That*, to me, didn't make sense. Buddhism was a better fit if only because its "all sizes fit one" philosophy, allowing, if not *embracing*, imperfections. I never joined any organized religion.

By contrast, Walt found Christianity early on, including practices that swung from browbeating cults to megachurches. He may still think that I'll burn in hell after I die. Am I really an abomination, or is it a "Love the sinner, not the sin?" kind of acceptance? In fact, I believe what many consider *beyond* belief: that everyone goes to heaven—to Home—after we die. *Everyone.* Hell is of our own making, and if *that's* the case, I'm pretty sure we'd choose not to spend much time caught up in Fork, Flames and Eternal Pain once we realize we're doing it to ourselves!

Through all of this, my brother and I kept our parents' politically liberal-minded proclivities.

This became a problem for Walt as American-style Christianity leaned further and further to the right. First, the "moral majority" claimed Ronald Regan as their own. Then after 9/11 George W. Bush became a Christian war hero. Obama was the anti-Christ, which finally led to preaching Trump as a veritable Savior. All this put Walt at odds with his religious surroundings. Suddenly he had to mind his political Ps and Qs. Talking freely raised eyebrows. People questioned his faith in Jesus based on his politics. Expressing concern to his pastor about endorsing *any* president from the pulpit (which is illegal) the man just shrugged. That's what his parishioners wanted to hear. Bottom line: they were paying the bills.

When we first arrived in the States in 1957, my parents were bewildered by the atmosphere of paranoia that hung in the air like the then-heavy smog over Los Angeles. (Coming from atmospherically pristine New Zealand, my assaulted sinuses often drained unbidden with *streams* of yellow mucus!) Though the House Un-American Activities Committee hearings had ended a few years prior, there was still a kind of toxic air of suspicion everywhere. My mother had to lower her hemlines. A neighbor asked, "Are you communist, hon?" after hearing her clear-eyed observations about America.

When she joined the PTA at our elementary school, a young mother, hearing my own mother's "foreign" accent, said, "You're in America now. You're free." To which my mother—a stranger in a strange land (stranger than she expected), stuck carless in the suburbs, away from lifelong friends and family, minding two young children while her husband was out beating the bushes—replied truthfully: "I've never felt less free in my life." The woman was insulted, taken completely aback. It wasn't long before my mother quit the PTA altogether. By age eleven, even I knew there wasn't "liberty and justice for all" and while people got all misty-eyed over the Pledge of Allegiance, I never said it out loud again. America has always had a self-delusional side, preferring the aspirations of that which *never was* to the less glorious *what is*.

Once I turned eighteen, my parents gave me all the space I required. As I started to be sexually active with both genders, I began to intuit that men (and probably some women) might be more sexually fluid than world culture cared to admit. That sexual attraction was *or could even be* on a gradient scale.

This came as a surprise. What meager "Sex Ed" we got in middle school never suggested that there was anything but male/female attraction. For those who were coming of age in secret, there were no reference points at all—no movies, no books that any school might reference for those questioning their identity. I'm not sure the term "gay" even existed back then. But dehumanizing labels like "fag", "queer" and "homo" certainly did. Many still grow up seeing themselves as nothing but a curse word.

Being raised, as most everyone, in a hereto-centric culture, I discovered that what was "normal" wasn't necessarily normal for everyone. Latin guys in particular seemed to have a confusing acceptance/denial thing going on that I could only explain as natural urges muddied by Roman Catholic indoctrination. They could say they weren't gay even sucking a cock! Large swaths of the United States had been instilled with a reading of the Bible so selective that it imbedded completely needless guilt, repression and self-loathing enough to ruin entire lifetimes—to say nothing of giving license to the haters who had it both ways with God on their side.

Much later, visiting Arab countries, I sensed a pernicious, and at the same time almost ironic denial of cultural proportions. Romantic friendships, especially in early adolescence, are completely natural. *Of course* there would be same-sex attractions when boys and girls—even grown men and women!—were so scrupulously separated almost from birth. With whom but their own gender would they have to discover and perhaps explore their sexual awakenings? The virulent homophobia, I surmised, came from adults assuaging their own memories of youthful, perhaps formative, affections. How powerful that guilty denial must be to claim God Himself justified—even to the present day—punishments like stoning, beheading and the tossing of people from tall buildings.

~

Gracie suggested that Tess and I visit an astrologer who specialized in compatibility readings. I jumped at the idea, and on the appointed day we took the bus to Fulham, which wasn't far from the flat. Her name was Mrs. Novak, and it turned out she was from, of all places, Prague, Czechoslovakia—somehow, I couldn't cut the ties!

We found her address on a tidy street of row houses, each with its own small, well-tended front garden. There were sheer white curtains in a bay window which extended up to matching windows on the first floor.

When Mrs. Novak opened the door, I was struck, first, by how very tall she was. Her no-nonsense hair was straight and black, cut square at the shoulder. Her smile was welcoming but equally no-nonsense. My first impression was that she looked more like a scientist than a woo-woo astrologer. She led us into the front room where there was a table in the bay window. Three chairs and three charts were ready. (Tess had submitted our respective birth dates and times when she made the appointment, her sign being deep in Aquarius, mine Aires on the cusp of Pisces, the dreamer, no doubt...)

After initial pleasantries, the reading progressed with information I more or less expected. First, a summation of Tess's chart, then my own, which mostly reflected that which we had already gleaned about ourselves. The only surprise was how accurately the stars reflected who we were. As for the future, Tess's stars suggested difficulty in the coming years, friendships rather than relationships, and new roots separate from her place of birth. (That would all prove true.) Mrs. Novak said if I had kids it would be a disaster *for the kids*! (Why did I suspect that that also might be true?) As for career development—my "success" if you will—was scheduled for very much later in life. That was truly disheartening. No indication of what the heck was waiting for me in the meantime except to confirm I was a creative soul with very Aries tendencies going off in many directions.

The third chart was akin to 3-D chess. There, Mrs. Novak had overlaid our astrological alignments to find an interplay between them—our compatibility—but it was at that point a mood shift occurred. It was as subtle as moonlight dimmed by a passing cloud as the three of us were quietly enveloped in a kind of psychic bubble. Again, much of what Tess and I had gleaned between us, the good and not so good, was mirrored in our stars. But very quickly we moved past the aspects, conjunctions, trines and squares into a place of deep intuitive divination.

Every detail of it is gone now but for one when Mrs. Novak said: "In a past life the situation was reversed."

I had no idea what that meant, but perhaps because it was *such* an enigmatic phrase, it stayed with me for years.

Overall, the reading's bottom line was what Tess and I had always felt: that Destiny had indeed brought us together, but it wouldn't be forever.

Now, flash forward several decades.

Tess and I *are* no longer together after a start and a stop and finally one last try-again before we separated for good. After eight years together, it was the right and painful thing to do. She would live in Paris (no surprise), and professionally dictated world travel aside I would stay based in L.A. It was there I met an elderly woman, a PhD psychologist who more or less founded—wrote a two-volume thesis on—the practice of past life regression as a therapeutic tool.

I submitted to numerous sessions, all of them profound in their revelations drawn from what I can only surmise as my akashic record, the storehouse of my soul's history embedded in my subconscious if not the quantum realms of my DNA.

"Just make it up!" she'd say as she guided me in deep meditation to a door which I would open. And behold, the entire picture of a time and place would arise spontaneously. I didn't "make it up" with forethought because the scenes were always so random. I couldn't have predicted any of them more than I could know which hexagrams would turn up when I consulted the I Ching or which cards would appear when consulting the Tarot. But similarly, the regressions were always uncannily appropriate to the answer or the clarity I was seeking. I cannot verify their "factual" truth, but every regression came with a powerful emotional validity. During one I suddenly burst into tears, re-experiencing the heartbreak I felt during a centuries-old time that connected with quantum immediacy to events and people in *this* time.

But seeking insight into my by-then decades-pastime with Tess, one regression was especially enlightening.

Through the usual guided meditation, the door in my subconscious opened on a room in Paris. The time was the late-1700s. There were numerous people seated around a long table, all of them younger than me. I was a heavyset woman in my late-forties beyond desirable marrying age. A beautiful younger sister was there as well: an actress, vivacious belle-of-the-ball; utterly cavalier about motherhood and her neglected son, a child, who was also seated at the table. Picking up my sister's slack, I was now my nephew's primary caretaker.

After gentle probing by the therapist, I realized that the vain sister and her neglected son were my mother in this life and my brother Walt.

The vision (if that's what you call it), gave sense to their story: After having an early taste of fame and glamour as a popular big band singer in New Zealand during World War II, my mother finally relinquish her dreams of making it as a singer in America and chose devotion to husband and family (especially my increasingly disabled brother) over personal ambition. To her great credit, that devotion *in this life* lasted until the day she died at ninety-five years old, revealing a kind of amends or balance-making for the former-life's self-centered obsessions.

As for *my* eighteenth-century self, at the point the regression started, I, the taken-for-granted spinster, had been left in the lurch after an off-and-on love affair with a handsome man—Tess in *that* life—who abandoned "me" and joined the Catholic priesthood.

Where else would an ambitious homosexual man of that time go?

In a past life, the situation was reversed.

Finally, I understood.

~

I resisted all the little distractions—the looks, his sociable charm, the ever low-burning sexiness—that were a constant in Sebastian's presence. Gracie, I suspected, was falling without resistance. In fact, her life had changed completely in the short time I'd known her. If she was more than Sebastian's Girl Friday... well, as I got to know Sebastian better I decided they *weren't* having sex. He just kept her dreaming that they might.

As for Finn, he'd found himself a patron, just what every artist needs. I actually hadn't seen him much but had the impression he and Sebastian were in the throes of the time-honored artist/model collaboration. Whether it had turned sexual, I simply couldn't say. But I did think that in Finn's World of Wonder anything was possible. How could he, of all people, resist the pull of Sebastian's beauty? Add my own new nocturnal rounds, and the whole flat hummed with excitement. When we did all share time in the sitting room, Finn seemed in very good spirits. Gracie told me that his late-night pacing had ceased entirely. Not, however, his double-edged wit. No one was off the hook, least of all Colin and Francesca. But Finn's bite-the-hand digs were often so smart and funny we could only laugh them off.

Gracie assuaged (again) my concern about the portrait. She had it on Sebastian's good authority that it was coming along nicely, though she admitted she hadn't actually seen it herself. "Not to worry," she said, confident that Finn would rise to the occasion. There was plenty of time.

Gracie had also taken over Tess's job collecting the rent and reporting to Colin. While discussing the generally rundown state of things, even a possible facelift, she had become privy to the details of his other property investments, including a well-situated, four-story building just off the Kings Road. He'd already sunk a lot of money into hiring a structural engineer and an architect, envisioning the quick completion of a small coffee house/cafe as the money-making anchor while renovations of the building's six flats were ongoing. From my level, it was all high finance, out of my league.

Meanwhile, I was suddenly experiencing London itself from a vantage I never imagined, certainly higher than the early days when I was sitting in a basement flat in Earls Court. My whole world was developing as quickly as a Polaroid! Tess watched as if from the balcony. She was interested, called out encouragement, whispered caution, but was basically removed. Nor would she be accused of cramping my style when her excitement didn't match my own.

Anyway, she had other things in mind.

Green buds were filling the barren trees on Sloane Street. I watched the seasonal transformation for the first time in my life, all from the upper deck of a London bus. I joined every Englishman's longing for the chill of winter to finally be over. Tess said it was time I saw Paris.

That I *hadn't* suggested a huge gap in my education. I couldn't have agreed more. Besides, France was literally Tess's home away from home. According to her, visiting Paris was simply a requirement for anyone living on Planet

Earth! Come the soonest three-day bank holiday she was determined to show me the City of Lights.

In preparation, we went to Leonard's salon for fresh haircuts. On Thursday after business hours, the too-hip salon (competitor to Vidal Sassoon), offered free cuts by their young stylists-in-training. One took one's chances (for the price of a £2 tip) but the cut was always finished by one of the instructors. Tess wanted to change her look entirely and went for a trendy asymmetrical cut, jawline on one side and mid-ear on the other. Style-wise, it was up to the minute and suited her perfectly.

My cutter was a very cute boy, barely eighteen, who I gave permission to simply do his best. I didn't need a makeover, basically just a trim albeit a trendy one, so I didn't think much could go wrong. But I quickly suspected I might have been his very first client as he kept spiraling around my head trying to get both sides even. In the end I had a too-short haircut with no style at all, and worse, it revealed the decidedly unflattering egg shape of my head. Not even the finalizing stylist could save me.

The "boat-train" relay entailed first an evening train from Victoria Station to Dover, where we'd board the nighttime ferry crossing the English Channel to Calais, then a second train to Paris. Once on the ferry, who did I see strolling the deck but my young stylists-in-training obviously taking advantage of the long bank holiday just like we were. We eyed each other but said nothing. I only hoped he quietly apologized seeing the damage he had wrought. It really was the worst haircut of my life!

Booking third class on the ferry meant we didn't have a proper cabin; instead we slept uneasily on reclining chairs in a large common room filled with budget travels. When things became a little rocky, we moved outside to a wide covered deck with more reclining chairs open to the sea air. Fortunately, that was all we needed to settle our queasy stomachs.

France revealed itself at dawn as our train sped through the countryside toward Paris. The farm houses and small-town buildings we passed had tall windows—actual in-

France French windows! I was already feeling the excitement. Then finally Paris. I was dazzled as London simply didn't dazzle. I was romanced as London had only pretended to romance when I was in fleeting love with my crazy Dutchman. Amsterdam had felt uncannily familiar, but Paris was something else. It was sensual. It was chic. Paris wore its bold beauty with the ease of a sophisticated lady. The Champs-Élysées cradled history down its long, gently sloping arms. Every cafe, every aproned waiter setting out sidewalk tables in the morning light, welcomed me. The monuments, the grand design and imperial proportions left no doubt about the presence of a culture all its own.

And Tess spoke the language!

The ease with which she bantered with our taxi driver, pointing things out to me on the way to our address…it was a side of Tess I'd never seen including slightly different mannerisms; Speaking French was not just a language but a way of expression. This was not the Tess I'd seen bottled-up by the confines of her family's routine. France revealed a freer woman than her Englishness allowed. It was the same Tess I was also getting to know from her eager lovemaking.

Our destination was a grand building on the Avenue Victor Hugo, just off the Etoile. The concierge greeted us with chitchat (all in French, of course) saying she was expecting us and gave Tess a key. We were directed to the glass doors of a marble-clad foyer across a wide cobblestone courtyard. Inside, a grand stairway curled around an Art Nouveau elevator framed like an oversized birdcage. This we took to the fifth floor. From there we had to climb a narrow flight leading to the top sixth floor and a door-lined hallway where our apartment was at the end, on loan from a friend. These rooms were once the building's servant's quarters; now each door led to a small apartment, pricy and desirable in such a good address.

Ours was a single, spacious corner room with two chest-high square windows on each exterior wall, all of them sloping at an angle under the mansard roof. A kitchen and enclosed bathroom were against one inside wall. There was a small dining table between the two windows near the kitchen area. The low bed lay between the two windows on the other wall. The view outside was of a gorgeous, classically Parisian French facade: five floors of windows, each with small, wrought-iron balconies. Because of the mansard angle I could not look straight down the exterior face of our building but had to lean my head and shoulders out to see the street. Far below, the building opposite had an arched entrance to what I presumed was its own central courtyard.

I was in heaven!

Paris was not only igniting my imagination, but my loins as well. Not just the City of Lights, but the City of Lovers was calling me, and I wanted to be part of that romance as well—right then and there! Before we even unpacked I was pulling off my clothes and Tess's too, as we fell on the bed to be one with the city's sensual essence.

We didn't venture out till mid-afternoon. Tess finally had to insist. We had lunch at a nearby cafe which included my first real French baguette. Buttery escargot! Onion soup! Light French table wine! Lemon gateaux for dessert, all of it so affordable! The Metro lines were still running decades-old wooden carriages with flip-latch doors. We went to the Louvre, crossed the great plaza years before I. M. Pei's glass pyramid, entering the palace with its endless halls and overwhelming collection. One could see the world and never leave Paris, or so it seemed. So rich, so adorned. Grandeur and picturesque at every turn.

And, no surprise, even more sensuality just below the surface.

A moment in the men's room proved as distracting as the galleries when, from the corner of my eye, I noticed a handsome young blonde seeking my attention with a very showy piece of personal art. *What to do?* It was impossible to ignore—an invitation, not a proposition—but very awkward timing. Tess had popped into the Ladies for her own little break. Dallying was not an option. I tore myself away to rejoin Tess outside. Later, as we left with the closing bell, I saw the boy again, a stoic glance between us, honor among thieves as we went our separate ways…life in the big city…paths to never cross again.

That evening we went to Montmartre to have dinner (more wonderful, affordable dining), and roam the narrow streets. Artists at easels were still set up in the main square, aping the scene of a century ago. We strolled among them, but there were no Lautrecs or Van Goughs to be seen.

I told Tess about an artist friend in Los Angeles who was offered the chance to make some extra money doing portraits at a local restaurant. A couple approached, and the woman sat down. "She had a nose like a potato," my friend said, presenting him with the existential question: does the artist draw truth or stoop to flattery? He chose the former, and when the woman's companion saw the finished work, he was outraged. "I'm not paying for this! You've made her nose look like a potato!" A few months later, another couple and the same dilemma. This time my friend took the safe road. But when the woman's husband saw the flattering portrait he said, "What kind of artist are you? Can't you see my wife has a nose like a potato?"

We walked up to the Sacre-Coeur, its very un-French architecture almost out of place yet iconic on the highest hill of the city. From the balustrade of the cathedral's wide terrace we could see below the backsides of a small buildings—apartments and their tree-filled gardens. How to know that one day Tess would own her own apartment in one of those very buildings, gathering with beloved neighbors under those same trees.

We took the Metro back to the Etoile, then a final stroll, arm-in-arm along the Avenue Victor Hugo toward our building. By then it was well after midnight, and the prostitutes were out in force. Approaching from a distance, the women were almost glamorous: tall and confident, some bundled in full-length fur coats. Passing up close, however, we could see they were mostly older women, weathered if not weary. One was severely pockmarked. Another had a tethered neck. Their makeup was too heavy, almost theatrical—probably best seen from the audience of slow-cruising cars than the sidewalk stage up close. As I stared, a woman, possibly younger than her looks, smiled cheekily my way and flashed her coat open, revealing nothing on underneath. Tess gasped out loud, and the lady laughed a throaty rumble.

Somewhere near a car alarm began a rhythmic pulse. It pierced the cold night like an insistent stabbing knife. It continued as we approached the door of our building, then on and on for hours, straining the nerves of the entire neighborhood up to us in the very highest floors, wearing us down finally into exhausted sleep.

Then BOOM!

A huge explosion sucked the air from our room like a quick inhale. We were nearly thrown out of bed. A long, eerie quiet followed, as unnerving as the explosion itself. Tess started shaking. I was completely disoriented, scrambling around for my underwear until Tess finally screamed, "Just get dressed! We have to get out of here!"

Someone shouted "Un bombe!" from the building opposite.

It was early Sunday morning. When I leaned out the window, the street was deserted, but I saw people in the building opposite, still in sleep attire, standing in their windows stunned and pointing. Directly below, I saw something lying in the street. I couldn't make sense of it at first until I realized it was a whole human leg in trousers, shoe still on.

Within ten minutes, after hastily gathering some things for the day, Tess and I were back down on the Avenue Victor Hugo. The sidewalk was littered with glass. I looked up and all the windows in our building had been blown out. Fortunately, the upward angle of our mansard roof had saved us from direct impact. And there was the leg pouring blood from its severed hip. It had been blown clean off from whatever force had detonated in the courtyard of the building opposite our own. Tess nearly vomited.

"We have to get out of Paris," she said, still shaking, as people started to gather and the distant sound of police sirens closed in. We made our way to the Metro heading for the Gare du Lyon. From there we bought tickets for an hour coach ride to Chateau de Vaux Le Vicomte, which was the closest retreat Tess could think of without consulting a guidebook.

Soon we were calming our rattled nerves on the grounds

of a stunning seventeenth century estate. Its chateau was completely surrounded by a mote. A wide bridge gave entry to many grand rooms where the old wood floors echoed underfoot. To me, the main attraction was beyond the tall windows. It was the garden that beckoned.

Le Norte's incredible landscape was a wonderland of wide terraces, patterned walkways and large round ponds spewing water from elegant fountains. A forced sightline rose into the distance crowned with a pavilion that looked back toward the chateau's dome and tall mansard roofs. Bisecting the long view were two narrow ponds that extended left and right out of view behind a wall of forest that defined the vast property's boundaries. Then more fountains, all of them a tour de force of gravity-defying, pre-electric engineering.

As Tess and I strolled in relative hiding from the shocking event in Paris, news was rippling out like a grim tsunami, creating waves of international headlines. The evening papers would report that it was a German terrorist cell that planted a bomb at a tour office doing business with Israel. An innocent bike messenger was killed as he happened to be in the wrong place at the wrong time. Tess and I were slow to realize that our firsthand experience of political terrorism would also mark the first serious fissure in our relationship. It began with lamenting the state of the world:

How impotent were our governing systems if they were impervious to stirrings at the vast bottom layer of society where change was needed most? All we heard about the 1970s oil crisis were the high-stakes negotiations between a handful of rich Arabs and oil executives representing their own company's equally untold wealth. *They* were the deciders. We the People, including millions of anonymous, working-class Saudis, were out of the narrative altogether.

Was violence the only catalyst for change? I refused to believe it. Bombs were a downward spiral. War solved nothing. Perhaps not, Tess said, but our maps were drawn from conflict. Greed and cruelty were part of our human nature.

I disagreed. "We have options," I protested.

"We're running out of options," Tess replied.

"Hating war won't solve things. Loving peace *will*."

Tess laughed. "We have no practice loving peace! We can't even imagine what a world at peace would look like or what we'd do *instead*!"

I had to agree that declaring peace as easily as we declared war sounded, if not radical, then totally naive. "But that's the goal as I see it."

"Well, we better get there fast," Tess concluded. "Now that we *can* blow up the world, somebody just might."

There was nothing more to add except a grim final note in the Chateau's information brochure saying King Luis XIV was so jealous of designer Le Notre's sublime garden he had the chateau's owner, Nicolas Fouquet, arrested and imprisoned for life! No good deed allowed to go unpunished.

As we savored our peaceful surroundings, we noticed a pair of young men about our own age strolling along the opposite side of the garden's long pond, their reflections distinct in the still water. I'd seen them earlier when we toured the chateau; heard them speaking quietly in German. Now I was following them with my eyes when they stopped, embraced and kissed tenderly.

It was a beautiful moment, but I must have gazed too long. I felt Tess studying me and turned to her. I'd been caught. Overcompensating, I said the words I'd never said: "I love you."

"No, you don't," she snapped, a catch in her voice that probably surprised even her, one so good at concealing her feelings as I was telling lies.

The truth was, I ached for something Tess could not provide. More than just sex (or a penis) it was the unexplainable, almost instinctive power of attraction, which was still as much a mystery as it was to me when I was ten years old.

On the coach ride back to Paris, I mused about taking up photography in a more serious way. Sebastian's name came up, of course. He'd said I showed real talent. Maybe he was right. He should know.

Tess flared. Now was not the time to be invoking Sebastian.

"You're just dazzled," she said dismissively.

"You said the same about Gracie, but look how well *she's* doing. It's like you don't want us to have anything but your idea of fun!"

"Can't you see what's happening?"

"Tell me," I demanded.

"I'm watching, and I'm frightened. Have you seen Finn lately? I saw him the other night when I was visiting Gracie. You'd gone out *somewhere*..." (Message clear.)

Actually, I hadn't seen Finn in several weeks. Occasionally I'd hear him passing on the stairs when I was in bed. If he was in his room, he was quiet, which I considered a good sign. Maybe he had some new commissions. Sebastian wasn't shy with introductions.

"Well, he doesn't look good, Terry. If I didn't know him better, I'd say he was on drugs."

"He's not on drugs."

"Are you sure?"

"Tess, he's not on drugs." I insisted. "And for what it's worth, Sebastian doesn't do drugs, either. He barely drinks. I'm sure they're working on something... having fun. Do you want to deny *everyone's* fun?" The words sounded pathetic the moment I said them.

She looked at me incredulously. "Deny you?" Tess shouted. "You do whatever you want!"

She was right, of course. Tess could read me like a book. I found it almost presumptuous. I hid behind compartmentalization. Nor did I read the warning any more than I had from the car alarm in Paris, a harbinger of probabilities straining the energetic field until they finally released their terrible dark blast.

By the time we left Paris, each of us needed some breathing room. We didn't talk much on the train to Calais; even less on the rocky ferryboat to Dover. We both slept in our seats on the train back to London. But pre-arranged plans dictated continued close quarters starting with, of all people,

Tess' parents. They would be picking us up at Victoria Station. We'd spend the night in Hampstead rather than lug suitcases on the Tube back to Notting Hill.

And there they were on the platform, waving and excited to see us. We piled into the back seat as Mister and Misses settled themselves carefully up front. Mr. Greenwald ticked all the boxes before ignition, then carefully looked in all directions before taking off.

"How was your first trip to Paris, Terry," Mrs. Greenwald asked brightly.

"Well, apart from the terrorist bomb, everything went well."

"Oh, yes," she replied, as if mentioning bad news skirted bad manners.

"But you came *through*," Mr. Greenwald said, all onward and upward as if, returning from the wars, we could now put all that behind us.

Tess remained quiet. She was deeply disappointed that our experience—sharing the city she loved—had been marred by such violence *as well as* its inescapable metaphor as it related to the issues between us. I also knew her father's *Carry On* tone was driving Tess crazy.

"What I could use now," I said, hoping to change the subject, "is a nice hot shower."

For once there was no perfunctory reply.

In fact, the silence turned positively weird.

Uncomfortable looks were exchanged between the grown-ups. I looked over at Tess. *What had I said?* Finally, Mr. Greenwald broke the ice.

"Well, it's like this, Terry. This is Sunday, and Sunday is Gerald's bath night. We want to make sure there's enough hot water, so if you could just hold off on that shower until tomorrow morning…you understand."

"Oh, sure," I said. "No problem."

But I was still confused. Setting aside my wondering if Gerald only bathed one night a week, the awkwardness seemed out of proportion to my request. I could tell it would be pushing things to suggest I take my chances and have a quick shower *after* Gerald's bath. There was more to this than hot water. In any case, there'd be no exceptions, even for weary travelers. My shower would have to wait.

When we finally made it to the privacy of Tess's bedroom (where we would break more presidents by me sharing her childhood bed), she explained the real issue. Sunday was not only Gerald's bath night, it was also when Mrs. Greenwald was tasked with scrubbing her grown son's naked back while he was in the tub. I immediately pictured her waiting to be called; Gerald covering himself with a washcloth, leaning forward as his mother entered. She would kneel beside the bath then enact the ultimate subservience, flagrantly unnecessary for a grown man, soaping up a soft brush and scrubbing Gerald's back, careful, I am sure, not to miss a spot.

My guess was that they'd never imaged having to explain themselves to anyone. This was the most private of family matters. And by their reaction, it was clear that even *they* knew there was something slightly *off*. But it was all part of shrugging helplessly as their willful son wielded his joyless routine upon the household; punishment ever due. Atonement had become a way of life.

~

One always remembers the worst times *first*. But mostly they were good between Tess and me. We truly enjoyed each other's company, helped each other bloom at a time in our lives when life is all about finding out who one is, what one wants—and *doesn't* want. To our friends, we were Terry and Tess. The words rolled off everyone's tongue like it was the natural order of things. And in most ways it was.

Tess had always wanted to learn French cooking. The big kitchen at Notting Hill made that doable. I'd help out by providing employee-discounted ingredients from the Food Halls that might otherwise have been prohibitive if not unavailable almost anywhere else. She not only became a great cook, but I, as her biggest fan, gained a vocabulary in French cuisine. When Blanche was not away on tour with her dance company, we had many little dinner parties with her and her very funny string bean of a boyfriend, Henry. He was just starting his first post-college job as a mechanical engineer. His goal was to design car engines. I'd never considered people actually studied for that; thought the matter was settled: you turned the key and the engine started. Once Henry set me straight, it gave new meaning to the words in "Little Duce Coupe" and "409"—all early Beach Boys songs—the ones not about surfing. But Henry said electric cars were the ultimate goal. I agreed that that was probably true, but it sounded like, you know, *the future*. Indeed, the year 2000 was a long way off—if we made it that far.

Part of Tess's busy post-graduate schedule was conducting supervised sessions with traumatized children, mostly those from abusive homes or even witnesses to murder. When she chose to talk about it (she internalized their pain, too) the writer in me found it extremely interesting; but this was serious work, which required decompression time. Fortunately, hearing about *my* day was almost like a holiday! We still saw each other two or three times a week; had lunch in Knightsbridge, dinner at her flat. We spent most of our weekends together. But the time apart gave us both room to consider our relationship.

The fact—the specter—of my bisexuality (not that we ever used the word) was never far from the surface. In fact, we didn't actually talk about it at all. But lines blurred one night after another enjoyable dinner with Blanche and Henry. Tess had triumphed over all doubts about the tastiness of liver and onions with a French recipe she found. Between the four of us we'd consumed several bottles of good wine (my contribution with indirect thanks to Sebastian). Then dessert and exotic cheese with apéritifs, probably Cointreau. Blanche and Henry retired to their room. Tess and I fell into bed, warmed, lusty and ready for sex.

But on this night I was a little more drunk than usual. I must have been more amorous, too, moving as I never moved with Tess. At one point I began to slide down past her breasts, below her stomach and in my drunken abandon ready to do what I'd never done. Suddenly, Tess was crying. She pushed me away as if she was being assaulted. I didn't understand. But Tess did. She knew. This was not me with her, but that other me with those other people she didn't know—or want to know anything about. She saw how I made love with a man.

Yet through the half truths and quiet disappointments, Tess and I had our own version of balance. We were making our own history; even talked fondly about "the old days" living together at Wandsworth Bridge Road, when we'd sometimes walk to our local on a Saturday night. She'd have a shandy, I'd have my usual bitter, and we'd just soak in the pleasure of conversation. Then back to the flat for a good screw!

Once Tess moved to Notting Hill, we did most of our socializing—and all our screwing—in the comfort of *her* flat. But even then we occasionally walked down to several local pubs. I had indeed discovered the valued place that pubs have in English life.

Before the 1980s, there was no such "third place" in L.A. No cafe-going as a way of life or streets for promenade in the European sense—or even the New York City sense.
Nobody walks in L.A.
Missing Persons wasn't half wrong about that. The citizens of Los Angeles had no practice being *among* people, brushing shoulders, feeling the crowd of a city. The reason was partly geographic. For over a hundred years, the ever-spreading suburbs had instilled a sense of isolation. Cars made the wide open spaces more accessible, but people were still in their bubbles, walled off by metal and shatterproof glass. Bus-riding in L.A. had always been considered mostly for the working poor. This remained true even in the early 90s when the first threadbare subway system finally opened fifty years late. (The Mañana Syndrome is imbedded in L.A.'s DNA.) Even then, it took most Angelenos a few years to catch on to the advantages of real mass transit.

Los Angeles County has eighty-eight cities including the

City of Los Angeles, so it's understandable that "L.A." as one thinks of it is not a defined place. It has no true center, and there's no signature style. One of its pleasures *is* the rich architectural diversity, which is to say that L.A. is not like San Francisco or New York or Paris or even London where, when you step outside, you know immediately where you are. L.A. *is* as genuinely cool as its reputation, but that "cool" is hidden in its enclaves: in the woodsy canyons and behind the manicured hedges, mostly on the west side. Its greater footprint, however, is largely an unattractive sprawl. A car ride from the airport to anywhere has been known to make people weep with disappointment. Don't visit Los Angeles for a few days thinking you'll get it. You just won't…it's impossible.

That said, for all its half-baked glamour Los Angeles has remained a prime source for Media writ large: movies, music, television, radio. But that's just L.A. doing what it does: projecting *out* from its insular core. That all changed forever when the 1984 Summer Olympics came to town. It brought an international tide of people flooding *in* and over the course of a single summer L.A.'s view of itself began to include the rest of the world. Most of the sporting and art events were programed in downtown venues because the city fathers were determined to make DTLA a *place* after decades of neglect.

As it happened (coincidence? I don't think so…) a few months before the Olympics I was forced to decamp from my Hollywood apartment after a fire in the building. Through a dear friend who was decamping back to Vancouver, I inherited two rooms (bathroom down the hall) at the American Hotel, a 1905-era boarding house, which also housed, at street level, the now legendary Al's Bar, where bands like the Red Hot Chili Peppers, Nirvana and Sonic Youth played early gigs. Both bar and hotel were at the bullseye center of an emerging new art and music (punk) scene. Suddenly I was in the eye of the storm!

One of my two fourth-floor windows gave me a perfect view west to the city's burgeoning skyline. The other was above the patio behind Al's. "Burning Down the House" was in constant play on the jukebox inside, and it wafted out to the patio and up to my window every night of the week. I never got tired of it.

Most Angelenos still didn't know downtown was even habitable. Our neighborhood didn't have a name. Thirty years later it would be officially designated as The Arts District, but by then no artists could afford to live there...least of all the starving ones. Rent at the American was so cheap ($270 a month for my *two* rooms), that my friend across the hall who rented just a single, said in words I'll never forget: "If you can't afford a hundred and thirty-five dollars a month you don't deserve to live!"

On my first night at the American Hotel, I was unaware that, with all the moving, my white cat Kitty (with her mismatched David Bowie eyes) had been inadvertently locked out, stranded in the hallway. The bar had closed. I was sleeping when there was a knock at my door. Answering it, Al's punk-haired bar-back held out his arm holding Kitty.

"Is this yours?"

She must have jumped from an open window in the hallway, her long fall softened by the trellis of vines over the patio tables and chairs. Then she jumped (or fell) to the ground and ran inside the bar. The story got around in a matter of days. Kitty's stunt had introduced me to the neighborhood! For the first time in my life I felt a sense of community surrounded with art and like-minded artists. That's where I began my real journey as a professional photographer, drawing, a decade later, on all the lessons and experience Sebastian had afforded me. The full-circle of it all still amazes me.

But with the 1980s came L.A.'s biggest change of all, which can be summed up in a single word: *Starbucks*.

Finally—collectively—L.A. had a destination besides home and work. It is no exaggeration to say that Starbucks changed the city's entire social way of being. We didn't have pubs, but suddenly we had coffee! Then one Starbucks begat a thousand, and seemingly overnight everyone was...*meeting for coffee!* People became *connoisseurs* of fucking coffee! An entirely new vocabulary emerged! In pre-

Starbucks days, people met at Denny's for coffee—pretty lousy coffee it was, too. All that changed in the 1980s.

~

Tess never knew the particulars of my subterranean life—where I went, whom I met, what kind of sex I liked. If "discretion" is the proper word, I was discrete. If "cheating", "lying by omission", "selfish" and "amoral" are more apt words, I was those as well. I never punished her for what I might have perceived as restraints on my behavior. I never intentionally hurt her pursuing misguided notions of "being free" (to quote Joni Mitchell again). I didn't want to lose Tess, not in a million years. We were right for each other on so many levels. At the same time, I pined for something else: for love with a man.

Tess picked up on my shifting moods; the restlessness, headaches and mild depression. Quite naturally she took my distancing as rejection. But we still met for lunch in Knightsbridge once or twice a week. We'd stroll back to Harrods, where Tess might do some grocery shopping. Of course, her purchases all went back to *her* flat. Trust Finn to comment on the diminished treats at *our* place now I was only providing for one. But the physical space between Tess and me actually strengthened our relationship; it gave time for the little wounds to heal. To my mind, there was nothing broken. I wasn't wrong being bisexual.

As for sustaining a heterosexual relationship, it was overly optimistic. Bless Tess for looking on the bright side. If not a card carrying optimist, she stuck at things, pushed through adversity with a determined nature. But her bravery was probably as naive as me thinking I could navigate unscathed living on both sides of the fence. We both wanted to keep what we had—the bird in hand, so to speak. But what was in the bushes would never really stop rustling.

There *was* newfound freedom with Tess's new situation. Besides more adventurous escapades in the kitchen, there were the pleasures of her bedroom in the form of a proper double bed. We finally had more play room, but equally rewarding, room for a comfortable night's sleep.

On nights I didn't want to stay over (because taking the Tube from Notting Hill to Knightsbridge the next morning was complicated), a map suggested that if I watched my time, it was actually easier to walk from Notting Hill to Earls Court, where I could catch the last Tube back closest to my place.

But that turned out to be the devil's road.

Taking it the first time, I recognized the narrow, high-walled sloping walk leading into Holland Park. It was the same cruising spot Pieter, and I had discovered by accident months before, where the shadows were alive against the long wall behind the trees. It was always a temptation, and sometimes I would linger, resigning myself to missed trains and a longer walk home. Or, if I brisk-paced to Earls Court, I might catch a last pint at the Coleherne. Otherwise, I'd fly down the open-air stairs heading for the Tube to catch the final ride before Doors Closing. I never missed it except by choice.

One night, having made it to the Coleherne and not yet ready to continue home, I thought I'd sample the notorious cruising street behind the pub. I'd checked it out once before but realized there was nowhere to actually go besides getting into a stranger's car heading to "your place or mine". Mine was out of the question, so I never went back.

But on this night, as I debated the cruising cars, a clean-cut guy about thirty pulled up and suggested *his* place. After assuring me that it was nearby, I got in. All I remember is that he was very pleasant, a nurse at some local hospital he said, and that his flat was one of many in a wide deco building with multiple floors. Details are spare beyond that for reasons I only deduced later.

When we got to his flat, he offered me a drink. The next thing I remember was being let out politely to find my own way home. Fortunately, I knew where I was, but as I walked, I felt a slight discomfort, even dampness, at my rectum. I was slow to grasp the unthinkable, but considering the hospital connection and a complete block of lost time, I realized I must have been drugged, fucked, then shown the door, all in time to never trace my footsteps back to his.

Who could I tell? There was no one.

If I were still with Carlos and Burt, I'd have told them everything. At least I could have vented my outrage, my disgust. Instead, I never told *anyone*. Forget the police. They were notoriously homophobic, and I'd have only subjected myself to their humiliating winks and snickers. *"It's your own fault, mate,"* they'd have said, and they wouldn't have been wrong. When living in the shadows, you take your chances. My "real" world never touched the parallel one of after-hours cruising and anonymous sex. But no encounter would be as depraved as meeting that sicko nurse who committed nothing less than rape.

~

Which, dare I broach it, brings me to the subject of penises.

I almost hesitate to speak the obvious, but it really is a wonder about cocks. Why do we risk so much in pursuit of them? Why are they so…*of interest*?

Across the ages they've been fetishized, worshiped and enshrined. Not surprisingly, gay men bring an added ardor to this adoration. I've seen grown men rendered weak in the knees—I've been genuinely rattled myself—at the mere sight of a big, beautiful cock. Just seeing the outline (or what my mother once described as an "undesirable contour") can be a goal in itself. For a photographer/voyeur (this one, at least), the blessed compliment, of course, is an exhibitionist whose own pleasure I'm only too glad to accommodate. In the modern era where cameras and videos are ubiquitous, there seems to be an endless parade of more-than-willing show-offs! What a blessing! I thank them all.

But visuals are just the beginning! Pressing one's face against a well-formed bulge can be as exciting as discovering what's cupped inside. Once released, there comes the surprise of variety. For sure, no two dicks are alike, but some distinguish themselves. Beyond mere length, there's shape, color and girth. (The really big ones *are* rare.)

Foreskin can be a newfound pleasure for mostly circumcised Americans (and Kiwis), and also comes in various lengths and thicknesses. Some foreskins are thin and veiny. Some are long and bunch at the tip. Some almost disappear at erection; a few are so tight the head is never fully exposed. One guy I knew had foreskin so thick it doubled the girth of the shaft inside. Truth be told, it was more alluring as a bulge *under* his clothes.

Then there was the guy I knew before *and after* his circumcision. He showed off both versions, bless him—a true exhibitionist—having the rare authority to know the difference in…what's the word… *lifestyle?* He deemed he was happier minus the "extra".

And balls! Don't get me started! I've known women who consider them as useless as a soft cock. For *their* purposes, I see their point. But balls are part of the whole package coming with their own range of variety, from tight and bunched to sweetly dangling to (rare again) pendulous and heavy, swinging like great bells.

Once at Catacombs, I saw a guy who showed off a hard cock that bent sideways almost a full right turn. Everyone looked as if only because it was so truly unusual. A few weeks later at work I happened to be using one of the public restrooms, a rare occurrence in itself. I preferred the employee's facility on the top floor; it was quieter, bright with window light and had all original wood partitions and white-tiles. Anyway, I found myself standing next to a young guy, and when I peeked over, it was the same bent cock!

"I know you," I said quietly, surprising him, nodding at his distinctive tool. "I've seen you at the Catacombs."

He smiled awkwardly. "Yes, probably," he replied. Then I realized I'd caught him actually cottaging at Harrods! I didn't even know that was a thing, though I suppose I shouldn't have been surprised. But cruising at work was not going to be *my* thing, and I made a hasty retreat back to the Food Halls.

On a final note, I'll share my theory as to why some straight men have a problem with gay men and their multiple partners: they're just a little jealous!

A straight guy's search for sexual coupling usually involves courting, dating and finally the woman's permission allowing her body to be *entered* by the male member. All this usually comes with the speed bumps of donning a condom or the shadow of concern, condom or not, that some mishap might cause an unwanted pregnancy. But the goal is penetration.

By contrast, gay male sex need *never* involve the dinner date or that ultimate breach—i.e. fucking. I can attest to encounters where the pleasure of oral sex and mutual masturbation were transcendently (if not drunkenly) pleasurable, be it with an intimate lover or a quick and busy TCB.

Ahh, but to each his own.

~

One day, Blanche's brother Timothy, the blonde charmer I met over Christmas, invited us—Blanche and Henry, Tess and me—to a fancy-dress ball at his Oxford college. It meant I'd have to rent a tuxedo (a first in itself), but I wasn't going to miss an opportunity to experience Oxford from the student's level, not just as a tourist. That the whole thing came by way of Timothy was icing on the cake. He was coming with his girlfriend, Angela, the unlikely mathematician.

The plan was that we'd all stay a night at the comfortable home of a recently deceased former professor, John Thomas, with whom Timothy had been close for several years. Along with the old man's sister, Timothy was helping to sort out the house. When we arrived, the entire place was in an obvious state of dismantling: bookshelves half empty, boxes half filled; framed artwork and awards leaning in stacks against the wall. More boxes filled with kitchen items and sundry nicknacks.

But even in disarray, the house resonated warmth. When I asked Timothy about our deceased host, he spoke of him with great affection. Professor Thomas had taught three generations of Oxford's youthful best and brightest, frequently welcoming small groups into his airy sitting room to discuss literature, poetry and music. He was a man ahead of his time, Timothy said, and from a time that will never come again. It was all so English, revolving around an academic world I knew nothing about. But if only for a day or two, knowing my own school days were well and truly over, I could revel in imagining I was an Oxford student myself. (In much later years, I had that same feeling staying several weeks as the guest of a Fellow at the American Academy in Rome...imagining how it might have been if I'd done what it takes to actually get there...but I was never that guy.)

With permission from the surviving sister, we had the house to ourselves for the weekend. Timothy assigned the rooms. Blanche and Henry took an upstairs bedroom next to Timothy and Andrea, whose laughter I heard even through closed doors. Apparently, he was still as amusing as he was when we first met on Boxing Day. Tess and I were given a room on the ground floor that the Professor himself had occupied after he could no longer manage the stairs. There was a bed facing the window, replacing a large desk that had been moved into the dining room...more boxes of books there, too.

"We're just making do," Timothy said, but he was being modest. He'd prepared all the beds himself with fresh sheets and clean towels in both upstairs and downstairs bathrooms. Space was made for candles by the beds. In fact, there were two gracious hosts looking after us. One whose nurturing spirit, even after passing, gave us warmth and shelter. And Timothy Haddock himself, looking after the real world amenities with his own preternatural charm. I was secretly thrilled and smitten all over again.

At the appointed hour we gathered for champagne in the sitting room before calling a taxi to take us to our first stop of the evening. Tess wore the low-cut, floor-length dress she wore on New Year's Eve, her wonderfully ample breasts on rare and glorious display. Andrea was dressed in early Chanel, flapper style: a black three-quarter length straight-line with three tiers of long fringes all the way round.

Blanche wore a simple black cocktail dress offset by a quietly spectacular choker borrowed from her actress sister, featuring a fan of five large rubies surrounded with diamonds. Henry was so tall and thin (and those pimples!) I doubt if he ever found clothes that didn't seem to just *hang* on him. Timothy, on the other hand, was clearly born to wear tuxedos. I'd never seen anyone so elegant. But his *way*—the tussled hair, his easy gestures, beautiful voice, as well as an air of kindness—was really beginning to rattle me.

After a very short taxi ride, we were dropped at a pub in the middle of town. It was probably a casual haunt—one of many—for Oxford's student population, but on this night it was crowded with young people all dressed up for the ball.

I'd seen enough Masterpiece Theater programs on American television to give the whole scene context. Even Harrods, a living thing, retained those echoes. But Oxford itself was like stepping deep into history, and a surprisingly well-preserved history at that. The old stone walls, ornate windows, heavy doors, even the college's empty courtyards still held the ghosts of centuries shared on the lovely shoulders of youthful promise.

As dusk turned to early evening, people started drifting out in animated little groups, and we more or less paraded casually through Oxford's timeless streets as everyone headed to the college (I don't remember which one) where the ball was being held. How grand we must have looked and how proud I was, the only American, being welcomed to drink deeply, literally and figuratively, of this uniquely English *way*.

The ball itself was a student-planned event, somewhat disjointed, modern to a fault if not overly-ambitious. First, there was no grand ballroom as I imagined it; no orchestra playing waltzes. Nothing like it. There was a rock band outside, a second one in a large, beam-ceilinged dining hall with large dark portraits on the walls. Elsewhere, a DJ spun records, which ended up being the best music of all. The two bars charged for drinks. But we danced and laughed through it all. Eventually, Timothy and Angela went off with their friends. Blanche and Henry found a corner of their own. Tess and I roamed the arched cloisters. I couldn't even say how we got back to the house. What I remember most is waking up the next morning and feeling the delicious afterglow. I put my tuxedo bowtie back on to cover my nudity, and Tess and I made love.

Suddenly the bedroom door, barely two feet from my side of the bed, flew wide open, and I was looking into the face of an old woman. We both froze, staring at each other with open mouths, me with bow tie affixed, bare bottom up between Tess' legs. She hid her face in my shoulder. Not a word was said. After an awkward moment, the woman simply stepped back and closed the door. It was as flagrantly *delicto* as it gets, but once we put our momentary embarrassment aside (and my instantly limp dick back *in*side), we finished the morning properly.

Laughing about it with the other couples over breakfast, we learned that the lady who discovered us was the sister of the deceased professor. She'd come over on a quiet Sunday to continue packing up her brother's things. She knew there were house guests, but thought we were all upstairs—not having sex in her newly late brother's bed!

~

It nearly killed me to not talk about my glamorous nightlife with my co-workers at Harrods. Sometimes I dragged myself in and must have looked like I hadn't slept at all. But no matter how late I stayed up, I could always slog through until my morning break—both of them. At lunch I'd crash in the large resting room on one of dozens of comfortable recliners that lined the walls. More than once I'd wake up to find myself the only one there and have to fly down multiple flights of wide marble stairs to the ground floor. When the store was busy, I'd just slip right in unnoticed. When it wasn't, Mr. Taylor gave me dirty looks.

He actually hinted that I had a drinking problem. When I laughed it off, he took my denial as further proof I *had* a problem. Saint or sinner, I was damned. Mostly, it bothered him that I seemed to have more going on than just Harrods. He was a corporate player, which meant one mustn't stray too far from the fold. I didn't know how true that was until a fellow employee once asked if I lived in a "Harrods house". I didn't know what she meant, then shuddered to learn there were flats in buildings where all the tenants worked at Harrods. The store could be one's entire community. Harrods could fill your life.

I deposited my weekly paycheck, as most employees did, at Harrods Bank on the fifth floor. This was also where the executive offices were located. Once I went exploring and found myself in a quiet corridor, carpeted, lined with narrow tables and artwork on the walls. There was no one around, so I opened a pair of important-looking double doors to peek inside.

And there was Valhalla! Harrods' boardroom! It wasn't overly large and curtains were drawn to cover the several tall windows, so the only light was that which spilled in from the corridor behind me. But there was no mistaking the gravitas implied in the long table and ten green leather high-backed chairs down each side. Well over a century of decision-making had happened here, and the room hummed with the quiet weight of power.

~

Between them, Gracie and Dee ran a tight ship. I'd started getting some good pocket money—always paid in a timely fashion—from publication fees for my pictures. It made all the difference to my date night options with Tess. We dined out every few weeks. Went to "the cinema" a few times. It was there that I encountered yet another example of England's class distinction. In America, you bought your movie ticket and sat where you liked. In England, seats closest to the screen were the cheap ones. The supposedly best seats (the pricy ones) were at the back—reverse from live theater, but the "sections" concept held over to maintain the "station" separation. Either way, it worked out fine for me. I always liked watching a movie from the third row.

Sebastian's name came up in most of Tess and my conversations. It came up again over dinner one night at a restaurant he'd recommended.

"It's all business," I said, rather naively. This after she voiced her usual concern, wondering out loud about what Sebastian's motives might be socializing so intrepidly, to say nothing of bringing both Finn, Gracie and me so tightly into the fold.

"We're all having fun," I said.

"Of course, you're having fun!"

"So, what's the problem?"

"I don't know, Terry, but when it's too good to be true, maybe it is."

"It's working out fine for Gracie."

"Gracie!" she said, throwing up her hands. "I hardly see her. She's become another person; like she's been...I don't know...*abducted!*"

"Why do you have a problem with that?"

"With abduction?"

"No," I laughed. "With change."

I could see her struggling. "She really wanted to be an actress, and suddenly she's left that all behind."

"She's twenty-two!" I protested. "It's the *perfect* time to be changing her mind!"

"But she wanted it so badly."

"Tess, I wanted something badly, too, remember? Then life hits you in the face and things just change!"

She nodded, still not settled. "But all that work, so much action required....her dreams..."

"And now she has different dreams. I actually think what she's doing now is a perfect fit."

It seemed hard to dispute, and I felt that tidily ended things, but Tess hadn't finished.

"What about you?"

"Me?"

"What do your actions say? Have you changed your mind too?"

"About what? I'm a failed student, Tess. Harrods is not my life. My visa's running out. When I'm back in L.A. I want to get serious about becoming a photographer."

Tess went silent. It was the first time I'd addressed directly that I had a visa which *would* expire—and, more to the point, I wasn't going to renew it. But I knew it wasn't only about that.

"I've never lied to you."

"You lie by omission, Terry. You always have."

Her words, though spoken quietly, drowned out the trendy restaurant buzz. She was right. I'd kidded myself into thinking we had a tacit agreement. I wouldn't talk about my after-hours and she, politely, wouldn't asked. The truth was that Tess had no references to imagine the places I went or the things I did—least of all her boyfriend being raped. It was literally unimaginable! As long as I showed up, everything was normal.

"You're the only one, Tess."

"I like to think that, but…" Her eyes filled with tears.

I took her hand. "It's true. There's no one else. My life is so full with you and with us."

"What about Sebastian? I can understand being…I mean, he's quite good looking."

I laughed out loud at her understatement.

"For the last time, Tess, we're not having an affair. For sure he's not *after* me."

"He's after the world, Terry, and everyone's lining up to give it to him."

She was right about that. "I keep a professional distance."

"I don't want details, Terry. I just want to know you're…"

She stopped.

What could she ask? That I be faithful? At least I wasn't seeing other *women*. But little trysts with men? That was play. Letting off steam. A guy thing. Apples and oranges. But fidelity? I couldn't promise that.

"I actually think he's asexual," I said.

"You mean like all *and* nothing?"

"Very funny," I said, taking a moment to consider my next words—which I hoped would clear the air once and for all. "I'm his *assistant,* Tess. Yes, we work as a team, but there's no more to it. Can you live with that?"

"Do I have a choice?"

I sighed helplessly. "Tess, I'm just going with the flow."

"Going where? That's what worries me."

"Stop worrying," I said. "I know what I'm doing."

Famous last words.

~

As for Finn, he and Sebastian seemed to be thick as thieves. True, I hadn't actually seen either of them lately. In those days everyone was busy. Gracie was clearly on a roll. I began to feel that even though she now had the big bedroom (and a phone!) all to herself, she wouldn't be long for the flat.

If I was being seduced by Sebastian I didn't see it. In fact, I thought I was doing a pretty good job keeping my head straight. I knew Sebastian as a person, not an icon. There were tangible perks, too. More than on-the-job training, I was getting respect as a photographer—not that anyone knew it by the photo credits, but *I* knew it. And it all came with the excitement of mixing with the A List crowd. There was *no* discernible downside. Meanwhile, I realized that the publishing of our nightlife escapades was helping to create the new decades's image of *post* Swinging London. We were the Next Wave! Sure, the town still practically shut down by eleven o'clock, but not in Sebastian's world. The cool places stayed opened late—very late. And disco was still the rage.

~

I arrived home from work to find Gracie and Colin in the sitting room going over papers spread out on the dining table. Francesca was making tea in the kitchen and chirped a hello. But there was a somber mood among them.

"What's going on?" I asked.

Finally Colin said there was no breaking it to me gently. "I'll have to raise the rent."

I was surprised but not overly alarmed. With the extra money I was making I could easily manage an increase.

"How much?"

"Nine pounds more a week."

"We'll manage," Gracie said.

I was about to concur when I heard that *we* again. She was speaking *for* me because she knew what Sebastian was paying *to* me. With Tess gone, Gracie was also privy to all the flat dealings. And now to Colin's other business as well, apparently, as he shuffled documents with quiet concern. What didn't add up was how our collective raised rent payments would ease the stress I could see on Colin's face. We were smalltime compared to the grownup wheeling and dealing of his other properties. At least, that was my impression. He must have seen the question on my face.

"I'm getting the squeeze," he said.

"Not from us," I replied.

Francesca came in with the tea. "Oh, not from you, darling. It's that big building off the Kings Road."

Colin nodded, though from his expression I think he wished she hadn't mentioned it. But Gracie was all ears.

"I thought you bought it," she said.

"Buying it doesn't mean owning it when you're still paying a mortgage," Colin replied. "And those big loans involved for the improvements," Francesca added. "Someone's nipping at his heels."

"Thank you, darling," Colin said, as if to say *that's enough volunteering*.

"Like a hostile takeover?" I ventured.

Colin swallowed. "Well, that's a little out of scale, but you've got the idea. It's all a bit of a mystery. New building requirements coming out of nowhere, slowing things down. The bank calling me as they *never* have, and believe me I've been a perfect customer. Now they want me to put this place up as collateral, which is exactly what I didn't want to do—didn't *have* to do six months ago."

"*More* collateral!" Francesca trilled.

"Darling, please," Colin said, sounding pained.

"To fight the marauders!" she added, unstoppable.

Gracie was running the numbers in her head. "Which means you don't own this place either?"

"No, I *do* own it, that's always been my best defense. But now I have to borrow heavily on its value."

"So that *is* a squeeze," said Gracie.

Colin nodded glumly.

Then we heard the front door open and close. A moment later, Finn walked in. I was shocked by his appearance. Tess was right, he looked terrible.

"Good God, darling!" Francesca exclaimed before anyone else had time to react.

"Hail to you, too," Finn replied. "I could use a cup of tea."

"I'll say you could," said Francesca, turning immediately back to the kitchen.

Finn looked at me and smiled sheepishly. "Long time no see."

"We keep missing each other," I replied weakly.

Then Gracie dropped the bomb: "The rent's going up."

Finn barked a loud Ha! "Welcome to my world," he said as if this news capped the events of a bad day.

"It's doable," I said. "Just nine pounds."

But my first instinct was to take him in my arms and hug him. Whatever was going on suggested he needed something more than tea. Hopefully, it wasn't drugs. I dreaded to think our beautiful artist was heading down the dark ladder.

"Sebastian's coming by later," he said as if this was something we should know.

"Are you hungry?" Gracie said. "Let's order something in."

"What a good idea!" Francesca called from the kitchen.

"Yes, let's do it!" Gracie said, casting a quick eye toward me as if to say *Agree with me!*

"I'm starving," I said. "What about Chinese?"

"Yes, there's that place at the end of Kings Road," said Gracie. "How about it, Finn?"

"Chinese sounds good. I think they deliver."

All these sudden imperatives seemed to rattle Colin further, but Francesca insisted on calling the restaurant right then and there.

"All right, let's do that," Colin agreed. He seemed too beaten to argue.

"That's right, Colin," Finn said. "Slum along with the rest of us."

What might have been amusing weeks ago fell woefully flat and hung in the air like an unpleasant smell.

Francesca broke the awkward silence by coming in with a fresh cup of tea.

"Here you are, darling," she said, handing Finn the cup. "Now, I want no more glib talk. We'll order in and that settles it. Go and sit down. Be nice."

"I'll call the restaurant," said Gracie, taking a phone book from the bookshelf.

"Just order one of everything," Francesca called out. "I'll take care of it."

Finn dropped onto the couch next to me. Gracie huddled at the dining table in the corner flipping pages.

"So, how's work, Terry?" Finn asked. "I know you've been out with Sebastian."

"Yes," I replied. "I'm on the night shift."

Gracie looked over. The mere mention of Sebastian's name pricked up her ears.

"Terry's become quite good with a camera," she said quickly, almost preemptively.

"I never doubted you," Finn said.

Before I could react or share the moment or I don't know what, Francesca called again from the kitchen.

"Who's Sebastian?"

We all looked up. It was Finn who spoke first: "Don't tell me you don't..."

"He's that fellow on the busses," Colin said. "They're all working for him."

Francesca stepped into the kitchen archway and looked at us one by one.

"All of you?" She sounded confused. "And you met him on the bus?"

Gracie laughed. "No, we met through the theater where I work."

"Used to work," I said.

"Well, yes…now….where I used to work. He owns the building right next door."

"But you said he was on the bus."

"His picture, Francesca," Colin said. "He's a famous model."

"*And he rides the bus?*"

I laughed. "No, Francesca, *I* ride the bus. Sebastian's picture is on the *side* of the bus. There's a big difference."

"Yes, I'd say there is," she said, finally putting it all together. "Well, it's good to have interesting friends."

We all digested *that* for a moment before Francesca turned to Gracie.

"What about your acting, then?"

I was stunned she remembered.

Gracie kept her eyes on the phone book. "Wait, I've got the number," she said, then ran the phone and the long phone cord into the hallway and called the restaurant out of earshot—a convenient exit, I thought.

Colin seemed confused, but Francesca was already counting heads. She turned to me.

"And you, Terry? You're working with this model fellow, too?"

"I'm his personal photographer."

"Yes, I'm sure," she replied slowly. "Writers *are* good observers."

She remembered that, too!

"Oy, what about us painters?" said Finn.

"Of course, darling, there's no comparison; photography is *objective*," which she made to sound positively distasteful. Then she looked around at all of us, including Gracie behind the door. "But it is curious."

"Why?" Colin asked. "He's just a model—isn't he?"

"Apparently not, darling."

When the delivery boy arrived with four large paper bags filled with steaming boxes, Gracie paid with

Francesca's cash, including a twenty-five percent add-on, because it seemed the very good Chinese restaurant *didn't* deliver. Gracie had coaxed them into it. That, too, was probably part of her job.

Once the warm bags were brought into the kitchen we all watched, fascinated, as Francesca dismissed any help and managed the entire serving herself. She ordered the coffee table cleared; brought out our mis-matched plates, and elegantly served—with chopsticks the restaurant provided—all the numerous dishes of our meal, naming each one. For the spring rolls she said "These you eat with your fingers."

We were all rather mesmerized. Colin not so much, but perhaps he was used to this heretofore hidden side of Francesca. There was no telling what worldliness the doors of class and money opened. I'd seen it on occasion with my Harrods customers: a famous name dropped casually, the mention of a yacht, a second home in Switzerland, an island in the Caribbean. For some, it was just the way of things, none of it for show.

Once the serving was finished, Francesca, inspired by the Chinese delicacies before us, opened up with stories of her debutant days in the Far East. She was actually courted by *two* competing suitors. One was a Hong Kong businessman who flew her to all the Jet Set cities in Asia and, when she arrived, stayed at his hotels. ("As soon as there were helicopters he'd land me on the roof!"). The other was an Italian movie producer who dressed her in couture ("Two fittings a week then glorious long lunches; we did that back then.") and wanted to put her in his films. She said yes for a year before she finally visited a film set and it put her off the whole idea completely. She finally walked away from offers of the silver-screen and life as an international hostess because, "you know, darling, I'm really a simple girl at heart."

We didn't know if we should laugh or groan.

Yet here she was with Colin, standing by her man, who listened to her stories with a Cheshire Cat smile. At the end of the day, he'd won the lady's heart, and they seemed completely devoted to each other.

I noticed, too, that Francesca had the good grace not to ask Finn about her portrait. But when she started to ask more about Sebastian, Gracie steered the conversation into vagueness. When we finished our meal, Finn seized the moment, saying it was time to go.

"Thank you, Francesca—and all of you—for a very nice evening."

It was the most genuine I'd ever seen him. Not a hint of spice; the unguarded Finn and I think we all took note. "Gonna catch a pint round the corner before closing," he said. Then, looking at me: "Come with? I owe you a pint or two."

Gracie chimed in almost too quickly. "Aren't you meeting Sebastian?"

Finn took a long moment. "He'll find me when he needs me," he replied.

Then back to me. "Ready?"

After thanking Francesca again, we grabbed our coats and walked the few blocks to our local—the same pub Tess and I frequented when she was still at the flat.

Over our first pint, Finn was relaxed, almost like the early days—before Sebastian came on the scene. Yes, he looked thin and worn down, but I had no sense of drugs or a fidgety addiction lurking in the background. Commencing our second round, I summoned the courage to ask about his portrait of Francesca.

Instead of the defensiveness I was bracing for, his eyes lit up.

"The old girl's got something, I'll say that for her."

After tonight, I had to agree.

"Is she actually sitting for you or…"

"No, no, not anymore. She sat for the pencil sketches at the beginning—that was even before you came on board."

So, yes, this had been dragging on for quite some time.

"We had two long sittings. I've changed the format several times. Now, I'm going deep, not wide, layering paint. Layers of color. With all we just heard, I may add a few more! At first, I didn't know where it was going. Actually, it wasn't going anywhere. Then Sebastian gave me that commission, and you can say I got sidetracked....kind of like the rest of us," he added pointedly, taking a long gulp of his beer. "But I kept thinking about what Colin was saying about the manor house, how the eyes were alive, following him around."

I laughed. "She's living history."

"Exactly! Not quite a relic, but that old blood's in her DNA. And *that's* all about layers."

I saw where he was going. "So, how big will it be?"

"Well, I won't pretend to compete with those wall size portraits they used to do."

"But the one of Sebastian? That's got to be big."

Finn stopped. He changed before my eyes. The momentary burst of excitement suddenly vanished. He finished his glass in two gulps then without a word got up and went to the bar for another round. I hadn't finished my second, but he plopped two fresh pints on the old wooden table. When he sat back down, he said:

"Yeah, that one is big." Then he looked right at me. "A lot of space to fill. I should never have taken him on."

"Is he paying you okay?"

Finn laughed out loud. "Very well. *Suddenly*, money is the least of my problems!"

I would have thought that was welcome news, but somehow it didn't sound like it.

Ah, but there's nothing like a third pint to loosen the screws.

"Money's definitely part of it for me," I said.

"Part of what?" His tone was sharp; he was back on the attack.

"Well, Sebastian, of course. He's opening doors *and* there's already money coming from the magazines. Gracie's on top of all that. She also said you're not pacing at night like you used to."

I immediately wished I hadn't gone that far; it was unnecessary. But Finn just chuckled.

"So, you miss me?" he said, smiling.

"I miss the old Finn."

"What's wrong with this one?"

"We're concerned, Finn, that's all I'm saying."

"'We' meaning you and Gracie?"

"And Tess, too. She said she saw you last week and..."

"And what? She didn't like the look of me?"

"She was concerned."

"Don't be," he said flatly.

"Is it the portrait? Is it Sebastian?"

He laughed scornfully. "Sebastian's doing you just like I'm doing him."

I didn't understand.

"Let me put it to you this way, mate. Art is like a rabbit hole. Maybe you're born to fall in, or you get to it by process of elimination because you're no fucking good at anything else. But once you get too deep, there's no turning back."

"And you can't hand back the money," I said, thinking that was somehow clever.

"Fuck the money, man!" he replied with a gesture of throwing the money back in my face. "I can whore myself for money if it comes to that. You as well," he said, shoving his glass in my direction, splashing beer on the table.

"I'm working for my perks, Finn, just like you."

"You're *stealing* for them just like me, Terry. You're stealing from Harrods and Tess *and* Sebastian. You're a liar and a thief *just like me*."

Then he held up his glass as a challenge. "Half full or half empty?"

"Half full," I replied.

"And at the end of this long night?"

"Still half full." I said with false bravery. "Even if it's empty!"

"Yet before the cock crows you'll disavow me!"

"It has to be full," I said as emotion choked my voice. "Or we'll have nothing."

Finn took a long breath. "You're an optimistic fool, Terry, bless your bleeding heart."

"Better than the alternative," I said.

He laughed ruefully. "Then maybe you'll come out of this unscathed."

"Out of what?"

"The rabbit hole, matey. That big blank canvas we're all trying to fill with some poor excuse for a life."

"I make no apologies," I said.

"And that's the fatal flaw," Finn said, downing his beer in one long gulp. "I'm off."

"Where to?"

"Same place as you, Terry," he said, smiling unkindly. "To thieving and lying. Isn't that what we do best?"

He stood up and looked at me hard. "Before the cock crows, Terry, mark my word." Then he patted my shoulder and headed for the door.

I held onto my glass, sipping slowly. I didn't like the half-empty turn things had taken. It was too glib, reducing everything to whoring survival. He'd taken a different tack entirely when we talked about Francesca. He was honest, optimistic, even magnanimous toward his subject in a way that actually surprised me. There seemed to be light at the end of *that* rabbit hole.

Less so, apparently, facing that huge canvas for the restaurant. He said it was deep. Maybe he was too far down to turn around. Or maybe just lost. I remembered him talking about the wonder—the distracting wonder—of creative options. Was he *still* struggling with choices? Finn had greatness in him. We all felt it. But if money was finally *not* a problem, what else was going on?

I finished my beer, bringing things up to a nice three-pint buzz. The night was still young, so I decided I'd see how quickly I could make it to the Coleherne; maybe catch one more pint before closing. Then a taxi came by, and I hailed it without thinking. Ten minutes later I was pressing through the crowd as last call was shouted over the din.

Fifteen minutes later and nicely topped off, I joined the after-hours crew ambling jovially round the corner to Catacombs. Lost myself on the dance floor for a song or two. Suddenly I was grabbed by the shoulders, opening my eyes to a beautifully tipsy grin. It was my old buddy Jamie, the ever-game Scotsman. We danced together for a while, then he suggested we go round to his place for a quick rocks off. I loved how he was so refreshingly direct and playful about his urges (and so ready to include me!). Besides, he had a big uncut cock and was happy as an exhibitionist to offer me another closeup look. No fucking necessary. Just some sucking and a wank. The best kind of no-strings sex between mates. I walked home at peace with the world when, from somewhere, I heard a rooster crow.

~

I'd started my "Dear diary" in high school because nothing I felt on the inside could I express out loud. All my male friends were thinking about girls, chasing girls, and by senior year dating girls. Sometimes, girls were all they really wanted to talk about. They could live their fantasies out loud, crude jokes and all, and the culture at large, parents included, celebrated their blooming heterosexuality. It was the natural order of things.

It wasn't so for people like me. Half my life was in the "Secret" file, buried in the pages of my journals. In another time and place I might have lived in hiding my entire life like a criminal waiting to be caught; cowed by the common narrative that my feelings, the love I longed for, was, if not quite an "abomination" then certainly "less than". One had to assimilate or "pass" in some way. Or over-achieve to blunt the pointed fingers.

When I was in high school, I fell hard for a beautiful surfer boy named Sam. He was actually my first love—or whatever you call it at sixteen. He had curly blonde hair, bright blue eyes and, again, (like Timothy Haddock) a ruddy blush on his cheeks that can still slay me to this day. He was two years ahead of me in school. Wore the same loose attire *then* as any surfer/skater kid today. Fortunately, Sam showed only kindness as I followed him around like a lost puppy. I wrote excruciatingly heartfelt poems about him (terrible), and soon began journal-keeping to wax in longer ways. Sharing any of this was out of the question because as a not-entirely-hetero teenager, there was no one I knew of like mind with whom I *could* share. Even my journal was a secret back then.

After high school, I started venturing further from the nest; first jaunts to the Bay Area to visit a female friend who was studying American literature at Berkeley; then to the desert and to Mexico for meditation retreats. My journal filled with glimpses of new people, new situations, sometimes pictures, ticket stubs, mementos I would tape to the pages. And dreams—not the sleeping kind, but page after tedious page as I plotted the imagined course of my future success. So tedious, in fact, that when, years later, home computers came to pass and I began a long-imagined transcribing of my handwritten volumes, I became so frustrated with the me then I finally had to put the project aside with an exasperating shout: S*top dreaming and get a job!*

I discovered fellow journal-keepers in Anais Nin when I lived in London, and later, Ned Rorem's five volumes of published journals. What emerged was a liberating revelation: journal writing had no form! I could write whatever I wanted! Journaling became my personal "third place." Unbound by storytelling, character development and the dictates of Beginning, Middle and End, I realized how freeing journal writing could be. If "I" was the main character—protagonist if not hero—the plot was *allowed* to be improvised, meandering, sometimes pointless, with a narrative arc that might not ever resolve. It was a catch-all for whatever I wanted to mentally sketch, mull over or rant in cruel ways I'd never voice out loud. I later realized that my writing and photography actually bled into each other. I wrote with a photographer's eye and took portraits as a storyteller.

I wrote numerous plays, movie scripts (ten in all) and novels which at times poured out of me almost fully formed. At those times, inspiration did indeed find me working! But I should hastily add that these creative efforts were all written "on spec": speculative writing for love first and hopefully money later. Literary agents to whom I pitched ideas said if I wasn't actually being *paid* to write I really wasn't "working" at all! No matter that with every effort I *was* becoming a better writer, honing my craft, discovering my style, my "voice". Still, according to some friends, I've spent half my life just *hobbying*.

No wonder an artist's biggest struggle is feeling he even deserves to live!

SUMMER

I was surprised just how bloody hot London could get. Crowded buses were worse than the Tube because they never moved fast enough to circulate the air. One day I saw a sweaty conductor lean over seated passengers to gape longingly at people splashing in a Hyde Park fountain. He was a dark-skinned West Indian man, and I imagined him dreaming of his tropical homeland, wondering why he ever thought sooty, congested London was the place he wanted to end up.

I was thinking of home turf, too. My London clock was now on the waning side, and on some levels, I wasn't sorry. The good part was that Tess and I were together and *growing* together. We had friends, met for lunch, made delicious dinners, and I'd spend comfortable nights at her place several times a week.

She rarely came to Wandsworth Bridge Road. Never stayed the night. The flat was *my* space. The secrets were *there*. Both of us were compartmentalizing because the good parts were so good. Neither of us were our best when we were apart. We started talking seriously about Tess coming to the States, making a go of it together in L.A. Just the thought added wind to our sails.

I was also out on the town with Sebastian *at least* twice a week. The pocket money was as welcome as the experience honing my skills not just as a photographer, but as a social animal. There was an art to casual mixing, especially in close quarters. For some, it came naturally. For others, particularly some of Sebastian's business associates, you could tell they were just putting on their nice face. I'd occasionally capture the unguarded one, and when Sebastian and I reviewed the photos at the end of the night he would laugh at a particularly revealing moment.

"You got that bastard just right, Terry," he said about one cruel-faced associate. "But this will *never* see the light of day!"

Later, the man's more flattering façade ended up on the

party page of a business journal—standing next to Sebastian, of course. We were all dealing in illusion.

~

Then came the arrival.

Daimler limousines began pulling up in front of Harrods. From them disgorged flocks of short, stout women covered from head to toe in black burkas, including face veils or beaked masks that only revealed their mascara-heavy eyes.

I suppose the men had been coming to London for ages, blending in, wearing Western-style suits, doing business and shopping at their leisure (though probably not for Frosted Food). Now they brought their women, their wives—their multiple wives! Most of us had never seen authentic Arab attire in person, yet overnight they were moving among us, paying cash in big wads of fresh bills drawn from their gold-chained Chanel handbags. Moving as they did in groups throughout the store, entirely covered, their presence was as conspicuous as it was just plain odd. Then they kept on coming until, years later, "the Arabs" would buy Harrods outright, alas with regrettable results. But that summer I was witness to the first wave, and it was a particularly remarkable phenomenon.

Equally jarring was the sight of backpackers dressed for trekking strolling around—even in the Perfumery!— with travel-worn kits the size of suitcases strapped on their backs. The degree to which this was so totally *wrong* was quickly noted (I, for one, was appalled), and management soon opened a kind of coat-check where bulky items could be stowed while the scruffies "did" Harrods.

American tourists came too, wearing someone's idea of the latest style. They called them Leisure Suits: a matching jacket and pant ensemble, usually beige, pale blue or insipid yellow, made of something that looked more extruded than any sort of woven fabric. Not only unflattering in a factory uniform kind of way, Leisure Suits just screamed "American", and I found them personally embarrassing.

~

Gracie called to set up another night out with Sebastian. It was all routine by now, usually a two or three day notice. He'd pick me up in front of the flat, prompt as ever; ask about my day. There was always one anecdote or another to tell; Harrods was all about stories. Sebastian enjoyed my little observations; he said it was what made me a good photographer.

But he rarely lifted the curtain on his own business dealing, speaking only in the broadest generalities. Still, over time, one catches on. I was never privy of the deals that were no doubt swirling behind the scenes. The game was as murky as the endgame. But by now I'd met the players, could even put names to the faces. A cold lot, I decided, almost bloodless despite the social niceties. Sadly, I realized Gracie was becoming one of those. Our dealings had become brittle. *Just the facts.*

She and Tess were becoming strained as well. Tess didn't withhold her mistrust about Sebastian. Instead of considering this as a friend's cautionary words, Gracie took umbrage and became suspicious of the accuser. She knew Tess was getting my side of the story, too, which in Gracie's eyes probably meant we were both loose threads she needed to keep an eye on. None of this was clear until the night Sebastian asked me about Tess—which he never did. Then I knew Gracie had been talking. I told him Tess was happy for me—meaning the opportunities, the extra dough.

"But how does she feel about me?" he asked point blank.

I was taken off guard. First of all, there were no discouraging words about Sebastian *anywhere*! Who were Tess or me to start dissing?

"She likes you," I said.

Sebastian chuckled. "I suspect otherwise."

"She's a shrink. Everyone's under the microscope!"

"Shrinks keep secrets," he said.

"So do big time fashion models," I countered.

There was a momentary pause until Sebastian said,

"You've been loyal, Terry. I appreciate that."

Hold on...*loyal?*

I'd never thought about our relationship in quite those terms. I was his trusty personal photographer; we were teammates. It's true I didn't gossip and I know Sebastian was glad about that. But talk of "loyalty" coming at that moment sounded vaguely like a threat. Was he threatening Tess as well?

Before I had time to weigh the nuances further, he said: "Just do your job."

"I'm at your service," I replied.

Then he looked at me and smiled. Such a beautiful, perfect smile. But his eyes were as unrevealing as a shark's.

~

It turned out that Blanche was the perfect flatmate because she was hardly ever there. When her dance company wasn't touring, she visited Timothy in Rome. It was reported that he had two large rooms in a stunning palazzo owned by the family of a friend he knew from Oxford. *Of course he did!*

With all the good cooking that Tess and I were both doing, we thought it was time, if not overdue, to invite Tess's parents for dinner as they'd had us over so often—always on Roast Day (which would be Sunday).

On the appointed Saturday night, they extolled the delicious smells that reached them coming up the stairs even before they entered the flat. Their tone changed slightly when they learned that I was cooling. It changed again when I described the unexpected mix of food groups: ground beef with mussels in the spaghetti sauce along with shiitake mushrooms, an exotic extravagance virtually unavailable outside Harrods. For dessert we severed my favorite Frosted Food offering: profiteroles (*"From Italy,"* as I would tell my customers.) These we served (per instructions) warmed from frozen so the whipped cream inside the pastry balls was soft and the chocolate sauce on top dripped down seductively.

I regaled Mr. & Mrs. Greenwald with stories about

Harrods. I think I even made frozen food sound glamours; this alongside my second job as the personal photographer of a famous model. The way I went on, it almost seemed I was too suited for the job. All of it was a world away from anything they'd ever experienced. By the time I got over myself to see me from their angle, it was too late.

"You're a real good-time Charley," said Mrs. Greenwald, speaking the phrase that she and Mr. G. probably both had on the tip of their tongues.

All in all, though, the evening was deemed a success.

SO successful, in fact, it led to us extending another dinner invitation several weeks later, this time venturing out to a restaurant Sebastian recommended.

Mr. & Mrs. Greenwald picked us up at Tess's flat. We piled into the back seat. Two minutes later we'd barely reached Notting Hill's High Street when I realized I'd left my wallet on Tess's bed. A quiet panic hit me, but I put it aside once we were seated in the sleekly modern dining room with its white marble surfaces, trendy clientele and beautiful wait staff. The Greenwalds looked decidedly out of place.

Sebastian and I rarely had proper sit-down dinners, but when we did, he always suggested I try something unusual—abalone or goose, say—if it was on the menu because "if you're going to have it somewhere it might as well be in the hands of a good chef." That seemed like good advice on this night, too. The house specialty was steak. I decided to order it prepared in a way I'd never had before: *rare*…to see how that was supposed to be done rather than the *medium* I might have ordinarily ordered.

When the plate arrived my steak was already sitting in a pool of crimson brine. Blood oozed out when I punctured it with my knife and fork. Tess looked doubtfully at it then at me. But it was too late to back out now. I ground what flesh I could out of each bloody, uncooked mouthful then had to put the half masticated remains back on my plate. I couldn't swallow any of it. The mash piled up. It reminded me of a Francis Bacon painting. When I dared to meet eyes with my dinner companions, I saw them, even Tess, quietly appalled.

Once the main course was concluded (not a moment too soon) replaced by a light sorbet for dessert, my panic from earlier began to rise. Coffee was served and the conversation dragged. It became clear that since I had suggested the restaurant—and by my own account was *in the money* from all my incredibly cool nights out with famous celebrities—that it was my turn to repay Mister & Misses for all their generous in-home hospitality.

How could I say in so many words that, oops, I left my wallet at home? How weak would that sound? If I *hadn't* forgotten it (accidentally on purpose? *Why would I do that to myself?*) I would have been pleased to pay the bill, especially after the awkward stalling suggested there might be a question of who *should* pony up. In the Greenwald's mind I don't think there was *any* question it was my turn.

But instead of making feeble excuses, I did the even worse thing by excusing myself to go to the restroom. There was no way out. I was utterly humiliated, and worse, I was sure I'd deeply embarrassed Tess.

When I returned to the table after a too-long absence, Mr. Haddock had settled the bill. His *there you have it* expression was clear. It wasn't about the money. It was about me. *Some boyfriend.*

But it didn't end there!

On the drive home, perhaps ignited by the alchemy of wine and raw blood, my intestines started churning, and I suddenly farted. It was a silent emission, but the smell was sharp and rancid permeating the enclosed confines of the car.

Who admits to farting in polite company? I certainly didn't. But everyone knew, it just wasn't a *family* smell. Had Beauty, their old Labrador, been with us, they probably wouldn't have even put the blame on her. I was the culprit. No one said a word but held their breath until Tess finally acknowledge the inescapable and wound down her window with an exasperated exhale.

We never spoke of that night again.

~

I was asleep in the employee lounge when I woke up and found the big resting room empty. I'd over-slept again! I raced out, flew down the stairs two at a time (I'd become an expert), double-timed through the Perfumery's heaven glow to find business as usual in Frosted Food, my presence hardly missed.

Someone said Tess had called and I should call her back. Now was not the time because we were so busy, but not long before closing Tess appeared. "We have to talk," she said, and we met a short time later at the employee entrance.

She was quiet as we walked to our usual lunchtime sandwich shop, which at this hour was practically empty.

"Where were you last night?" she asked as we took a table of our choosing.

"Finn and I went out for a pint," I lied.

"How's he doing? Gracie said he looked…"

"He's thin, but he's fine," I said quickly.

"Well, I'm not, Terry."

"How do you mean?"

"I'm uncomfortable…down there."

"You're late?"

"No, I'm not pregnant, if that's what you mean," she said impatiently, as if I was already missing the point. "I'm just…something's not right."

"Oh," I said dumbly, because any other words would have rung with the guilt that suddenly washed over me.

"I'm seeing my doctor in an hour."

"Well, that's good," I replied.

"And maybe you should, too."

I was silent. Or went silent. All the words that could be said, the accusations, the fears, distrust, disappointments, the hurt she felt was left unsaid. Yet, even in the silence, I was guilty as charged. No matter that I'd never knowingly put myself at risk; my extracurricular sex was virtually contact-free—except maybe a few blowjobs. No fucking. No kissing. A moral crime, perhaps, but I didn't think it put me or Tess in *physical* danger. Unless it did. Nothing I could say would change what was. Then she handed me a piece of paper.

"What's this?"

"Call them," Tess said flatly. "I've already made an appointment. They'll be expecting you at six thirty. I have to go."

Then she got up and walked out.

The clinic wasn't far from Wandsworth Bridge Road...on my way home, essentially. Tess had thought of everything. And I *was* expected.

A young doctor took me to a private room. He poked a swab into my urethra. I peed into a small plastic cup. Results would be back in an hour if I cared to wait. The tests were negative, so I hadn't been wrong about my reasonable caution. But it was hardly good news.

I called Tess later. She asked about my visit. I said I was fine. I asked about hers. She said they diagnosed a yeast infection (nothing too serious), but not before she detailed the entire invasive procedure, including the part about hiking her legs up on the stirrups to expose her vagina to the inquisitive male doctor. She wanted me to feel the humiliation, and God knows I had it coming. But I couldn't tell her that. An entire quadrant of my life was lived in secret. Yet even that was not entirely true because in certain places I was, indeed, a familiar face. But worlds did not collide.

Until a week or so later they did.

~

I hadn't seen Sebastian in several more days than unusual. No sightings at the flat, either. I assumed whatever work Finn had to do finishing the portrait he was handling by himself. *Sebastian*, the restaurant, was scheduled to open right about the time my visa expired. Tess and I were talking seriously about the future. Suddenly it felt like we were all on a deadline.

Then Gracie called. Sebastian wanted me for another evening out. I was glad for the extra money, but mostly I was glad I hadn't blown it somehow considering all the stuff going on behind the scenes between Gracie and Tess, all of which I now assumed got back to Sebastian eventually. I didn't think I'd mis-stepped, but now I wondered if I knew too much or was somehow deemed not loyal enough. Like so many things in all our lives, much was left unspoken.

The stars were out in a cool, clear sky as Sebastian turned off Kings Road into the poshest section of Chelsea. I could see the Thames Embankment at the end of the street. It was remarkable how, in big cities, the character of neighborhoods could change from block to block. I knew the general Chelsea area, but whizzing by on a double-decker bus I realized I'd missed the atmospheric details—that which gave Chelsea its vibe: still dripping in money but hipper than stuffy Mayfair or Belgravia.

We pulled up to a corner address. There was a man, smartly dressed in a dark suit, waiting discretely, almost in shadow, at the top of stairs leading up to the front door. When he saw us he turned to knock at the door, then came down to meet us.

"This is it?" I asked. The place looked like a private home—a deserted one.

"Evening, Sebastian," the man said quietly as Sebastian stepped out of the car, leaving the engine running. Only as the handsome man slid into the driver's seat did I realize he was our valet, though there were no other cars around.

As the car pulled away I joined Sebastian on the sidewalk. We were totally alone. He gave me a wink as I followed him to the top of six stairs, where the black front door had the number '29' in brass numbers, but no suggestion of what was inside. This time, it was the *lack* of commotion upon our arrival that seemed to be the point. Then the front door opened, and another handsome doorman greeted us.

"Good evening, Sebastian," he said quietly as we stepped inside a small vestibule with a heavy curtain blocking further entrance. Once the front door was closed behind us the doorman pulled aside the curtain, revealing a large, mellow-lit entry hall where an older, very tall, very thin black woman was approaching to greet us. She was dressed in a gold lame column dress that dropped from shoulder straps to the floor. Her hair was pulled back in a tight bun, like a dancer's, which she had surely been in younger days.

"Hello, darling," she said to Sebastian with an accent (African? Middle-Eastern?) I couldn't place. The entry hall had heavy curtains at intervals around the walls, revealing nothing about what was behind them. I heard soft modern jazz muffled in the background.

"Ara, this is Terry," Sebastian said. "He's my mate for the night. I'd like him to get a few pictures...for ambience."

"Not a problem," she said, her voice like honey. Then she turned to me.

"Just none of the other guests, Terry, all right?"

"Not a problem," I said.

When she heard my accent, Ara's eyes lit up. "You're American!"

"Yes, I am," I replied.

"We love Americans."

I should have stopped there, less being best in unfamiliar circumstances, but then more words spilled out: "I work at Harrods."

So stupid! So apropos of nothing! I was trying to imply that I wasn't just an American tourist, but wouldn't that have been obvious? *Here?? With Sebastian??*

Ara laughed, the deep, rich sound of a purring cat, putting me at ease.

"We love Harrods, don't we, darling?" she said to Sebastian.

He put his arm around my shoulder. "Ah, but we have bigger things ahead, don't we, Terry?"

"Ever the optimist," I said to Ara, trying to make the best of it.

She purred again: "We love optimists, too," she said. "Just mind the rules."

"Thank you," I said. "I will."

"This way, please."

She led us across the entry hall, pulling aside a curtain that revealed a large sitting room where a dozen people were either seated on comfortable couches or standing in small, huddled groups. The decor was all plush, muted grey and burgundy tones. There were more heavy curtains drawn closed on the two tall windows. Everyone was older than

Sebastian. I was by far the youngest and felt the heat of scanning eyes as we crossed the room heading straight to the bar against the opposite wall. A doughy older man with blotchy red skin, tall, wearing an immaculate three-piece suit and heavy, black-framed glasses raised his whiskey glass discreetly. Sebastian nodded back, not breaking stride. The handsome bartender in black-tie tuxedo was already mixing drinks.

"Good evening, gentlemen," said the barman.

"How are you, Rudy?"

"Very well, sir. The usual?"

"Yes, for me," Sebastian said then winked in my direction. "And something light for my friend."

"Ah, yes, I have just the thing," he replied.

I leaned in toward Sebastian. "Do you want a picture?"

"Later, Terry. Let's settle in first."

He was right. The flash would have been entirely disruptive. This wasn't an art opening or even a party. It was more like a prelude, but to what I still wasn't sure. There was almost an equal mix of men and women. They all looked pretty expensive. One was familiar—I'd photographed him on other occasions. Two I recognized from the newspapers. The blotchy older man with the heavy-framed glasses kept casting his eyes Sebastian's way, almost begging for attention. Sebastian looked without expression.

"Who are these people?" I whispered.

"Art dealers, businesspeople, politicians," he whispered back. "Very useful."

I still wasn't getting it. The background music from discrete speakers was some abstract impressionist jazz; a frenetic saxophone wailed; the stop and start 5/4 rhythm rattled more than soothed. My drink, though mild as Sebastian had ordered, somehow had the opposite effect. If this was "heady company", I was beginning to feel it.

"What's the name of this place?" I asked, still whispering.

"There's no name."

I let that sink in, looking around. "Yeah, I guess that's the point."

"*Now* you're getting it," he said behind his glass. "Want to mingle?"

Just as we stepped away from the bar, a beautiful older woman came through the curtain from the lobby followed by a tall, much younger man, ridiculously handsome, with exaggerated Roman features—the nose, the dark eyes, olive skin and a rich head of wavy auburn hair—whom I immediately recognized as the current face for Valentino. When the woman saw Sebastian, she and her young companion came over, warm and smiling, ignoring everyone else in the room. They air kissed, and I was introduced.

"Carla, this is Terry, my assistant."

"Oh, darling," she said to Sebastian. "I'm sure you don't need any help."

They all thought that was amusing.

"I'm just taking pictures," I said.

"Really?" Carla turned to Sebastian, her expression aghast. "Here?"

"He's with me," Sebastian replied as if that was the only explanation necessary.

"Well, then," she said, looking me over. "You must have something *quite* special."

The innuendo needed no explaining.

"How about a...," I began, and reached under my jacket for my camera bag.

"Later, Terry," Sebastian said.

"Later!" Carla said, laughing again. "That's what Luca always says, don't you, darling!"

She brushed the lapel of her handsome companion's Valentino jacket. "And I've been assisting *him* for years."

Luca just smiled. I wondered if he spoke at all. I was getting the impression that the woman was his agent—and, from her joking, probably a lot more. He didn't seem particularly bright, but with Carla managing his career, it may not have mattered. They were a team. It seemed she had the impression that Sebastian and I were the same kind of team. He said nothing to change her mind.

As they chatted, I stood by quietly, marveling at the rare beauty of the *two* men before me. Luca's was almost as compellingly freakish as the monster cock I'd seen at the Catacombs. All he had to do was show up, and everybody noticed. But in terms of normal functionality, like that giant cock, Luca was impractical, a distraction, rendered almost useless by his exaggerated attributes. He needed Carla like a pet needs an owner. But he was her golden egg. By contrast, Sebastian's looks, while startlingly handsome, were also disarmingly earthbound. When he smiled, you felt included. He was almost approachable—in no need of a handler.

A waiter approached offering refills: the same "usual" for Sebastian and me, and two glasses of champagne for Carla and Luca. It seemed that their drink preferences were already known as well.

Sebastian waved the waiter off, but I quickly exchanged my half-empty glass for a full one. I needed a prop more than I needed more alcohol, but drink I did, feeling like a fish out of water. The *oh, darling* chatter wasn't putting me at ease. Nor was the music, which had begun to prickle my ears like slightly irritating static.

I watched as if from the sidelines, not exactly ignored, but nor was I one of them. A third suggestion of picture-taking was declined with a quick shake of his head. I slowly gleaned that whatever the night was about, it wasn't vanity portraiture. Only a real Andy Warhol could have gotten away with photography in this rarified setting. Something else was going on, though I still didn't know what. I finally shifted my camera bag behind my back and out of mind.

More people trickled in, including several more of Sebastian's political types, who had beautiful women on their arms, probably not their wives. Some nodded a discreet hello. Solo guests were quickly absorbed into one group or another. The room was never crowded because people seemed to come and quietly go. More than cigarette smoke, the smell of secrets was in the air. And money. The abstract music, as much as the drinks, was starting to make my head spin. I seemed to be drifting in and out of focus like the guests. I decided it was time for a break.

I excused myself on the pretext of needing the restroom. Take your time, Sebastian said. I went back out to the entry hall and saw our feline hostess ushering two lovely young women from the front door to a curtain across the hall. Then she turned to see me.

"Terry!" she said, warm and familiar. "Are you enjoying yourself?"

"Yes, thanks," I replied. "But I was looking for…"

"Of course, darling. This way." She walked to another curtain and pulled it aside, revealing an elegant circular staircase.

"Up and first left."

Could she tell I was a little woozy?

With a gentle touch of my arm she led me through.

"Explore," she said with gentle amusement as the curtain fell behind me. I was suddenly alone on the unexpected staircase. The quiet sounds of music and voices were completely muted. The stairs curved up to the first floor where I stopped to get my bearings. I found the first door to the left and the private restroom I needed to gather myself. It was tiled all in black, including a black toilet and matching bidet. I peed, washed my hands and face, drying myself on small white hand towels, which I then dropped into a basket under the sink. Refreshed, I stepped back out into the hall.

"Explore," the lady said.

There were closed doors along the hallway. More than beckoning, they seemed alive with promises. I now needed no guessing to imagine what this no-name club was all about.

The first door was on my right. I leaned close, listening. Music pulsed quietly. Almost soothingly. I turned the door handle slowly and peeked my head inside. The room was draped in Indian fabric, including numerous gossamer veils suspended from the ceiling surrounding two low beds, one on each side of the room. Indistinct figures, naked bodies, three on each bed, were writhing in the dim light. No one noticed as I listened to the breathy moans of women and men completely engaged. It was like a movie: removed, untouchable, voyeuristic. I eased the door shut and ventured down the hall.

White light pulsing through a space at the bottom of

another door caught my attention. As I came closer, I saw it was not one light, but fast blinking lights, and the quiet, thumping bass of very modern electronic music coming from inside. I eased the door open and was blasted by the rapid bright and pitch darkness of a strobe light. The room was painted entirely black, and there were more thin veils suspended around a large round bed in the center of the room. As my eyes adjusted I saw the naked bodies, maybe six or seven, it was impossible to tell. They were pressed together into a single form, strangely animated in the fast-flickering light. It took a moment to realize they were all young men; a primordial cluster entwined like snakes in a writhing orgy. I stepped in and closed the door behind me.

As I watched unnoticed it didn't take me long to become aroused. No one seemed to notice as I took off my jacket. Only then was I reminded of my camera. I quickly pulled it out and aimed at the bed. The flash was swallowed by the pulsing strobe; the quick whine as the picture ejected blended with the music. I tucked the camera and single frame back in the bag and undressed completely. I pulled the veil aside, and as I did, someone looked up. A face freeze-framed in the strobing lights, our eyes connected. It was Timothy Haddock!

His hand reached out. Someone mounted him from behind, and he winced with sweet pain that quickly melted into a kind of satisfied exhale. He gripped me harder and drew me in. I was instantly entangled, kissed by one, sucked by another, stroked and tongued. Timothy gripped my hand for a long time until the tide of shifting flesh pulled us apart and we were swallowed in the undertow.

~

Hours later I watched a gloomy mist hovering over the cold, dark water of the River Thames. Where was Sebastian? Where was Timothy? I had left the no-name club in a drug-like haze. If I saw Ara before the night air hit me, I don't remember. Exhausted, almost shell-shocked, I followed the Chelsea Embankment until the road turned in toward Kings

Road. Then I walked familiar streets back to the flat. I fell into sleep, then woke out of habit just in time to call the Harrods operator and tell her I was sick and wouldn't be coming in.

It was about noon when I heard a distant ringing telephone. Then the thud of footsteps.

"Phone, Terry!" It was Finn. He knocked twice as he bound past my door back up to his room.

Christ.

It was probably Tess. On this day of all days, she was the last person I wanted to talk to. She'd probably called me at Harrods, hoping to meet for lunch. They'd told her I was sick… more lies…

I dragged myself downstairs and took the phone at the dining room table, holding my head in one hand. "Hello," I said, hoping I sounded like death's door.

"Is that you, Terry?" said a man's voice.

"Yes," I replied, "this is Terry."

"It's Timothy Haddock."

I went dead silent.

"Hello?"

"Yes, I'm here, Timothy."

Another long pause as I gathered my addled brain.

"Why am I surprised to hear from you?"

He chuckled uncomfortably. "Right," he said. "It is all rather…" His words trailed off.

"'Rather' is right," I said.

"You're not at work, apparently."

"No, I called in sick."

"So they said."

I let that sink in and Timothy caught my surprise.

"I remembered that's where you worked," he said. "I had to find you. It's about last night."

"Yes, I imagine it is, but…?" I was at a loss.

"I wonder if we can get together right away?"

"You want to meet?"

"Is that a problem? I don't want to cause any…"

"No, no, it's not a problem. It's just….this is all very…"

"I know, Terry. But it's important. Alone, of course," he

added. "I mean, if that's at all possible."

What was all this? And Christ... *If that's at all possible?* For Timothy, *anything* was possible, but enough of the English niceties, please! We were so past that! Suddenly I was back where we started, smitten by this tousle-haired wonder, his beautiful voice, our perfect host in Oxford. He even played the fucking piano! Now, bonus of all bonuses, we were partners in sex! What stood in the way of us finally...couldn't we...?

"Terry, are you there?"

"Yes, yes, I'm here. I was just..."

It all left me wondering what Timothy could he possibly want to talk about? What was so urgent that he tracked me down at Harrods and charmed someone into giving him my number? Did he now intend to blackmail me for my nonexistent fortune? Or worry that I'd out him to his "girlfriend" or even his sister, who would immediately ring Tess? More likely it was about a sexually transmitted disease. Or worse: maybe I gave him crabs!

One factual thing I could say was that I'd just had my first gay orgy; it was probably as good as it was *ever* going to get, and I'd die in relative contentment if it never happened again.

"When do you want to meet? I'm off work anyway—recovering."

He chuckled again. "Yes, I wouldn't mind a little hair of the dog myself. How about the Gloucester? It's on the street that runs parallel to Sloane Street. On the Belgravia side."

He paused. I waited. "Look," he said. "I know this is sudden. Even a little awkward under the circumstances, but it's time we met."

"Is it?"

"Well, I think so...under the circumstances."

I wasn't sure exactly what circumstances he was referring to, but...

"Sure, I'm game," I said. "I know the place. What time?"

"Great. Well, let's see; it's just gone twelve. Best we act now before they close after lunch."

"Right," I said. "I can be there in an hour."

I hung up the phone, then just as I was getting up from the table, it rang again. It had to be Timothy following up.

"Hello?"

"How are you feeling?"

Christ, it was Tess.

"Not great, but I'll live."

"They said you called in sick."

"Yes," I replied, non-committal.

"Can I bring you anything?"

"Actually, I'd like to come over to your place later. I could use a change of scenery."

"Is everything all right?"

"I'd just like to see you," I said, and meant it.

"I'm home early. I'll cook you something proper."

"That would be wonderful."

"Come when you like," she said.

Timothy was at The Gloucester when I arrived an hour later. It was a smaller, cozy place with all the old, dark-wood charm one imagines that an English pub should have—in other words nothing like the Coleherne. Timothy was seated at a small table, a half pint of lager in front of him. When I approached and extended my hand in greeting, he gripped my shoulders and kissed me on both cheeks.

Well, didn't that set the tone!

"I'll get you a glass," he said.

"Half bitter, thanks," I said, letting him do the honors, which gave me a few moments to observe him standing at the bar.

He wore a chocolate brown Burberry trench coat over jeans and a bulky, cream-colored kitted pullover folded high on the neck. That beautiful sandy hair covered his ears nearly to his shoulders. He stood not more than five foot seven, a very cuddly height. In a word, as delicious dressed as (now I knew), undressed.

"Thank you for coming," he said, setting the beer down in front of me.

"I'm intrigued."

"I knew you might be. But I had to see you. Warn you."

I was raising my glass when my hand froze. "Warn me? About what?"

"About who," he said.

"Well, who, then?"

"Sebastian," he replied, giving me a moment for that to sink in. "I don't think you know this, but he was my boyfriend."

I studied him for a long moment, not sure he was serious. "He's everyone's boyfriend, Timothy. The whole world loves him."

He chuckled. "I know what you mean, but it's more complicated than that."

"Yes, I'm sure it is, but..."

"Once you're close..." He paused.

"We're just mates, Timothy. Sebastian's opened some doors. *Lots* of doors, apparently," I added.

"Our meeting last night wasn't a coincidence."

"No?" I said, weighing his words. "What was it then?"

"Think, Terry. I'm a student at Oxford, nothing more. I'm not one of his power brokers."

"Neither am I?" I said, confused. "I'm his photographer." Was this a jealous ex-lover thing? "We're not having sex, if that's what you're thinking."

"Well, that *is* some good news," Timothy said, sounding genuinely relieved. "Keep it that way."

Okay, so this wasn't about sex. Where was he going?

Then, as if I'd asked the question out loud:

"You're a piece on his chessboard, Terry. So was I. But Sebastian plays to win. He *always* wins."

Suddenly, Tess's words were ringing in my ears. I started itemizing the connections—and some immediate concerns.

"Does Blanche know about...?"

"Yes, but it's all been very hush-hush, practically a state secret."

"So Tess may or may not know," I said, mulling the potential complications. "Will you say anything?"

"Of course not. But you're flirting with trouble, Terry. That's what I'm trying to say. Sebastian will eat you."

"And you say this as his *boyfriend*?"

"His ex-boyfriend. We were together for nearly a year, but I finally had to….if I don't leave England now, he'll ruin me."

I scoffed at the exaggeration. "How can he do that?"

"He can. I just don't want to find out how. Everything he touches, Terry, everyone…"

"Oh, please," I said. I'd heard about enough. "You're free, I'm free. We can walk away from anything!"

"I know it still looks that way now…for you, Finn, even Gracie."

I looked up, surprised he mentioned their names. But he hadn't mentioned….

"What about Tess?" he asked.

I demurred ruefully. "You mean the voice of reason?"

"Is she involved?"

"*Involved?*" That was a strong word. "No, not at all. In fact, she's said more or less what you're saying."

"Well, that's some good news."

I thought his reply was presumptuous. How well did he know any of us? And what of *his* choices? Timmothy was obviously living a double life just like me.

"What about Andrea? Isn't she your girlfriend?"

"We've been friends—just friends—since high school in Switzerland."

"So, she's not…?"

He chuckled. "Hardly. Were soulmates, like siblings, not lovers. I'm gay, Terry. What about you?"

I had no answer.

Tess and I were soulmates, too. And lovers.

"I loved *you*, last night," I said quietly.

Timothy smiled…so kindly. I could have taken him—or him take me—right there.

We locked eyes. He raised his glass. "Hair of the dog?" he said with a twinkle.

Maybe he was getting hard, too.

I gulped my drink and let things settle.

"I don't know what to do," I said at last.

"Just be careful. Keep your distance."

"Can I see you again?"

"Don't, Terry. It's impossible."

"*Why?*" I said, throwing my dignity out the window.

"Because I'm leaving for Italy the day after tomorrow. I won't be back anytime soon."

"What about Oxford? What about your family?"

"I'll finish my schooling in Rome. My family will visit. They'll just have to understand."

"Understand what?" I pleaded. "I'm ready to fall in love with you, Timothy—idiot that I am. I'd do anything if you'd have me."

"That's exactly what I said to Sebastian."

"But he's not gay."

"Wrong label, mate; he's a chameleon. He's the face staring out that everybody wants to see staring back. He's the dream come true if he touches your life. Why do you think they pay him so much? Why he always gets his way? He's not just a pretty face, Terry. He's a siren. Follow at your peril."

"And where was he leading you, I ask, now that we'll be saying goodbye forever?" I took a long breath. "You know, for a minute there, last night, I really thought we had something."

He smiled a pained expression. "As my dear sister would say: *She will love them when she sees them; they will lose her if they follow.*"

"Joni Mitchell."

"The one and only."

"You're not that guy, Timothy," I said. "Not to me."

"But Sebastian *is*. I was almost ready to let him have me body *and* soul."

"Until?"

"Until I realized that the face I wanted to see in the mirror was mine, not his. And he didn't like that."

"So what happened?"

"You might say he threw me to the wolves—the wolves of my appetites. And yours, too, my friend. Neither of us could have been in that no-name club without Sebastian's entrée. As soon as I saw you, I knew he was behind it."

"But..." I hesitated. "You held on to my hand."

"Like a drowning man."

"And now..."

"Sebastian has bigger fish to swallow. You won't see me again, Terry."

"Maybe at Christmas, then?" I said, grasping at straws. "In Hampstead? Playing Bach?"

I knew I sounded desperate. Would I even *be* in London next Christmas? Would I be with Tess? This beautiful man, whom I hardly knew, had stolen my heart, but the possible was impossible.

"I'm sorry," he said, and I knew there wasn't any more to say.

Later, at Tess's flat, after a meal she made with so much love, I fell asleep before she even came to bed. Then in the night a dream: The great facade of Harrods loomed up in front of me, rising higher and higher, about to topple over on top of me as I raised my hands to protect myself. I awoke with a shout then burst into tears, sobbing in Tess' arms.

~

Something definitive changed after the swanky sex club affair. There were no more calls for my personal photographer services. I assumed my Andy Warhol days were over. Tess noticed the change in rhythm (and probably my mood) and asked me about it one day when we were having lunch in Knightsbridge. I gave her the answer I knew she'd appreciate: "It was fun while it lasted. I guess I'm no longer useful."

What I really felt was that I actually *may* have seen too much. Yes, I'd come to know the names and faces, but I still didn't know any of the particulars. I was sure there was a circle of intrigue, but I couldn't connect the dots. I finally decided to heed Tess's cautionary words. Timmothy was probably correct that our encounter, seemingly so random, was no coincidence. Rerunning the evening over and over in my mind, I decided Sebastian *hadn't* wanted me there to take pictures. Cameras would never be allowed in a place like that. Ara was just playing along. The suave bartender probably spiked my drink. Sebastian was showing off to demonstrate his reach: *I, too, can connect the dots, and I know where you live.*

It *was* all about power, just as Timothy said. We were useful pawns to play or be promoted to last rank and ultimately be removed—or routed out—from the board. At least I'd averted being eaten.

Gracie gave no clue as to what was (or wasn't) up. She was flat-hunting, a complete decampment imminent. I did miss the glam nightlife, seeing my photos (if not my name) in the magazines. The extra money had allowed me more than window shopping at the Way In. I had another Daniel Hechter jacket, a few more fitted shirts and trousers. To put it all to rest, I tossed my camera bag on the floor of my wardrobe behind two new pairs of shoes.

Sebastian was nearly open. Another guest list was being compiled. That meant Finn's artwork would be installed very soon—the restaurant's splashy icing on the cake.

I began to see Colin more than anyone else. He was still wrestling with the finances of his other properties but, to my surprise, now seemed to have an even greater concern for our flat. He said, "against his better judgment" he'd solicited bids from painters, plasterers and carpet companies to give the place a makeover.

Then I came home one mid-afternoon to find him standing alone in the kitchen. He was staring out the open back door, deep in thought. He looked so in need of cheering up I suggested a cup of tea and some comfort food. I took a box of frozen profiteroles out of the fridge and put them in the oven for a quick thaw.

"We can sit outside in the sun," I said.

"What's left of it," he replied, the gloom heavy in his voice.

Indeed, autumn was in the air. But Colin seemed so grateful just to have a friend to talk to that it finally sank in—the burden he was under.

I made the tea; split the profiteroles onto two plates, and

we planted ourselves on each of the only two folding chairs on the barren patio, which we *still* euphemistically (aspirationally?) called a garden.

Of course, we talked about the flat, its future now that everyone, including me, was making leaving noises. He wondered if upgrades weren't like rearranging deck chairs on the Titanic. I also heard it first when he told me Finn was moving out once he got final payment for Sebastian's portrait.

"It's the end of an era," Colin said glumly. "We were like a family."

Okay, now he was getting maudlin.

But deep down I had the same feeling.

Then, out of the blue, he said: "I think talent is instinctual. Not like that other chap."

"What other chap?" I asked.

"You know. The model."

"Sebastian?"

"Yes, him; the one on the buses. Nice guy on the surface, but…" He trailed off.

"Why would you bring him up?"

"Francesca got me thinking. And Gracie leaving those magazines open on the table. I find it strange he's everywhere…even here."

"It is strange, Colin. And there's more to him than busses, I can tell you that."

He sighed. "And there's more to me than this wretched flat, but it may be my only way to solvency."

"How do you mean?" I asked.

"To ward off the marauders, as Francesca put it."

Then I remembered. "The hostel takeover?"

Colin nodded. "Even if I fix this place up it'll only be to let it go."

"You're going to sell?" This *was* leading things further than I'd thought.

"I may have to, Terry. The bank likes *their* offer—whoever 'they' are. It was such a good deal when I bought it, but suddenly I'm being priced out. How did that happen? I'll be back to square one. All the deal-making…I almost don't see the point."

I wasn't sure whose point he was talking about, but no doubt *somebody* was profiting.

~

Amidst the late summer crush one early afternoon, I heard loud voices coming from the Perfumery; not shouting but raised and insistent announcements. Then Harrods' uniformed security personnel, and some stealth plain-clothed ones I recognized, came quickly through the Food Halls in a wave. "Please move to the exits immediately!"

They were directing people toward the Produce Hall, which I knew was the nearest way out through the loading dock. You could tell from their faces that this was not a drill. Times being what they were, everyone instantly feared the worst. The calls to exit immediately persisted. I heard one security person whisper, "There's a bomb warning." My stomach turned.

It wasn't unexpected. The IRA had probably never *not* had Harrods in their sights. There was no doubt Security would have made contingency plans for something exactly like this. Now, the worst *was* actually happening.

I was at the cash register when the moment turned serious. I was about to give change to a well-dressed Italian man, but he turned and immediately followed security's directions heading toward the nearest exit. I ran after him, pressing the change from his purchase into his hand. He looked up with a quick smile, appreciative, but ironic. *What good was money if we were all going to die?*

I was still in the building, many walls and a floor away from the front of the store when I heard the deep, bass drum BOOM. The whole world would soon learn that a firebomb had been placed in the women's clothing department. The IRA had given short warning, and store security were able to seal off the bomb-blast area and begin evacuation before a massive explosion gutted the room. It blasted out windows and sent debris all over Brompton Road, a planned and very visible statement of whatever it was they were trying to say—and using Harrods to say it. No one was hurt, but the assault on our besieged dowager would make global headlines in time for the evening news.

Though my terror-bomb experience in Paris was much more direct, it was couched in the quiet of a Sunday morning. No one was prepared and thankfully, no one was around besides the unfortunate messenger who lost his leg along with his life. Tess and I were already hightailing it to the peace of a French chateau before the police even arrived on scene. In Knightsbridge, because of the forewarning, police cars and ambulances, horns blaring, blue flashing lights everywhere, were already converging before the actual blast. By the time I got outside, all the local streets were being cordoned off. People were scattering everywhere.

Amidst all this, I heard someone calling my name. It was Dermot hurrying toward me, pale as ash.

"Oh, Terry, it's so good to see you," he said, taking my arm. He was shaking and didn't slacken his pace as he led me briskly away from Harrods and the crescendo of activity that was overtaking the entire neighborhood.

"I was up on the first floor checking a delivery," he said, breathless. "Suddenly, in comes security shouting something. But I was in the stockroom and didn't hear what it was about. They found me just in time, Terry. Ran me out, shut the door, and the fucking thing blew! Knocked us right down!"

"Christ," I said. "That was lucky."

"More than lucky, mate. The bastards almost killed me!"

He was nearly in tears, continuing to grip my arm, pressing tightly against my shoulder.

"Are the pubs open?" he asked. "I could seriously use a pint."

"The Gloucester," I said without hesitation as we'd already reached Sloan Street. "Just a couple of blocks down."

I could hardly believe I was heading back to the scene of my recent heartache. Then things turned doubly strange when, with shattered nerves and a pint of beer in him, Dermot poured his heart out, confessing his lack of courage for not being more friendly on the loading dock, not following up on everything he'd felt for me. "I think I'm in love with you," he said.

Oh, no!

I had no idea!

Dermot told me that he'd never been with a man. He wasn't even positive *I* was gay. But he did know I was the right guy to come out to. I chose to take that as a compliment. I chose *not* to say that if all this had happened six months ago, we might have had an entirely different story to tell. That's what the shy looks had been about, his coy friendliness. Dermot was just too scared to break the ice. And I was suddenly learning that his "right guy" was me!

Over a second pint he told me more about his growing up in a small Scottish town, always having to keep his head down, eyes averted in case someone knew the real emotions that were churning behind his shyness. He'd come to London out of desperation, and couldn't believe his luck to get a job at glamorous Harrods. (This time I didn't tell the joke about the guy shoveling elephant shit at the circus.) Everyone seemed so open and free in London, Dermot said, but old habits die hard, and he still didn't know how to meet people—a "special person", he corrected, looking at me.

It was all so genuine, so surprisingly unguarded. Add the gentle Scottish accent and I was nearly a puddle on the floor.

He went on like this—how I started showing up regularly, but Sammy was always watching—he watched everything. Meanwhile, Dermot started to think about me more and more, which forced him to examine his feelings...on an on, all ending with: "If you'd have me."

Good God. I was an expert in fatal longing, hang-dog pining, grateful for the slightest acknowledgment, scared of rejection. Now, after looking death in the face, I guess Dermot thought he had nothing to lose. I was getting the whole dam-burst of his pent-up feelings. I hardly knew how to respond. On one hand, his vulnerability was giving me an erection. His dark brown eyes were as plaintive as any heartsick boy's could be. It was all I could do not to wrap him in my arms and comfort him.

But how could I say his timing was atrocious! Or

mention the double irony that only a fortnight ago at this very table it was me pouring my guts out in the face of my own true love that was *never* going to be!

I realized that Timothy—even sweet Dermot—were like intoxicating scents one passed as through a cloud: engulfing but ephemeral, the stuff of poetry not novels.

I was saved from the urge to make my own confessions when the barman called, "Drink up time!"

So we made our slow, slightly intoxicated way back to Harrods. They'd closed the store, but the employee entrance was open with extra guards double checking everyone—for whatever good that did. We went back to our respective departments to wait out the day, tidy up, tell tales about our brushes with death.

Ah, but this was nothing, I said. In Paris I'd been thrown out of bed! Saw a guy's whole leg lying in the street! And as I had with Tess, we wondered about the tense and violent state of things. Every county seemed to be a target of one fanatical group or another. None of us imagined a world becoming *less* prone to violence. Peace was just a dream some of us had.

I called Tess when I got home. She said she'd tried to reach me at Harrods, but the lines were completely tied up. No surprise. The whole terrible business had brought back the frayed truths of our Paris experience. Now we were *both* ready to seriously consider living together in L.A.

(Spoiler alert: my soon-to-expire visa did not end our relationship. Tess *would* come to America. We actually got married, but it was more a marriage of diplomatic necessity. We couldn't have continued as a couple in the States *without* being married. Mainly, we just weren't ready to call it quits. We still never used the word *love*.)

~

After our collective brush with world-class terrorism, Harrods immediately began mending its wounds, repairing the damaged showroom and getting back to the business of keeping a stiff upper lip.

Tess came in one quiet afternoon shopping the adjacent grocery department for a new teapot. The one we used at her place was chipped and stained; it was time to upgrade. She chose one and brought it to my cash register. I rang it up with the usual "friends" discount, when suddenly, in a blur of commotion, three people from security pounced. The tea pot and the cash register receipt were yanked from our hands, then we were both hustled across the floor like shoplifters nabbed in the act—which we kind of were.

I knew all the plain-clothed security people on sight, but I hadn't seen them hovering: professionals in the art of hiding in plain sight. It all happened so quickly, so out-of-nowhere, we were both taken by complete surprise, busted without a doubt. I looked over at Tess, who was doing all she could to not burst into tears. After that, I kept eyes front allowing myself to be led past shoppers who probably didn't know what they were seeing. But my fellow employees most certainly did. I'd never been so embarrassed, all the worse involving Tess in the security team's little perp-walk show of power.

We were led down to a maze of narrow corridors I didn't even know existed, and into the office of a man I'd never met. He was head of store security, "employees' division", he said. The teapot and receipt were already on his desk. He asked if we were connected in any way and I replied over-dramatically, that Tess and I were lovers.

He chuckled, making a note on the form in front of him. "So, she's your girlfriend."

"Yes," I replied, deflated.

He looked at Tess. She nodded, already beginning to gather herself.

"How long you worked 'ere at Harrods?" he asked me.

"Almost a year," I said.

This actually seemed to sit well. I wasn't some new hire whose sole purpose was to rob the place blind. I had no idea what kind of hardened types he normally dealt with, but we must have seemed particularly unlikely. He looked at the selling price of the teapot (not much compared to, say, a watch or jewelry), then the forty percent below market I'd rung up. After a few more questions, a verdict was rendered.

"Let's just say you pushed the wrong buttons, shall we?" he said, completing his report. "Of course, if this happens again, you'll be out of a job and quite likely reported. Consider this a caution…to both of you."

And that, most fortunately, was all there was to it. Yes, we were co-conspirators, but the blame was officially all mine. Now it was just a matter of returning to my department and toughing out the sidelong glances and a final word from Mr. Taylor: "That was pretty stupid."

At least I still had a job.

Tess and I never spoke of that day, either.

~

In summer's last days, there was a letter in the post addressed to me. Inside was an invitation from Colin and Francesca to a barbecue. Coming in a beautiful envelope and written in a formal hand it was amusingly out of scale to the occasion and its proposed setting: our scrappy back "garden". But we all got one. Mine had a line extending the invitation to Tess as a "flat alumna". I had the impression that Colin and Francesca were already feeling nostalgic as we all contemplated the end of our short-lived era. Selling the flat was now a foregone conclusion.

On the appointed Sunday afternoon, with the summer heat behind us and the days already shortening, we all looked forward to what would probably be our last reunion. Colin and Francesca seemed to have gone all out. They brought a small hibachi barbecue and a bag of coals to cook lamb chops—lots of the small, expensive ones with a bone sticking out, allowing one to eat with fingers. Francesca provided the ingredients for a big salad, announcing proudly that the greens were all taken from the manor house's kitchen garden. She also provided several bottles of really good red wine "from daddy's cellar" (that would be the Baron). Finn brought beer. I provided Harrods' cheese and ice cream for dessert.

Tess arrived, pleased to see everyone again but

especially Gracie. At one point I watched them huddling together, giggling like old times. Gracie said she'd invited Sebastian as her "plus-one" (she had the lingo *down!*), but I could have told her that was a bad idea. Sebastian may have thought so, too. He'd have sucked up all the oxygen even without meaning to.

Finn was in good form—definitely on the lean side, but with his stinger sheathed if only because his armor seemed so battle-worn, bruised from bumping into things. He didn't even poke at Colin!

But I was most surprised by Francesca, who seemed to be more relaxed every time I saw her. Yes, she was literally to the manor born; anachronistic in almost every way. But her inbred airs and culture were as authentic as Dolly, the Cockney retiree who came into Harrods every Friday reminding me with a twinkle not to forget her discount. Both embodied England's long history and I adored them equally.

There was another layer of excitement as well. Finn announced that he'd be presenting Francesca with her long-awaited portrait. She was tingling with anticipation. I think we all were—or maybe it was relief.

When we pressed our luck, Finn said no, we were *not* allowed to see the big portrait of Sebastian until it was finished. Then, with the authority of an insider, Gracie said that the only two people to have seen it were "the artist and his muse". She was making a joke, and she wasn't quite wrong, but I saw Finn wince. If the artist-muse relationship between him and Sebastian implied some kind of reciprocity…well, this was not that. But none of us knew what was really going on. And it went without saying, Finn wasn't going to volunteer.

At one point Tess went upstairs to use the bathroom. After she'd been gone too long, I went up to find her. She was in my room, sitting on the bed in tears.

What could be the problem?

I saw beside her my sling bag, camera removed, resting on the Indian bedspread. I immediately guessed she'd wanted to take pictures of the gang and went to find the camera. Not a problem.

Then she thrust the Polaroid toward me.

I froze.

"This is *Timothy!*" she said through tears, utterly incredulous.

Having not shot anything since that fateful night, I'd forgotten all about the single frame I'd put back with the camera and tossed in the wardrobe. I took the photo from Tess and stared at it. There was no mistake; veiled but *unmistakable,* it was Timothy surrounded by the arms and legs of naked male bodies. I'd never even seen the fully-developed photograph myself!

"Were you sleeping with…*oh, my God, Terry*…were you sleeping with my best friend's *brother?*" She made it sound positively incestuous.

"No!" I said emphatically. "I mean not like that…it was just…it was an accident!"

"Really? An accident at some…" She struggled for the words. "Some sexual *free for all?*"

"It was Sebastian, Tess, before Timothy went away to…"

"I know where he went, Terry. I know all about it."

"Actually, you don't, Tess. I doubt you know *anything* about any of it."

"And that's probably the *only* thing I can thank you for," she zinged back,

sobbing some more.

"I'm sorry, Tess," I said weakly, looking at the picture again.

"I warned you, Terry."

"I didn't even know he was gay," I protested weakly.

"Then you're not as bloody observant as you think you are, are you?"

"Apparently not," I sighed ruefully.

"Blanche warned me, Terry! She told me about Timothy and Sebastian. She told me to watch out."

"Timothy warned me, too…the day after…this." I tossed the Polaroid onto the bed.

"Tess, it was…"

"*I don't care, Terry!* I don't want to hear any of it! So

many lies…" She sighed heavily, wiping the tears from her cheeks. "And we've been having such a nice time. How can I ever trust you?"

"You can't," I said bluntly. "You've always known the score."

She nodded sadly. "I don't know if I ever want to see you again."

As she stood up, the door opened. It was Gracie.

She saw Tess's tears. "What's going on? What happened?" But her demanding tone wasn't out of concern for Tess.

Tess looked at her, then back at me. "I don't recognize either of you anymore," she said, and pushed past us out the door.

Gracie and I looked at each other. Her eyes darted to the Polaroid on the bed. Then she saw my spark of panic.

"What is that, Terry?" she asked.

Suddenly we both lunged lunged for the photo. But I was closer and grabbed it first.

"It's Sebastian, isn't it?" she said. "We can't have those sorts of things getting…."

"No!"

"Yes, it is!" she yelled and grabbed for my arm.

I pulled back. "Please, just let it go, Gracie. It's not about you. It's not about Sebastian."

She was ready to lunge again when I heard the front door slam shut at the same time someone running up the stairs. Finn poked his head in. "Everything all right? Was that Tess leaving?"

"Yes," Gracie said coldly and moved toward the door. Finn stepped back as she stormed out.

"Just getting my camera," I said.

I quickly tucked the photo under my pillow and tossed the camera to Finn. "Here. You do the honors."

"What was that all that about?" he asked as we headed downstairs together.

"Tess had to go," I said.

"Already?"

"Guess so," I replied.

When we entered the sitting room, Finn continued out to join the others. But Gracie was waiting for me.

"We can't have any compromising images floating about."

There was that "we" again.

"Put it to rest, Gracie."

It was all she could do to not frisk me. I was shocked by her fierce gaze.

"I think we're through," I said.

She took a deep breath. "I'll talk to her," she said, meaning Tess.

"No, Gracie, *I'll* talk to her. Whatever *you're* on about has nothing to do with Tess."

"It's just that Sebastian is very…"

"Enough!" I said too loudly, cutting her off immediately. "I get it!"

Gracie looked nervously over her shoulder toward the patio. "We better join the party," she whispered.

When we stepped outside, Francesca addressed me: "Did Tess leave already?"

"She wasn't feeling well." My tone suggested there was nothing more to say.

"Poor dear," Francesca replied and very diplomatically left it at that.

Colin was demonstrating the radical addition of raisins to the green salad.

"It's Mediterranean," he said to Gracie. "Do you like olives?"

"Oh, no, no, no," she protested.

"How about a picture," Finn said, waving my camera. "Come on everyone!"

"Oh, yes, a picture!" Francesca trilled. "Come along, Colin, darling, Finn's going to make us immortal."

"If I live that long," he replied, his dark clouds showing.

He put down the oversized spoons he was using to toss the salad (olives on the side) and we let ourselves be arranged by Finn, our back toward the kitchen's open door.

"Cheese!" he said when we all lined up. He took the picture, catching the frame as it came out of the camera.

"And another," he said quickly, stepping closer. "And one more..." he said, stepping nearer still as he fired off a third shot. The way he held the camera, setting up the next shot without a beat, handling the frames as they ejected....there was something practiced about it which I recognized immediately.

"Now, just relax," he said. We all took a breath, and he got off two more shots.

"I'd like one of those," said Colin.

"I want one, too," Gracie said, and Finn handed out the still unexposed images, including one to me.

"And one with Finn," said Gracie.

"I'll do it," I said. Finn and I changed places, and I took two more shots, putting one in my pocket and handing the other one to Gracie.

"Last one of Finn and Francesca." I said.

"Oh, yes, please! The artist with his other muse!"

I stifled a chuckle and caught Finn's quiet grin as well. I could tell he was about to say *something,* but in the spirit of bonhomie decided to give the girl—the lady—a pass. The photo session ended when Gracie screamed about the smoke and Colin leapt to rescue the lamb.

After the main course, Finn excused himself then came back with a wrapped package and handed it to Francesca. She tore away the paper and carefully studied the framed painting. We all crowded around to have a look. It was small at only 12 x 14 inches in a simple gold frame. The likeness was there, but submerged under heavy layers of paint just as he'd explained to me. He had painted History first, with the face of Francesca.

She said she'd have to find a special place for it or it would be swallowed up by the other near life size paintings at the manor house. Colin said he was relieved the eyes didn't follow him around. This time Finn couldn't resist and joked that when they finally *did* notice him they would.

All in all, however, after the incident with Tess, the whole afternoon was anti-climactic. I knew I'd fucked things up right proper.

~

I called her later that night. I had to beg that she not to hang up. Told her I was surprised as she was about Timothy...about me and Timothy. She said again that she didn't want details. For sure, I wasn't going to draw her a picture. Mainly, I wanted to assure her that I wasn't having an affair *with her best friend's brother.* That it wasn't...we weren't...it *was* an accident. It was Sebastian making a weird kind of threat. For sure Tess was the wronged party and I was so sorry. But I promised I wasn't *seeing* anyone!

After a while we both calmed down. I agreed that she'd been right about Sebastian all along, and I promised *again* that I was done with him. Timothy was gone. There was no one else to be concerned about.

"Can't we still be Terry and Tess?" I pleaded.

She said she'd have to think about it, which at least wasn't a *no.* She had the right.

We had an odd, paradoxically reasonable balance, Tess and me. It shuddered precariously at times (all my own undoing), but when we focused on only us, we remained surprisingly sound. Through it all we still liked each other. I knew *I* wasn't my best when we were apart. I only hoped she felt the same and in time could look back if not misty-eyed, then fondly enough.

To make up I bought tickets to see the great mime Lindsay Kemp in "Flowers", a powerful (and wordless) theatrical retelling of Jean Genet's classic first novel "Our Lady of the Flowers". In hindsight, I might have chosen something decidedly less queer. Was I being passive-aggressive? I don't remember asking Tess if there was something *she'd* like to see. Oblivious people don't know they're being oblivious because, well....*they're oblivious*.

But because I well knew the novel on which "Flowers" was based, and if I was going to have one last London theater experience (reviews said the play was a triumph), to my mind at least, it had to be this. In fact, I was so bold over by the dreaminess—the theatricality—I went back to the book inspired to write a movie version. To make it contemporary, my idea was to set it in New York in the time of Stonewall with Divine as one of the fighting (in her case doomed) drag queens. I envisioned a Warhol-era Joe Dallesandro type as her hustler boyfriend, Darling. I'd call it "Saint Divine".

Trouble was, I hadn't read "Our Lady of the Flowers" in quite a long time. Meanwhile, others had picked up all its cues, rarely, alas, for the best. It had always pained me that John Waters appropriated the name of Genet's seraphic heroine in the form of a fat, shit-eating Baltimore drag queen. Nothing could be further from Genet's poetic vision. Then there was Fassbinder's *Querelle*, based on Genet's 1947 novel "Querelle de Brest", with all the same homoerotic iconography: the sailors, the jail cells, the shadow cruising. Indeed, there were references to Genet in all the cool style corners. When I went back to actually re-read the book, I realized the imagery had been totally coopted—desecrated even—rendering Genet's queer dreams a series of cliches. I put my notes for a screenplay aside, another dream over the dam.

~

As the opening of *Sebastian* drew closer, Gracie was eagerly flat hunting, but she was still around. As "head prefect" I found her huddled with Colin again. They were running the numbers for that long-imagined upgrade to the flat, which I now *did* think was too little, too late. But Gracie had plenty of two pence to add, as if she'd been planning changes all along. The term "American kitchen" came up, which I could only guess meant hot water *not* coming from some contraption above the sink, or where both hot *and* cold water came from a single faucet—imagine! Maybe even a stove that didn't require matches! My only suggestion was a new floor in the toilet that didn't foster the propagation of mushrooms.

I stopped seeing Sebastian on the stairs. Nor was I called

to action, so it seemed my personal photographer days were well and truly over. Perhaps it was just as well. I couldn't deny that I missed Sebastian's smile, which I could never decide was flirting or just being nice. But after the swanky sex club business and all the follow-up, I was ready to mistrust him on every count. I knew The Face was also a mask. Besides, I'd promised Tess that I'd keep my distance.

It was hard to tell if Sebastian knew *I* knew the real story about Timothy. I finally decided he had to know. Sex was power, and in his hands, information as well. They both came easily to the rich and famous—and to those with rare beauty. I'd seen it firsthand: people practically threw themselves at him. The adoration was currency, but money and power were even *better* than sex!

Word was, too—no longer just from Gracie; it was in the papers—that Sebastian's modeling agency, a business he knew better than anybody, was absorbing several smaller agencies. "The Face" was on its way to becoming one of the top model managers in the country. But I kept thinking about those *other* faces; the out-of-place businessmen and politicians who were always on the periphery. They probably had more in common with Sebastian than all the beautiful people put together.

As for Timothy, he'd refused to see Sebastian's face in the mirror; he'd refused to be devoured. But he'd had to flee to get away. I was leaving too, so I only had my pride to protect.

Then Gracie called. Could I pop by the office after work?

Dee waved me up after I was buzzed in. The place was more finished. There was new carpet on the stairs; large, glossy photographs of Sebastian on the walls. Looking along the central corridor, I noticed that all the plain doors on the left side had been replaced with more important-looking ones with nameplates bearing names I didn't recognize. Below each name in small letters was engraved 'SEE, Ltd.'.

The light-filled open space opposite was busier than my first visit. There were more stylish young booking managers, mostly women, in several more cubicles. I saw no lounge lizards sprawled in the seating area down the other end, but a new panel was entirely covered with 8x10 headshots of the agency's growing stable of models. Dee was wearing a draped ensemble, burgundy so dark it was almost black, made of the same knotty silk I'd seen before. Her hair now had an asymmetrical cut similar to Tess's, but a much more radical version, probably cut by Leonard himself (at full price!). The hair around her left ear was shaved high revealing the tattooed arc of barbed wire. I didn't know it yet, but punk was just around the corner. Dee was gonna fit right in.

When I commented on the improved look of the office, Dee smiled and nodded.

"I have something for you," she said in her awkward deaf speech. She gestured for me to follow her over to the Art & Archive area. I waited by one of the big, glass-topped worktables. Spread out were sheets of color slides, a few large prints of Sebastian obviously shot by a studio photographer, numerous proof sheets and a Lupe to view them. There was also paperwork—several letters that weren't my business, but what caught my eye was the letterhead on each official page. They had the same letters that were on the doors along the corridor: SEE, Ltd. When Dee returned, I pointed to the letterhead asked her, "What's SEE?"

"That's the umbrella company," she said, gathering them up quickly.

I must have stared back blankly.

"*Sebastian Entertainment Enterprises,*" she said. "Everything is under SEE...including *this*," she added, smiling, handing me an envelope. Inside was a check for £480! I studied it for a moment, letting the number sink in. Then I noticed that the check was under the usual name *Sebastian, Ltd.*

I pointed to the title questioningly. "Not SEE?"

"Sebastian Limited is the pictures and publications. SEE is property and other businesses—and the restaurants."

Restaurants plural?

There really was more going on than I knew about.

Before I had time to ask more questions, Dee explained that the payment was for the re-publication of my images, several months of them, in Vogue Brazil and Vogue Italia. Apparently, I was more international than I dreamed—not that anyone would know. Sebastian, Ltd. still got all the credit. But I was thrilled with the windfall.

~

I was walking my last leg home from the above-ground Fulham Broadway Tube stop. The calendar had just tipped into Autumn and the days were already getting chillingly shorter. The flat was still half a block ahead when I saw a taxi pull up and Finn get out. My first instinct was to call and greet him, but I hesitated, shocked, when I saw how frail he looked, as if he'd been punched and was catching his breath to right himself.

I gave him time to go inside. When I went in, he wasn't in the sitting room. The house was silent. My urge was to go up and check on him, but it just wasn't done to knock on his door. A week later the flat was silent again when I came home. I went straight into the kitchen to make a cup of tea. I opened the back door to let in the fading light. There was a weird stillness in the air, like earthquake weather in L.A. minus the Indian Summer heat. Carrying my tea upstairs, I felt the old carpet soft under my feet. I looked down and realized the entire first landing was soaking wet. Water was seeping from under the closed bathroom door. Then I heard the sound of softly running water. I couldn't believe someone had left the bath unattended. Teacup in hand, I went to open the door.

It was locked.

Suddenly my skin went cold.

"Hello," I called, hearing the quaver in my voice.

I put my cup on the second step of the stairs and rattled the door handle with two hands. I knocked again.

"Oh, God," I said out loud and rammed my shoulder against the door. Two more body slams and it burst open.

And there I saw him. Shirtless, his face submerged below bloody water that flowed in a gentle cascade over the lip of the bath.

"Finn!" I yelled and lunged forward, pulling him up, holding him to my chest. I wanted to hug him back to life, but his body was already getting stiff. I knew he was entirely gone from his body.

"Finn!" I kept saying. "Finn, no, no, no!"

The red water splashed in waves onto the floor. When I went to turn off the tap, I saw a razor blade bouncing on the surface. I eased Finn's body back down into the tub. His face was a literal death mask. I reached down and felt for the plug. When I pulled it, a bubble of bloody water exploded on my shoulder. I started shaking and realized I was soaked in the cruel, tepid water. This snapped me out of my initial shock and I grabbed a towel from the hook on the door. Gave myself a quick pat-down, then threw the towel on the floor to soak up the overflow.

I kept staring at Finn as the tub water slowly drained revealing his frail body inch by inch. He was naked except for boxer shorts. Both forearms had clean lengthwise incisions. He looked incredibly delicate. "*Like virgins to the grave.*" I said out loud, a line from Joni Mitchell, which I would forever associate with this tragic moment. I backed out and closed the door.

What to do next?

First, I ran up to my room to change into dry clothes.

Then I ran down to the sitting room and called the police. I called Gracie, Tess and Colin. I could hardly get my words out. No one pressed for details because they could tell I was too distraught to be coherent. The police said they were on their way.

Not ten minutes later I heard sirens. Then a firm knock at the front door. I ran to let them in, a Bobby in dome-topped uniform and another who looked more senior in a cap rimmed with checkerboard black and white. Out on the street, another police car and an ambulance were pulling up.

"He's in the bath…" I said, pointing. Four men bound past me up the stairs, followed quickly by two paramedics.

More police cars arrived, stopping in the road. I heard bits of conversations but mainly held back, letting the experts take over. I had the sense that there was "routine" imbedded in every action I was witnessing, all in the service of quick disposal (an official "taking custody") of the body.

Then the expected questions: Did I live here? Did I find the body? Had I called the police? A black woman with CORONER across the back of her jacket came in and went straight up like it was her place. For the moment, this was *their* place. A crime scene!

I very much needed to sit down and led the policeman asking questions into the sitting room. Even in dry clothes, I was still shaking. We sat at the dining room table and forms were laid out. They'd need information, he said: the deceased's ID, next-of-kin. I told them his family was in Canada; they were welcome to go up to Finn's room and look for a passport.

For a minute I was clearly a "person of interest" but as long as my whereabouts checked out (Harrods was even my *alibi*!), and considering the estimated time of death six hours earlier, I shouldn't worry. Well, thanks for small mercies!

A few minutes later, the cop with the Bobby hat came back waving Finn's passport.

"I was here before," he said to me. "At Christmas."

It took me a moment.

"He was some kind of an artist, then? I remember that room."

I actually couldn't believe the coincidence. But the very fact that he'd been here before seemed to prompt suspicious glances.

"He was an artist, yes," I said. "A very good one."

He sniffed. "I wouldn't know."

I wanted to scream.

Then I heard Gracie's voice calling me from the front hall.

"That's our other flatmate," I said to the cops. "I need to…"

"Go on," the senior man said, remaining seated and already preparing forms. "We won't be too long. But we'll need everyone's information, if you could have that ready."

"I'll tell her," I said.

Gracie called again, and I went out to greet her. She was standing by the front door, her face stricken, aghast at the grim comings and goings. We fell into each other's arms. She started crying, then I did, too, finally releasing the shock I'd been managing to contain. All I could think about was Finn's frail white body, a gruesome pentimento beneath the crimson veil of bathwater.

"He was our angel," I said. "If only I'd known."

Gracie drew back to look at me. "Known what?"

Suddenly she was all business.

"Known what?" she asked again. It was the same demanding tone I'd heard when she tried to wrest the Polaroid from me.

Then: "Excuse us, please!" It was the coroner lady coming down to wave in a couple of men wheeling a gurney through the front door.

"Terry, what are you talking about?"

I led Gracie back into the short hallway so we could talk privately.

"He drove Finn to this, Gracie." I was starting to feel enraged.

"Who? Sebastian?"

"How could you not have known?"

"Hold on," she said. "Are you blaming me?"

"Not *you*, Gracie," I replied, letting that hang in the air.

I saw the wheels turning. Perhaps for the first time she, herself, was finally putting the pieces together.

"We could have stopped this," I said. "It didn't need to go so far."

Suddenly, Colin burst through the open front door, looking around with frantic eyes. He saw us and froze. "So, it's true?"

I nodded. "They said he'd been dead six hours. I came home from work and he was in the bath; bloody water all over the floor."

"Christ," he said, continuing into the sitting room. Gracie and I followed as he dropped onto the couch. I realized he hadn't seen the policeman seated at the dining table behind the door. Colin curled himself up like a ball, holding his head in his hands. "It's all coming at once. I can't believe it!"

"What is?" I asked. He was as distraught as I'd ever seen him.

But when he looked up, he saw the policeman seated across the room suddenly looking on with interest. Colin immediately changed his tone. His private business had nothing to do with outsiders.

"I didn't see you there," he said, standing; his manner as much as his posh accent indicating that the officer was dismissed.

"Sorry, sir; I'll just wait outside."

It was the power of class rule in action, and without another word policeman left. I was quietly amazed that even in the midst of chaos...well, there would always be an England.

After the door closed, Colin started pacing. "I don't know how I'll tell Francesca."

I looked at Gracie, who dropped onto the couch, her face inscrutable.

"It's all coming at once," Colin said. "I can't believe it."

"What are you saying?" I asked.

"I've been cleaned out. All my holdings!"

"How can that be?" I asked. Surely he was being overly dramatic.

"Developers I didn't even know existed. My building, the cafe, even this flat! Everything I own was taken right out from under me."

That was a pretty big statement. "Who can do that?" I asked.

He barked a grim laugh. "Who indeed? All very 'just business', mind you. The bank, the local council spinning ordinances, some big developer winning Eminent Domain. And here's me juggling my investments like a sodding chump. I thought everything was...no one said a word about...and now poor wretched Finn," Colin said. "I'll get back my equity—thanks a lot—but that's a pittance."

"Can't you sue?"

"Paying a solicitor to fight my way back will cost me everything I've got. Of course, they know that, too. Oh, they're good." He looked around the room—almost fondly, I realized. "All the years of work…"

"This place, too?" I asked.

"Everything! Someone's been paid off; that much is clear. Puts me back seven years! And now poor Finn…Christ. You'll all have to be out by the end of the month."

"Just like that?" I asked, truly surprised.

"Well, you're all leaving, anyway. Pretty good timing all round, I'd say?"

"Yes," I said. "Yes, it is. Very convenient timing."

Gracie remained silent, staring at the floor.

Then a knock at the door and the coroner lady stuck her head in. "We're taking him now if you want to…"

Yes, we did, so we followed her out and huddled in the entry hall as attendants carried the gurney down, straining to keep it level on the narrow stairs. Wide straps secured Finn's lifeless, sheet-wrapped form—another faceless casualty of city living. Flashing lights from the ambulance outside pulsed on our solemn faces. They loaded Finn up, shut the door, and he was gone.

When the policeman spoke, we all jumped.

He was behind us, coming down the stairs, waving a notepad.

"I'll need your names."

"Oh, right," I said. So we all trooped back into the sitting room to give the man our information.

"And you're the landlord," the policeman asked Colin, just to confirm assumptions.

"Yes, I am…for the moment," he added grimly.

"There might be some calls to finalize our report," the policeman said. "But it all looks pretty routine."

"Jesus," I said, relieved on one hand, but not hiding my disgust at the pitiless efficiency.

"We'll be available, of course," Colin said, speaking for everyone in the most proper tones, asserting his station.

"Thank you, sir. So, we'll be off, then. Sorry for your loss," he added perfunctorily, tipping his hat.

"Thanks," we said in quiet unison as we all followed to see him out, closing the front door behind him.

The flat was so quiet. Suddenly, the stairs looked like the gateway to, this time, an *actually* haunted house. It was chilling.

Colin took a heavy sigh, which caught in his throat, and then he burst into tears. I put my arm around his shoulder.

"Let's have a cup of tea," I said, and we started back toward the sitting room.

But Gracie hesitated. "I can't stay."

I looked at her, stunned. "Really, Gracie? A cup of tea?" I couldn't believe she'd just walk out now.

"I have to get back to the office."

"But your office is upstairs," I said.

"I'm practically moved out, Terry. You know that," she added coolly. "I'd rather tell Sebastian about all this in person."

"You mean about *Finn's tragic suicide*," I said, pointedly.

"Yes."

"I'm sure he'll be devastated."

"He will, of course. *Of course!* This is terrible...terrible what's happened."

"It is," I said, holding her gaze. "Terrible. Who'd have seen it coming when he was doing so well?"

She looked at me with a cold stare. "I really have to go."

"Of course," I replied.

"I'm so sorry, Colin, about everything."

"Thanks, love," he said, wiping his eyes. "We'll talk later."

She nodded and walked out. Colin and I went back into the sitting room. When I turned to look at him, he was staring back at me.

"What was all that about?"

"All what?" I asked.

He pointed to the door. "All *that*, Terry."

"I'll make some tea."

He followed me into the kitchen. "Do you know something I should know?"

"Colin, I don't know anything."

"Are you keeping things from the police?"

"The police have nothing to do with this."

"Because if you are…"

"The police are not our problem, Colin. Case closed."

I immediately regretted the leading words.

He stepped closer. "What's going on?"

"I don't know."

"*What* don't you know, Terry?" he pressed.

"I don't know anything, Colin…not for certain."

I was loathe to say more, afraid that talking would open the floodgates. But the chilling reality of Finn's desperate act was beginning to sink in. As I fussed with the kettle I could feel Colin's eyes boring into the back of my neck. My mind was racing. When I poured boiling water into the teapot, I realized my hand was shaking.

"What's wrong, Terry?"

I finished pouring the tea, choosing my words. "You mentioned the local council and some developers. That group moving in on your investments?"

"Yes," he said slowly.

"Do you know who they are? Is there a name?"

"Actually, I just found out the name, though it took some teeth-pulling. But what would *you* possibly know about…"

"Was it SEE by any chance? SEE Limited?"

Colin froze.

"How…?"

He looked at me incredulously. Then more suspiciously. Yes, how *would* I know about such things? But he was thinking. He looked toward the front door, then he said another word: "Gracie?"

There was disbelief in his voice.

"*Sebastian*," I said flatly. "SEE is Sebastian's holding company; maybe one of many, I don't know. But there could be a dozen different business under that one umbrella."

Colin digested that for a moment. "She was feeding him information?"

"Probably everything, whether she knew it or not."

Now Colin was racing to connect the dots. I was, too, remembering something Sebastian said the first night we went out. *There are sharks around every corner.* I just never thought he was one of the sharks.

"Good God," Colin said quietly, no doubt remembering all the huddle time he and Gracie had shared over his papers.

"So, we were all…?" Another silence. "Surely not Finn."

"He was useful, *too*, besides me as his *personal photographer*," words I almost spat. "There's one other guy I know as well."

"Who?"

"Tess's best friend's brother."

"*Tess is involved?*" Now, he was almost shouting.

"No!" I said. "No, she's not, Colin, I promise! Not Tess. That other guy was just a weird coincidence—or maybe it wasn't. My point is Sebastian finds people, insinuates himself, uses their gifts, talents, connections…"

"And property," said Colin.

"Yes."

"And he *eats* them."

"Like a shark."

"Good God," Colin said in a whisper, his mind racing over all the details, piecing together the whole scheme.

"He's very.…"

"…enticing," Colin said.

"That's the word," I replied. "All those rare good looks, the shine, the glamour and fame…"

"It's currency," Colin said quietly, still counting the ways he inadvertently fell into Sebastian's web. "And he's on the fucking busses big as life!"

"Bigger than life in the Tube station ads," I added. "And my arty photos of him are in the magazines. We all had something he could use."

Colin went silent, staring at his tea. His next words were almost a whisper:

"And she never said a word."

"She may not have known the extent of things, but he got her, Colin, hook, line and designer wardrobe. Changed her life." Then something else occurred to me. "What do you bet Finn's portrait is ready right on time?"

Colin sniffed derisively. "He actually finished it?"

It was an understandable reaction to all the unkind ribbing. Then he immediately reconsidered.

He looked at me.

We both looked towards the ceiling.

In the next moment we put our cups down and ran for the stairs.

Even in deep shadow, we could see immediately that the room was a disaster—almost the crime scene it *hadn't* been when the burglars came. There was debris covering the entire floor, which I recognized immediately as Polaroid film boxes, hundreds of them, their bright square rainbow logo popping out amidst empty, black film cartridges and the thick white paper sleeves protecting them. I reached for the light switch floodlights clamped to Finn's work blasted on.

Suddenly, a bold, extreme closeup of Sebastian's face nearly exploded toward us.

"Good God," Colin gasped. "It's not a painting at all!"

Indeed. Gone was the Wall of Wonder. In its place was a wide patchwork image made entirely from Polaroids. It had a mosaic quality that sometimes included, sometimes overlapped the white outline of the Polaroid frame. I knew at a glance the piece was sized to the proportions of the standing wall I'd seen at the restaurant on New Year. The tight cropping stopped at Sebastian's mid-forehead, the bottom edge to the bottom of his chin. The wide side edges stopped just past his ears, framing his face with those long corkscrew strands. We were slow to recognize the depth of it until we stepped closer.

"It's his body!" I exclaimed.

"His entire body to make his face," Colin said, looking closer, suddenly in awe.

We walked the length of the panel, and it was true: every frame was a detail from Sebastian's body—his entire body! No detail had been unscrutinized, but every moment was carefully put together to make a face: "The Face". Finn had burrowed into the quicksand of Sebastian's beauty and immersed himself completely. Up close, the facial aspects disappeared as each Polaroid pixilation became a sensual moment in itself—the minutiae of wonder! Only from a distance were Sebastian's features, the nuances of an expression, discernible. Finn had even managed to capture the opalesque colors in Sebastian's eyes from refraction caught on a fingernail.

"It's almost painterly with all the different mocha tones," Colin said. "And the white edges give it a kind of jerky animation."

I was surprised by Colin's insight. He'd always given the impression that it was Francesca who had the eye for art. Now I suspected that Colin, too, had a soft spot not only for art but possibly artists—and in spite of everything, this one in particular.

We both stepped way back to take in again the full impact.

"Mind you, I'm no expert," Colin said, breaking our long silence. "But this is a masterpiece."

"Yes," I said and nearly burst into tears all over again.

Colin started pacing the large room, shuffling aside the debris at our feet that spread like fallen leaves. "We can't let him have it," he said at last.

"Who?"

"*The bastard stole this right out of him*," he said angrily, pointing to the artwork.

"It's already paid for, Colin. Finn told me himself. Sebastian paid him good money."

"Finn paid with his life, Terry. That's not a fair trade."

"Well, we can't destroy it," I said. "That would be criminal on too many levels."

"Good God, no. We're not destroying *this*."

"So, what do we do? Steal it?"

After a moment, Colin said: "*Yes!*"

I turned to look at him. He was serious.

"The bloodless bastard has stolen everything—my investments, *this damn flat!* He seems to have stolen Gracie's decency. Now, it's our turn."

He looked hard at the portrait. "We'll steal his face."

Oh, my God!

It was a totally audacious idea, but the irony was too delicious. It was the last thing "The Face" would think *could* be stolen.

Suddenly, Colin was all business.

"How is it mounted?" He walked back to the portrait checking its side edge. I got down on the floor to look along the bottom.

"It's on two boards," I said. "There's four brackets under each panel."

"Yes, and across the top, too," said Colin, feeling with his fingers. "That's good."

"Will we damage it if we split the parts?"

"He made it to be moved," Colin replied. "But we'll have to be careful."

Then the next logical question:

"Where will we put it?"

Colin thought for a moment. "My place in Shepards Bush is too small."

"And too obvious," I said

Then lightning struck.

"I know somewhere no one would look."

I was suddenly caught up in the idea of a caper, a royal prank! Because I knew the absolutely most secret place in all of London! I'd always thought that a gay bathhouse was where I'd hide if I ever killed the president. But now I had an even better place. And it was hiding in plain sight!

"Where?" Colin asked.

"Harrods!"

He looked at me like I was crazy. "Harrods?"

"In the deep freeze, Colin! I'll bet barely a dozen people in the world even know it exists!"

Colin went silent, thinking with his mouth agape.

"A deep freeze? Do you really think…? What about…? How would we get it…?"

"I have a friend on the loading dock. He'd do anything for me."

It was a flippant disrespecting of Dermot's tender

feelings, but neither Colin nor me were thinking straight, both suddenly caught up like ten-year-old amateur detectives.

"We'll have to act fast," Colin said at last.

"You're right. Gracie's going to be on top of this in no time."

I followed Colin downstairs. He went straight for the phone and called Francesca.

"Darling, I have some very sad news," he began, and gently explained what had happened. "The coroner just left with his body."

There were long pauses. Colin looked at me pointing to his eyes. Francesca was in tears. Once she gathered herself, he explained our big idea.

"We're going to move Finn's portrait where no one can find it."

Suddenly he pulled the receiver away from his ear. Apparently she wasn't as caught up as we were. No, he wasn't going to tell her anything more; she shouldn't be involved. There were more pauses, nods and *Yes, darlings*. At one point he said, "Terry and I just think it's all so wrong and…yes Terry, he's here with me…yes, the American…"

Clearly, Francesca was dubious, but Colin kept emphasizing the outrage, the need for quick action. In the end she came round, if not with enthusiasm then a sense of duty, ready to stand by her man. The old girl had pluck, I'll say that.

Then Colin called the construction foreman he'd had to abruptly let go when he realized his financing had collapsed. The man said he'd bring a lorry over early the next evening after his new job ended and after he'd gone home for his tea.

The plan was that we'd take Finn's portrait down the following night—in a little more than twenty-four hours—but time enough for Colin to round up cleaners to have the landing mopped, the bathroom scrubbed down, *and* to round up the help we'd need to transport the panels. It would also give *me* time to talk with Dermot, whose cooperation would be crucial.

Once the plan was decided, Colin left, and I suddenly found myself alone in the flat. Never had silence been more unsettling. That lasted as long as it took to call Tess and tell her I needed to get myself up to Notting Hill as quickly as I could.

As I described the scene, tears filled her eyes. It was all such a tragedy but at the same time so chillingly dispatched: the cops, the coroner, the forms, the ambulance whisking Finn's body away, page turned, end of story. We decided to give Gracie the benefit of the doubt. I'm sure she was as shocked and heartbroken as we were, but her alliances were totally skewed. Protecting Sebastian was now a knee-jerk response. Tess said I got off light. It was true. I seemed to have been abruptly let go as Sebastian's personal photographer, but without any further consequences. Tess also had the good grace not to say *I told you so*.

There was nothing left of Finn but the artwork, and as far as Colin and I were concerned, Sebastian had to pay. As for our plan, Tess made her thoughts pretty clear.

"Now, you're stealing art?" she asked, sounding utterly incredulous.

"It's not *stealing* exactly."

"I'd say it is, Terry. The portrait belongs to Sebastian."

"But he stole it from Finn!" I insisted.

"I don't think the courts would see things through your moral outrage."

I knew she was right...damn voice of reason.

"And if pressed," she added, "I don't think Sebastian would be nice about it, either."

That was probably true as well. Beauty and fame may have opened doors, but skullduggery kept him in the room. He knew people. And they knew people. That's how it worked. That's how he ruined Colin.

Then, apropos of nothing (but really everything), Tess said: "Blanche finally told me *why* Timothy moved to Italy. You were right; I hadn't known the details."

My whole inside reacted at the mention of his name, but I just nodded, pokerfaced. I had no idea if Tess knew the extent of my feelings for Timothy, but that his name came up at all suggested she'd gleaned something.

"I didn't mention to Blanche about the Polaroid," Tess added.

"Best not," I replied, and quickly changed the subject: "I don't understand what Sebastian wanted with *me*. I don't have *anything* to steal!"

"You have talent, Terry. You were useful. Count your lucky stars that's *all* of you he used. If it was a power play, I'd say you won."

"I won because I didn't lose," I chuckled ruefully. "Somehow, it doesn't feel like winning."

We both chose to believe that I actually had *not* succumbed to Sebastian's charms: the playful sparks of sexual availability he scattered around like magic dust. Still, he never gave without an expectation of return. He was the bone he tossed to everyone, we, the hungry dogs he'd been baiting since he was a pubescent teen; since he realized his face—and sometimes the promise of his body—was not just his power but his weapon. The more permission he gave his admirers, the more they wanted more. Sebastian didn't offer himself to pose as a model for Finn. He summoned Finn, gleaning his weakest spot, to feast with abandon on his physical perfection. In the end, as emaciated as Finn was, he died of gluttony, a slave to his hunger for beauty.

I kept seeing him half submerged in the bloody water, pale and wan like a modern pre-Raphaelite Ophelia. In my mind, I willed it not to be so.

"I'm meeting Colin after work," I said.

Tess looked at me, amused. "You can't win, Terry."

"Well, at least I'm going to go through the motions—for Finn."

I stayed the night with Tess and got up very early the next morning, leaving for work in the same clothes I'd worn the day before. I arrived before my day started at nine and caught Dermot in time for his morning break. We had tea in the employees' dining room, taking my usual spot by the window that overlooked Harrods' unglamorous rooftop.

I laid out my idea minus any mention of characters or plot. All I wanted was early-morning access to the loading dock and a four-wheel dolly. I'd have my own help unloading the two panels of artwork. I'd get them up to Frosted Foods' small office and into the deep freeze under my own steam.

He studied me with a furrowed brow. Anything outside procedure was a risk, he said, and there wouldn't be much time. If he thought the whole idea preposterous, he didn't say.

"Sammy arrives at six-thirty sharp. I'll have a cart ready at six."

"Six it is; I'll be there. In and out with time to spare," I said, waving off his obvious doubts with a "Thanks."

~

The doorbell rang at four in the morning. Colin, who had fallen asleep on the couch in the sitting room, was the first to answer. I came awake with a jerk, so I must have been asleep, though it felt like I hadn't slept at all.

Two unshaven men, probably early forties but looking older, were coming up the stairs when I opened the door of my room. One was carrying a long roll of plastic with which we were going to carefully wrap each panel before moving it. This would not only protect the work, but hopefully obscure its very recognizable subject once we arrived at Harrods. I led them all the way up to Finn's studio without a word. It was just too early for conversation.

The job required all four of us. We removed both panels from the wall, triple wrapped then carefully maneuvered each one down the narrow flights and around the tight angles of the stairway. Outside, there was a work-weary cube truck double parked and waiting. The roll-up rear door screeched loudly as it opened. The metal floor was gritty with gravel and rust. The roof had a flat skylight clouded yellow with age. The one streetlight above cast no more light into the interior than the moon.

Nor was there anywhere to secure the panels vertically. They were too big to fit side-by-side laying flat on the floor.

There was no alternative than for two men to stand in the back holding them up. Colin and one of the workmen were chosen as I needed to meet Dermot when we arrived at the loading dock. It wasn't that far of a journey. I caught Colin's eye as the door came down. It was like we were seeing each other for the last time.

London was a different city in the wee dawn hours. I was reminded of my long walks with Pieter where what souls one saw were best to avoid. It was a world where only the rats and the rubbish men belonged.

The route along Kings Road was the same as my usual #22 bus ride, turning left at Sloan Street then straight up to Knightsbridge. Except this time I directed the driver to go left onto a side street that would put us at the back of Harrods.

We arrived just before the designated hour. Dermot was there to meet us, already looking at his watch. He reminded me that Sammy-How's-Your-Ring would be arriving promptly at six-thirty. There were already two big lorries backing in. Dermot played tarmac controller with practiced waves turning us around, guiding the lorry in backwards to the edge of the loading platform. I jumped out of the cab and ran round to raise the roll-up door. When I did, poor Colin was actually sweating, more strained than I'd ever seen him.

Beside and all around us, workers were maneuvering pallet jacks to unload a long shipping container packed tight with bulky furniture wrapped in heavy plastic. The four-wheel cart was ready, low and flat with support rails on its long edges. Colin and his guys carried the first panel out of the lorry and set it carefully onto the cart. It stood securely lengthwise, but was too tall and without support leaned precariously beyond the side rails. Dermot, Colin and I looked at each other with obvious concern. Suddenly, it was clear that actually getting the artwork upstairs and wheeled through the darkened showrooms, not to mention make it look like business as usual if anyone asked, was a two-man job. And we still had a second panel to load. Also, seeing them "in space" as it were, I realized that there was also a very real chance that the panels would be too tall to fit through the thick, insulated doorframe of the deep freeze. I'd never thought to measure. Worse still would be to get them up there and find they *didn't* fit. There was no time for thinking further, and there'd just be no explaining our misadventure to Sammy. It took only an instant to know that the whole idea was preposterous. In our haste, I *hadn't* thought it through. Colin caught my dubious expression, to say nothing of Dermot, whose own job would be on the line in about twenty minutes.

"Abort mission?" Colin said.

Dermot and I looked at each other and said, "Yes," in unison.

We scrambled to load the panel back on the lorry. Before the roll-up door rolled down again, Colin told the driver, "Park on Sloan Street."

Yes, I thought. *Now, that's a good idea.* We needed to rethink immediately.

I shook Dermot's hand, saying *thank you* and *sorry*, and we pulled out to the street, at least one disaster averted.

Once parked just two blocks away, we, including our workmen, stood on the sidewalk coming up with Plan B. If we were going to move the artwork anywhere else, it needed to be properly secured. Padded blankets and straps were required, and a vehicle with hooks or slats or something to which we could secure the pieces in transit. The workers told Colin that they had everything back at their garage, but it would cost him. By now they'd caught the smell of fish, saying they didn't want to "get stitched up in anything dodgy". They had Colin by the balls and started to squeeze.

In the end he got back into the back of the van, had them drive back to Wandsworth Bridge Road where he'd left his car. He said he'd work things out from there and call me later with an update. I walked back to Harrods, came in through the employee entrance and went straight to the staff lounge to catch up on my sleep.

~

I had a day's work ahead of me and could barely keep

focused. Just after lunchtime, Mr. Taylor approached, saying I was wanted upstairs in the employment office. *Oh, shit.* I knew I was only guilty of dubious intent, but I'd learned firsthand how stealth Harrods' security could be. Maybe they were watching the entire time. Mr. Taylor's dour look said *What have you done this time?* He hadn't forgotten the black mark on my rap sheet, though I'd certainly minded my p's and q's since then. Tess hadn't shown her face at all. I *had* continued helping Dolly-Don't-Forget-Me-Discount. I was almost ready to go down with *that* ship. I really had no idea what they wanted me for upstairs.

So, taking off my white Food Halls overcoat and wearing yesterday's clothes, I went up to the fifth floor, found the office and made my presence known. While I waited I thought that now might be a good time to put in my notice—that is, if I still had a job. I was about to depart England, anyway. No need to fire me, I'd just quit.

Then I was called. A very pleasant woman of middle age invited me to sit down opposite her desk. Her tone was warm, which surprised me.

"We've been reviewing your employment history," she began, and I braced myself. Then the surreal happened.

It seemed I'd never received two raises I had due. "Somehow, you slipped through the cracks," she said with an awkward little laugh. Then, with Harrods' sincere apologies, she handed me a check for £280! On top of the four hundred quid I'd just received from Sebastian, and with what money I'd saved, I could now return to L.A. with almost as much as I had when I left—and a cool wardrobe to boot! In fact, I had enough to avoid doing the one thing I was most afraid I'd have to do when I returned to L.A.: take two steps back by moving in with my parents. *That* would be the biggest mistake I could ever make!

~

The department phone was ringing as I arrived back from the office. Mr. Taylor wasn't around so I picked it up. It was Colin.

"Terry," he said immediately. He recognized my voice, and all I'd said was "Frosted Food"!

His words came out in a breathless stream as he laid out a new plan that was less costly and involved just the two of us. He'd rented a smaller van fitted out to safely move the artwork. When I asked where we were going, he said the manor house in Gloucestershire.

"*To Francesca's?*" I almost shouted before lowering my voice. "Are you serious?"

"I know, I know," he said before I had time to say more. "She's being a damn good sport about it," he said, adding: "Good old boots."

Old boots? Wait. That was a new one. I'd never heard the expression before, though the tone suggested a term of endearment. God help me, I was still learning something *English* every day!

When I asked where Gloucestershire was, Colin said it was west of Oxford. That much I could envision. The manor house was near a town called Cheltenham. I had no idea where that was. I could never afford to "do England" like a tourist. The scruffy backpackers "doing Dubrovnik" probably saw more of the UK than I ever did.

Colin said he'd meet me after work back on Sloan Street, where we'd parked before.

In mid-afternoon, Dermot walked through Frosted Foods heading home. I was busy at the cash register with a line of customers, but our eyes connected. This time we had something to say. I mouthed *thank you*, and he nodded a conspiratorial smile. We'd saved the day, maybe *both* our jobs, by aborting the mission. If that was going to be our secret affair, I guess we'd had it.

Now, I was looking forward to visiting the ancestral home of a real life Baroness!

Perhaps Plan B was no more sensible than Plan A, but by now Colin and I were committed. On a mission! Dusk fell quickly to nighttime as we settled into our rented transport van and slogged through rush hour traffic. It took us over an hour just to get out of Greater London. Everything was made grim under the orange haze of sodium lamplight lining the motorways. I'd never seen such street lighting before and found it totally depressing. Even as the M10 wound its way northwest toward Oxford then due west into Gloucestershire, the orange haze stayed with us mile after mile.

Eventually, after eight o'clock, Colin turned off the four-lane highway and we were soon down to two-lane roads lined with trees and low stone walls. Every now and then I saw lights in the distance. Colin said that most of England's countryside was scattered with centuries-old grand houses. At one time there were as many as three thousand.

"Now, there's less than a thousand. All the really big ones with hundreds of rooms have been torn down or are practically government owned, even with people living in them. They have to be open to the public to cover taxes."

I asked about Francesca's place.

"It's not one of those enormous piles if that's what you're thinking. It's still a private home. The current Baron has tenants who farm, raise pigs and milk goats. It almost pays for itself, which is quite remarkable. Been in the family since Francesca's great, great, *great* grandfather was awarded the estate in the 1780s. Georgian style outside with modern updates inside. Big, of course, and formal. But generations—entire families—have come and gone there. Quite remarkable when you think about it. I joke about the big paintings and that way of life, but really, the house is doing what houses are supposed to do. It's a home. It always has been. I was most surprised about that."

I caught a wistfulness, as if Colin felt he'd missed out somehow. It only occurred to me then that I knew little of his background. Where exactly *had* he grown up? Was he from a big family or an only child? His aspirational airs (Finn wasn't wrong about that) suggested he was *not* from the manor born. He screamed "public school" (which is to say *private* school), but I doubted it was one of the "right" ones. It certainly didn't matter to Francesca, least of all their twelve-year age difference. Mostly, Colin was a good egg—and obviously a damn good sport right alongside Francesca herself. He certainly didn't deserve to be financially ravaged by Sebastian.

Finally, we turned off the main road and, in a few minutes came to a large open gate with a gatehouse, an actual small stone house with a slate roof, at its entrance. Colin drove straight through, and we curved around a low hill when I saw the house up ahead. Colin was right, it wasn't a king's palace; more of a mansion, albeit an imposing one, with tall windows that spanned the wide, two-story facade. For all its Georgian stateliness, it actually had the feeling of a home. Perhaps it was the lights in some of the windows. A third floor was a combination of mansard roofs and smaller arched windows that jutted forward to align with the front facade. Driving into the wide gravel entry court, I counted five wide steps leading up to the house's central front door.

As we pulled to a stop, the door opened and Francesca came out. It was the first time I'd seen her in trousers—dark yellow capris at that, which tapered to the ankle. She wore a crisp white oversized shirt tucked in under a wide belt. Her hair, which was usually coiffed, now fell casually to her shoulders under a loosely draped Hermes silk square swept side to side instead of knotted beneath her chin. This wasn't the in-town Francesca I knew suited up for London, or the Francesca of Finn's portrait, her likeness almost obscured by layers of history. This was the modern Baroness, informal and at ease. I hardly recognized her.

"Welcome, darlings," she said. "Isn't this exciting!"

Colin and I exchanged glances. Without admitting it we'd both become entirely nervous about the wisdom of our little caprice. What we were doing *was* dodgy, probably illegal and most likely futile. At this point, we were just making a statement.

"Let me have a look," Francesca said, and we went around to the back of the van. Colin swung open the two hinged doors. There they were, each wrapped panel covered by a thick quilted moving blanket and strapped securely to the opposing walls. I was pleased and relieved to see them so well protected.

Francesca was too. "Safe and sound," she said. "Now, let's all go inside and have a cup of tea. You've had such a long drive. I've prepared a light supper. Jones and his fellows will bring the panels into the sunroom." As she spoke, three men in workman's attire came round from the side of the house. How nice to have people to put things places.

I decided to put my own tensions aside and see how the other half (my Harrods customers!) lived when they were at home. As we approached the open front door, I caught myself whistling Joni Mitchell: *Everything comes and goes.* She had words for every occasion.

The entry hall was floored with beautifully worn white marble squares. There was a round table with an enormous spray of flowers under the curve of a burgundy-carpeted stairway, its ebony bannister leading up to the first floor. High ceilings; walls a muted white. Grand, yes—it was assumed—but restrained, eschewing opulence.

The two rooms I glimpsed from the entry hall—a large sitting room and a smaller library—had that same restraint. I also saw some of the large family portraits that Colin always joked about. But against pale blue walls in a room full of windows, even at night they didn't look as shifty as he'd depicted. Quite the opposite. Here were the families and children—pets, too, as faithful footnotes—all of whom passed *through* this house generation after generation. Personal ownership yielded to the duty of stewardship. The current Baron and his daughter, the Baroness Francesca, were caretakers as were their inherited titles, to be passed on or, perhaps in Francesca's case, die with her.

"The powder room's in there," Francesca said, pointing to a short corridor off the entry hall with a single door on each side.

I followed Colin's lead as he pointed to one door, which I entered, and he took the other. *Ah, so there were two powder rooms! Perfect for entertaining.* Mine was clad entirely in gold-streaked dark blue marble. The patina suggested it might have been original. *Kings may have stood before this toilet after a long carriage ride from London,* I thought, as I took a much-needed pee. It was almost beyond grasping the two centuries of events, peeing and all, that had transpired in that house.

Emerging from the powder room, I was impressed again

that the house was neither an over-accessorized museum or some uncomfortable faux French showcase. *Those* I'd seen in Beverly Hills! Most memorably in the Palladian-style mansion of a famous fiction writer whose great round living room was scattered with stiff, museum-quality French furniture that was impossible to sit on comfortably.

Francesca led us down a corridor at the end of which was a large room with windows on three sides, the end ones, being French doors, were open to the night. This could only be the aforementioned sunroom. I imagined how glorious it must look in daylight. A cart with tea was already being managed by a maid wearing a black-and-white uniform. And I guessed that was Jones coming in with his workers carrying the second panel, leaning it carefully against a table next to the first.

I'd never been in a house with servants. Considering the late hour, I assumed they *lived in* somewhere, perhaps behind the small windows on the top floor, Parisian style, which I'd seen on approach. Colin told me later there were ten small servant rooms on the top floor, but times being what they were in *this* century, there were now only two full-time attendees in residence.

I had no idea how to address the maid who served us—if one addressed her at all. I settled on saying *Thank You* whenever she did anything for me I could have done myself. Francesca seemed to float above it all, sometimes a word to the help, sometimes not. Everything seemed to move with age-old efficiency. Before Jones and his men retreated he asked: "Will there be anything else, Miss?"

"No, thank you, Jones. Have a good night."

After he left, she told us that Jones was the estate manager. He lived with his wife and aged mother in the gatehouse we'd passed coming in.

"His parents and my father have know each other since they were children," Francesca said.

The appreciation, if not affection, was clear, but I still found it strange that one's standing at birth automatically put parallel lives on such different planes—and that *that* was just the way of things!

Our light supper was served at a casual table with water, not wine. We ate cold chicken, small roasted potatoes and *haricots vert* (another term I learned at Harrods). Francesca said both the spuds and green beans were grown in the manor's kitchen garden. For dessert there was sweet and tangy strawberry ice cream made with cream from the farm's own goat's milk—so rich and delicious I thought I'd died and gone to heaven.

Because of the hour, we were invited to stay the night. The Baroness herself showed me to my room called The Green Guest Room. It had two tall windows opposite twin poster beds with canopies. The pale green walls were silk, she said, hand-painted in the 1920s, with a widely spaced web of thin vines accented by dark green leaves and tiny orange berries. The view from my windows faced the rear of the estate. I saw no lights in the indeterminate distance, but I marveled to think of the wildlife—deer, bore, foxes and rabbits—that had lived undisturbed in this peaceful landscape for countless critter generations. I'd never stayed in a room so beautiful. Nor bathed so luxuriously in my own marble tub. Or slept so well on Porthault sheets.

When I came down the next morning, freshly showered and shaved, looking forward to a hearty English breakfast, I suddenly froze at the top stairs. Gracie was standing in the entry hall below! I couldn't believe my eyes! She had three stone-faced men with her whom I'd never seen before.

We were *so* busted!

After a deep breath, I continued down the rest of the staircase, hoping for a moment that I came off like I belonged there and she didn't.

"So are you the good cop or the bad cop?" I called.

Outside the open front door I saw a small moving van—one a lot nicer than ours.

"Don't mess about, Terry," she said, all no-nonsense. "You're lucky we don't press charges."

"There's that 'we' again," I said, approaching her face to face.

"Sebastian is ready to forgive and forget."

"Is he? That's big of him."

"It is, Terry, considering how complicated things *could* get." She indicated our surroundings, implying the scandal it was in her power to ignite. I had my eye on the three goons behind her.

At that moment, Colin walked in, followed by Francesca.

"The jig is up, Terry," Colin said.

"Jones is moving them now, Gracie," said Francesca, ready to make light of the situation. "All quite an adventure, I'd say."

"Best to say nothing, darling," said Colin quietly.

"I'm told it's a marvelous piece," Francesca replied, ignoring Colin. You can't tell a baroness what to do.

"I wouldn't know, Francesca," Gracie said coldly. "Nor does Sebastian. I think that's what gripes him most."

I saw her point.

Then Jones stuck his head in at the front door. "All done, Miss," he said.

Gracie and Francesca turned and said *Thank You* at the same time.

Heads spun round.

They glared at each other, a clash of the classes arm-wrestling over authority, neither ready to be usurped. In the tense silence that followed, Colin and I had to hide our smiles. It was one of the most priceless moments of my life.

After the van left, we had an uncomfortable breakfast in the east-facing morning room. Francesca said this wall paper was designed by her grandmother. The rich dark color was called Bishop's Plumb. Colin and I were barely listening, still feeling the sting of losing an unwindable war. As we departed, Francesca summed things up philosophically, echoing Tess's words:

"There was no winning this, chaps. What's done is done."

A few hours later Colin dropped me off outside Tess's flat. I knew I'd see him only one more time when I handed over my key to the flat. But the moment still felt like an ending.

"Thank Francesca for everything," I said, my voice

unsteady. I think Colin was feeling misty too. We shared an awkward hug and went our ways.

~

Back in the comfort of Tess's arms, relating events that had just transpired over the previous twenty-four hours, I promised again to swear off Sebastian once and for all. That is, Tess *made* me swear. It seemed like an easy proposition. I was leaving in less than a week. With my two recent windfalls, I was looking forward to restarting myself when I was back in L.A. And in all truth, no small thanks to Sebastian, I actually had a plan. I was going to be a photographer.

"Count your blessings," Tess said.

That was her way of telling me to put the past behind us. I knew that my "legitimate" late nights hinted at all the other ones that weren't—even if Tess *didn't* know the details, which I knew she did not. That was the other blessing: how scrupulously I'd deceived. Mostly, she didn't want to hear Sebastian's name ever again. Either way, we still weren't finished being Terry and Tess.

Gracie was all but moved out when I got back to the flat. I heard her on the stairs; caught her carrying arm-loads of clothes down to someone waiting in a car outside. A few times we exchange pleasantries over tea-making in the kitchen. She said she'd found a beautiful one-bedroom in Kensington—through a Sebastian connection, no surprise. Recent events were all too raw to rehash. What was the point? No discussion would have ended well. I was angry and sad about Finn, who I felt went like a lamb to the slaughter while the best of him—his artwork—remained to be gloated over by his executioner. A few days later, I came home and saw Gracie's favorite mug gone from the cupboard, and I knew she'd left for good.

Suddenly, I was all by myself again. If the flat was once the answer to my prayers, it was that no longer. The whole place had the air of a beat up boxer. Maybe it always did. I knew Tess and Gracie would never look back. Colin, bless his heart, was only waiting for me to move out before, under threat of eviction, he had to forfeit at no profit. It was never made clear *to whom* exactly. We surmised the no-name purchaser was a business entity entangled in the Gordian Knot of SEE, Limited. Colin told me he'd even decided to sell his flat in Shepards Bush in order to "reset everything" as he put it. Call the loss for what it was. It was wiser than paying lawyers to untangle shadows. And finally, the most sensible decision of all: he was moving into the manor house with Francesca—"until I get back on my feet," he concluded. If even I was relieved, I imaged how Colin felt.

I went up to Finn's room to have a look around. The bed had been stripped down to a mattress. The two work tables were gone, the wardrobe empty. The heavy easel was gone as well—maybe Colin gave it to Francesca as something she might bequeath to one of the other young artists she nurtured. Only the heavy curtains remained, probably the most luxurious feature in the entire shabby place. Below, Tess and Grace's room was entirely empty save the twin beds and bulky wardrobes. It was all swept out as mine would be soon, ready for the next generation of drama, joys and misadventures. Like the Manor House, we were only passing through. Strangely—perhaps most disappointingly—I harbored more of a grudge toward Gracie than Sebastian. She'd made a choice, whether *I* liked it or not. Sebastian was the snake that ate the frog after promising he wouldn't because that's what snakes do! As Colin said: *he eats people.*

~

I decided to make one last visit to the Coleherne—join the lads for a farewell pint and some tribal ambience English style. I was finishing my first round, standing at the bar waiting for the bartender's attention to order a second, when someone called my name.

It was Carlos!

I hadn't seen him in many months. We greeted each other with pleasure. By now, bygones were truly bygone. I ordered beer for both of us, and we pushed back through the crowd to catch some fresh air by the door. He looked about the same: American, yet with the seasoned veneer of an expat that even he probably didn't know he had. It was more than the clothes—by now his entire wardrobe, like mine, had been purchased in London. Or the haircut, which was more modern than most American guys his age. He still had the accent, but his Americanisms were softened and included naturally adopted English phrases.

"How's work?" I asked.

"Still in my hole," he said. "At least I get my music free."

"And Burt?"

"He has a boyfriend, a big Irish guy he's with half the time. Still works those long hours. I hardly see him these days. What about you? Still at Harrods? Did the new place work out?"

"Yes, still at Harrods. The flat's near Fulham. Good flatmates, all straight. But my visa's up so I'm going back to the States."

He nodded quietly. It was a moment before I recognized my words cast light on his *stuck* situation. I wished I hadn't mentioned it. As for my work, life at the flat, "vague" was about as specific as I wanted to get. No need to mention Tess or Sebastian. Carlos had probably seen my photos in music magazines, never imagining they were mine. I was so *past* the person I'd been when we were living together. Carlos was the same, only lonelier.

There was something else, too, impossible to define except in hindsight.

He was only five years older than me, still a young man. But Carlos had history. More to the point, a long and active sexual history. He and Burt had *lived* the Wharfs, the Trucks and the Rambles in their New York City days. Their promiscuous behavior continued when they came to London. None of us could predict the future, but Carlos had shadows in his eyes, the kind only an experienced sailor might read on a seemingly normal horizon but foretold a storm to come.

"There's a private party on Saturday if you want to go," he said. "Pretty wild."

Just then, shouts of "Closing Time" rose from behind the bar. We got caught up in the motion of quickly downed drinks and people heading past us to gather on the sidewalk. I had a moment to consider Carlos' invitation. Once outside, I knew my answer.

"It was good to catch up, Carlos," I said. "Say hi to Burt."

He got the hint.

"Yeah, I will when I see him," he replied. "I'll see you 'round, Terry."

I watched him dodge traffic and cross to the quiet side of Old Brompton Road. It was a ten-minute walk back to Nevern Square. Practically a straight line. I knew the path well, but never went that way again.

~

I started gathering things I'd be packing to take back to L.A. Of the hundreds, maybe thousands of Polaroids I'd taken, I had six. I lined them up on the mantelpiece in my room. First, the only one of me and Sebastian, the one Gracie took with me wearing my brand new Daniel Hechter jacket. I looked so happy. The only shot of Sebastian alone was the one I took that same night in his car on our very first outing. Technically, it was a bad photo but somehow the too-close blast from the flash spoke of our shared excitement. Sebastian was smiling. All his features were there, but his face had a mask-like quality—more telling than I knew at the time. Regardless, he still looked good. He always looked good.

There were two group shots from the barbecue: one with Finn, Colin, Francesca and Gracie, which I had taken; the other group shot with me included, taken by Finn, had me looking tense, sad and distracted. Tess had just run out the front door crying. Fortunately, there *was* a beautiful one of Tess, which was shot, minus the flash, in window light at her flat in Notting Hill. And finally, the one with Timothy. I kept it hidden for years, like the song you love but never play because it might break your heart all over again.

Did Gracie ever learn about that night at the swanky sex club? It was hard to imagine how Sebastian would describe things if he *had* told her. I chose to think she had no clue, blinded by the light. But I still got a pang in the pit of my stomach every time I thought of Timothy. He was right about everything. But I still didn't see the endgame. Sebastian was the giver and the gift; a mixer, a player. Most played willingly, some were just played. I took quiet pride that I'd never fallen down the rabbit hole.

Tess and I resumed our unspoken kind of peace. In spite of everything, we were making plans. The good between us was just too good. Even if we had to get married for her to immigrate to America, that's what we'd do. The rest would just have to play itself out.

We knew that having children wasn't in the cards. Considering how my life played out, it *would* have been a disaster for the kids. No regrets. Tess said as much decades later. No small relief to me, but it was still no excuse for bad behavior. Eventually, our past lives reversed enough to come full circle—at least, that's how I saw it—and, while remaining distant friends, we went our separate ways.

Meanwhile, I was reminded of Sebastian every day. There was a new ad campaign spread all over London. Chic eyewear, very expensive, by an Italian label I'd never heard of. Fashionably large frames, a very close angle. Once again, it was all about the eyes.

Then, on my last day at Harrods—two days before I'd be out of the flat, three more before Tess and I would kiss goodbye and I'd head back to L.A.—a call came in on the Frosted Foods phone line. It was Gracie. I couldn't have been more surprised. She got straight to the point: "Sebastian needs you," she said—meaning, of course, my services as a photographer.

I thought of everything Tess and I had talked about. My resolve; the promises I made.

I thought about Finn, felled on the altar of art.

Would I be available tonight? We'll pay you double for the short notice.

I thought about Colin, who was handed back his investments at a loss.

Sebastian really wants you with him.

Would I even tell Tess?

Then I said yes.

~

It was nearly eight o'clock. I was in the doorway as usual, waiting for Sebastian. He arrived promptly as ever, and I settled myself, camera deftly concealed, into the low seat of the XKE. If he was feeling awkward, it didn't show.

"New jacket and trou?" he asked straight away.

I chuckled. It was true. I'd wasted no time spending some of my *two* windfalls at the Way In, cashing in my modesty to negotiate a second Daniel Hechter jacket. I wanted to look like a new man when I returned to L.A.

"How's Tess?"

"Tess?" I said, surprise. He hardly ever mentioned her; that he was doing so now seemed on purpose.

"Not happy," I said.

In fact, she was profoundly disappointed that I'd agreed to associate with Sebastian again.

"Shit happens, Terry," Sebastian said, seeming to dismiss both Tess and the whole incident surrounding the portrait—and maybe Timothy, too. Blood under the bridge. By now, I assumed Finn's artwork had already been mounted in its designated pride of place—Sebastian at the center of everything.

"You're going to miss the opening," he said.

"I know all about openings," I replied, an edge in my voice.

"That you do," Sebastian chuckled, patting me on the leg. "Big night tonight, though," he said. "I'm glad you could make it…for old time's sake, eh?"

But I was pretty sure "old times" had little to do with it. I told myself (and Tess) it was for the money. I'd spent months gathering fruit but declined to bite the apple. Suddenly the old sweet tension between us was coursing hot again.

"Gracie said something about an art opening?"

"Trust me, it's not about the art. Even the gallery used to be important, but this show is purely commercial."

He explained that the featured artist painted oversize portraits of Elton John, The Beatles, Jimi Hendrix, David Bowie—England's version of Hollywood Boulevard caricatures: Elvis Presley, Humphrey Bogart, James Dean and Marilyn Monroe. I agreed that it all sounded painfully hokey. Sebastian assured me he'd never want to be commercialized *like that* (his emphasis).

"I'm doing Ronnie a big favor just showing up. Favor for a favor sort of thing," he added cryptically.

In earlier days I'd have let it go at that, but now I had nothing to lose. "What kind of favor?"

Sebastian paused for only a moment. I presumed he was quickly weighing the cost/benefit of revealing trade secrets. Maybe he thought he owed me one. He knew I was leaving in a matter of days, so what did matter?

"I'm acquiring the building; poor Ronnie's a bit hard up for cash."

I'll bet he is, I thought, as Sebastian gave me the same quick nod I'd seen between him and his co-conspirators circling other prey at social events. Spelling things out even that much implied, too, that now I was on the inside and he *could* divulge trade secrets.

"No need to say anything, just do what you do," he said, patting my leg again.

The gallery was in Camden, slightly north London, with a creative legacy that went back to Dickens and Keats, minus the upscale aura of Kensington or the West End. We approached the address, which was on the opposite side of the street. The sidewalk was crammed with people, including half a dozen ever-hungry paparazzi. Surely they'd been notified that Sebastian was on the list.

"Business as usual," he said as we passed, eyeing the crowd. Then he swung a sharp U-turn, coming back to stop in front of the gallery facing against traffic. Famous people can do that.

Two valets leapt into action, running to open doors. When Sebastian stepped out, I was nearly knocked over as the ill-dressed scrum of photographers surged past me, all vying for their best shot of the night's biggest star. I headed straight inside (where the headhunting paparazzi were not allowed), giving Sebastian plenty of room to do what he did best: being The Face. I didn't even bother taking my own camera out; I'd get exclusives inside.

As I walked into the crowded room, someone put their arm around my shoulder and said, "You must be Terry."

When I turned, I was looking into the face of a man I recognized immediately. He was wearing heavy, black-framed glasses, last seen tossing a wink and raising his glass to Sebastian in the swanky sex club lounge.

"I'm Ronald Headly-Jones," he said as he cleaved us toward a long table that served as the bar. (And, oh, look, the two handsome bartenders-of-color were from Sebastian's agency!) Ronald was a tall, doughy man in his fifties with skin gone blotchy from too much good wine. His dark navy suit was impeccably tailored. I had no doubt he was homosexual, as these mannerly, buttoned-up types usually were, posing as impudent and slightly daring upstarts. But really they were as stogy as an English fruit cake....pardon the pun. Called to account, they'd probably whimper—which maybe Ronald did under the whip of a stern master. He was just the type.

"I'm with the gallery," he said. "Anything you need."

"Ronnie!" I said too loudly and familiarly. Then I pretended I was trying to place him. "Now, where did we meet? Chelsea was it? I know...yes, it was that *club*! You know the one I mean. I don't think it even has a name!"

Mr. Ronald Headly-Jones blushed full red.

He fumbled for a moment then said that, well, no, we hadn't actually been introduced. "You were with Sebastian," he said.

"I'm *always* with Sebastian," I said conspiratorially. "We work as a team."

"A team?" He eyed me again, suddenly considering the possibilities.

"Oh, yes; thick as thieves," I replied, noticing how his blushing skin was blending with the alcoholic blotches. I turned my gaze to the very crowded room.

"Business looks good, Ron," I said, speaking over the din of the crowd.

"Yes," he said, sounding unsure. "Yes, it is."

"But Sebastian tells me you're closing after this show? That's too bad."

Ronald's eyes locked on mine. His instinct was to challenge me immediately for asking such impertinent questions. But I held my gaze, and he just caved.

At that moment I could have done anything, said anything, and he would have complied. It wasn't that I had power. It was that he relinquished his so easily.

Then, as if on cue, there was a commotion at the door. Sebastian entered, a tall silhouette against flashes of exploding lights. It was the *arrival* Ronnie had been waiting for. He quickly excused himself and barged back through the crowd. Handshakes and air kisses were exchanged. The sole in-house photographer swooped in, too. He was an overweight tangle of shoulder straps and clattering 35mm cameras, each with different size lenses. A book-size battery hung on his belt under a party-worn jacket. He was the kind of event photographer Sebastian cringed at accommodating, and whom I knew at that moment I would never be.

So, I let *him* do the heavy lifting as his rapid-fire shooting got all the expected groupings. I eased in after the rush just as Sebastian was looking around for me. Now, it was time for the money shots. He and Ronnie were shoulder-to-shoulder. I stood back for a loose three-shot including the featured artist. He was too young: an ambitious hustler bursting with misguided talent, already stuck in a creative rabbit hole—if not a reputational one—he'd never squeeze back out of.

Everyone smiled. FLASH. Then some approved others stepped in for the coveted moment with Sebastian. Another small group shot. I kept things tight. No one was interested in anyone's knees. FLASH, FLASH. Each frame slipped into the pocket of my jacket. Then Sebastian pulled Raymond close, and I stepped forward.

FLASH.

Then another step.

"You're so close," Ronnie said, grimacing.

I bore in even closer, not being nice. Sebastian gripped Mr. Ronald Headly-Jones so he couldn't get away, but The Face kept his eyes on me. He knew what I was waiting for. We were hunting together. Ronnie glanced around unnerved. He turned his frightened eyes to Sebastian then back to me. There was no way out.

FLASH.

Sebastian's next move surprised me. He reached for the frame just as I was about to spirit it away. Took a pen from his pocket and, as the Polaroid's chemistry did its magic, wrote something on the back. Ronnie waited, curbed like an obedient puppy. I saw what Sebastian wrote: *Thanks for everything*...because that's probably what Sebastian got: everything. The developed picture showed a curly-hair'd devil's mask smiling mirthlessly next to poor Headly-Jones, whose blotchiness looked like bruises, his eyes frightened, mouth half open almost pleading.

Who was the host here? Who was the master? *Comes as a guest to take a slave,* I thought, another great line from my *Summer Lawns* soundtrack.

The autographed Polaroid, a poisoned gift, was a reminder of who was really in charge. Ronnie probably gave the store away for the privilege of having the shit regularly beaten out of him by one of the most beautiful people in the world. Sebastian obliged as easily as he'd conspired with Colin's bankers and the politicians on his payroll. It was chilling how normal everything appeared; how they could play it all out in public, just another party night. The horror was there *was* no horror.

When valets, one on each side, closed the doors of the Jaguar and we sped away, the sudden silence was almost a shock. We'd been to plenty of crowded openings, but never had work seemed more like play. Cruel play. We both enjoyed every minute of it.

"You really got him with that last shot," Sebastian said once we were underway.

"I know. For a second he looked like a frightened puppy."

"He begs like one, too."

I looked over at him. The amused smile said more than I wanted to know—*but I knew*.

"And you, Terry," said Sebastian, putting a congratulatory hand on my leg *and leaving it there*, "You've got some new moves."

I knew what he meant. We'd tag teamed poor Ronnie. It was a side of me Sebastian had never seen. I wondered if he thought my skills were a missed opportunity? Either way, his praise was for all the wrong reasons. Not so the hand on my leg.

We drove in silence for a minute or so. At a red light, his hand moved inches from my crotch. In spite of myself, my fashionably tight trousers began to swell. I didn't want to say a word in case it broke the thrilling tension. Then the curving road required both hands on the steering wheel and Sebastian's focus returned to driving.

But a line we'd never crossed had most definitely been breached. I was sure it had to do with knowing this was our last gig together. I was gone save for the packing; moving out of Wandsworth Bridge Road the very next day to spend my last few nights at Tess's place. Every cautionary word she'd ever said was ringing in my head. But this…this was our last hurrah. There was nothing left to lose but my principals. His hand, his *advances*, weren't a question. Sebastian never had to ask for anything.

We drove in silence for a while. I was still nervous about crossing professional lines. He may have removed his hand, but I still had an erection.

As for the next move, our power positions did not need to be spelled out. Evelyn Waugh's "low door in the wall" was finally open. Even as I feverishly rationalized—*We were both adults! Isn't this what you've secretly wanted? People dreamed of being in this exact situation*—I knew I was about to walk through.

Then, as if I'd spoken these things out loud, Sebastian turned to me, smiling.

"Nothing to worry about, mate."

It was almost tender. Then he brushed my cheek with his hand, letting it drop slowly to rest again on my thigh.

All the parking spots on Wandsworth Bridge Road were taken. I expected Sebastian would just drop me off in front as usual. But this time he kept going, driving to the next corner, turning right, then another quick right which put us in the alley. He stopped at our back gate and turned off the engine.

"Not too late for a cuppa?" he said.

I hesitated, knowing my next words would change everything.

"No, no. It's not," I said.

We stepped out of the car. The sky was cloudless, cool and very dark. Suddenly, I was all thumbs fumbling nervously with the gate latch. I'd only ever come in that way on the night I discovered the flat had been robbed. Now, the back door was closed. No light in the window of my room. There was nothing left to steal. We were totally alone.

I closed the gate behind us. When I turned around, Sebastian was standing close, blocking my path to the flat. I looked up at the remarkable face and he was staring at me. The instinct to flee was as strong as the one that kept me rooted to the spot. Our eyes locked. I was beyond turning back. He took me as I reached for him, and we kissed, gently at first but only for a second before we fell into the timelessness of devouring and being devoured. I was lost on the lips of a beauty and charisma so powerful there was nowhere to go except deeper into submission...the rabbit hole.

I felt him pressing against me as he eased us around so his back was leaning against the wall. He drew me closer, then I felt a gentle pressure on my shoulder. My hands on his back came around to his waist. And, oh yes, dear readers, down I did go.

He helped me as I fumbled with his belt buckle and the top button of his pants. I rushed to shift them down past his hips, revealing trendy red Bonds briefs that bulged out to the left just inches from my face. I could have stared at the beautiful (desirable!) contour forever, but I had to feel it, rub my face against it, nuzzle, sniff, rake my teeth along the stiffening shaft. Sebastian let me linger. I looked up briefly, and he was smiling down. Did he know I was in heaven?

Finally, I hooked my fingers on the waistband, a moment of supreme anticipation, before I pulled down slowly and Sebastian's cock sprang out toward me. It was large but not massive; a player's cock, not a porn star dick; beautifully uncircumcised, darker than his caramel skin, with large balls that hung down begging for my hand to clutch them. I took the shaft in my right hand, slid the skin back, unsheathing the bulbous, shiny helmet.

"Go on, kiss it," Sebastian whispered, and after getting a proper eyeful, sliding the foreskin back and forward several times to savor its folds and texture, I put my lips on his cock then opened my mouth.

After that, our instincts took over. Twice he drew me up for air, locking eyes, tasting his own cock on my tongue, affirming his domination. I was prey for the taking. As we kissed, I unzipped my own trousers. He never reached for me, but once my pants were lowered, he gently pressured me to turn around. Eye to eye, I nodded *no,* unsure of his response. Might he have taken me by force? Or others? I was certain he was capable. One way or another, the whole world was ready to be fucked by Sebastian. But in this moment he demurred; we were friends; I had limits. Then I was back on my knees, holding Sebastian's perfect cock in one hand, my own in the other.

We settled into the shared goal of orgasm. But even here, as familiar as we'd both become, I felt a gloating thrill: *I was having sex with Sebastian!* It only made me hungrier, quicken my pace, suck his cock more eagerly, concentrating on the swelling head.

When I could tell he was going to come, I knew I was coming, too. I felt the first blast in my mouth then leaned back to see a second white stream shoot out. It landed on the shoulder of my new Daniel Hechter jacket. Then lesser pulses of creamy pearls which covered my hand. I kept stroking then eased my pace, pulling his foreskin forward to coax out the last drops, lost in the beauty of his orgasm, knowing, as a man, his pleasure, tasting his cum as I stroked my own cock; grunting breathless as I spent a load onto the patio concrete between us.

When we caught our breaths, I stood slowly, and we did up our trousers. We hugged, but there was no more bonding; it had the feeling of goodbye. All that he could give or that I might take was taken, or I gave away. We said goodnight, and Sebastian smiled a distant smile.

He gently closed the gate behind him. I heard the Jaguar start. Its headlights briefly lit up the alley, then both engine sounds and headlights crept away. I unlocked the back door and went up to my room. Time to start packing.

The End

The End

Stephen Jerrome was born in New Zealand but raised in Los Angeles. Minus higher education he has always juggled three creative callings as, essentially, a self-taught writer, photographer and accomplished pianist/composer. He has also maintained a voluminous hand-written journal all his adult life....almost a fourth calling!

In the mid-1980s through the early 90s, Stephen was a widely-published Hollywood society photographer (not a paparazzi) covering the art and underground club scenes during a particularly transformative time in L.A.'s social history. As a portraitist and documentarian at heart, photography has taken Stephen all over the world.

The London Year is Stephen's third published novel.

He resides near the coast in Southern California.

Excellent LGBTQ+ fiction by unique,
wonderful authors.

Thrillers
Mystery
Romance
Literary
Young Adult
& More

Visit us at
www.spectrum-books.com

Or find us on Instagram
www.instagram.com/spectrumbookpublisher

www.ingramcontent.com/pod-product-compliance
Lightning Source LLC
Chambersburg PA
CBHW011420070526
44584CB00026BA/3777